HECK THOMAS ★ *Frontier Marshal*

The Story of a Real Gunfighter

HECK THOMAS

★ *Frontier Marshal*

The Story of a Real Gunfighter

By GLENN SHIRLEY

CHILTON COMPANY · BOOK DIVISION
Publishers
PHILADELPHIA AND NEW YORK

For his daughter, BETH THOMAS MEEKS
who inspired this work

Acknowledgment

While much of the material for this work came from my private collection of books, pamphlets, newspaper records, and memorabilia on the Western peace officer and outlaw, I express my sincere thanks to the following:

To Miss Bess Glenn, Archivist in Charge, Justice and Executive Branch, General Records Division, The National Archives, Washington, D.C., for copies of correspondence, clippings, and documents from the Department of Justice.

To the staffs of the Oklahoma State Historical Society, Oklahoma City, and the Division of Manuscripts, University of Oklahoma Library, Norman, Oklahoma, for placing at my disposal certain collections containing material on Henry Andrew Thomas.

My appreciation goes to his daughter, Beth Thomas Meeks, of Tulsa, Oklahoma, for the use of family records, letters, voluminous scrapbooks, marshal's records, personal memoirs, and recollections; to his grandson, Colin S. Monteith, Jr., of Columbia, South Carolina, for enlightening correspondence and valuable photographs; and to his son, the late Albert Thomas, of Anaheim, California, for the details of many of the exploits of Henry Andrew Thomas in his lifetime.

Without this assistance, I would not have been able to interpret him in a book.

THE AUTHOR

Contents

Contents

Introduction

Within a quarter of a century, Oklahoma was transformed from an almost primeval wilderness into one of the most metropolitan and progressive states in the Union. From 1875 to 1900, it was a lawless land which bad men had made their stalking ground.

Strange as it may seem, here in the very heart of law-regulated America lay this great tract called Indian Territory, where for years the newly organized forces of law seemed weaker than the elements they opposed, and the roving bands of outlaws were the chief topic of conversation and apprehension as they swooped boldly down upon trains and banks, committed robbery and murder, and carried off great sums of plunder.

On the east side lay the wild, undeveloped lands of the Five Civilized Tribes. The herds of the great cattle barons roamed the prairies of the west side, finally to be usurped by the home-seekers, who were beginning in a crude way to organize the society that has reached such advancement today.

Of all the brave men who enlisted in the cause of law and order and who risked their lives by day and night to rid this land of its desperate bands, none won higher regard in his time and will be longer remembered for his most unbelievable deeds of valor than Heck Thomas.

He seemed an officer born. At the age of eighteen, at the close of the Civil War, he served as a policeman in Atlanta, Georgia, and from that time held the position of peace officer in some capacity well after the turn of the century.

He was an express messenger in Texas and put the Rangers on Sam Bass; he operated his own detective agency at Fort Worth and tracked down and killed the notorious Lee gang. From 1886 to 1892, he rode out of the court of the famous "Hanging Judge" Isaac Charles Parker at Fort Smith, Arkansas, and from 1893 to 1900, he served under every United States Marshal appointed for Oklahoma Territory. He became Chief of Police at Lawton, the first time after the opening of the Kiowa and Comanche country, and, after several terms, served as deputy United States Marshal again for the Western District of Oklahoma until his death.

An able Pauls Valley minister said afterward: "He did more to Christianize the Indian Nations than all the ministers who were sent there."

Thomas rode the range alone most of the time, rounding up men for whom he had warrants and bringing them to almost every court in the Territory. Invariably he picked out the most dangerous desperadoes to pursue. He gave them the opportunity to surrender, and thus live; if they resisted, he shot—and shot to kill. He sustained a half-dozen gunshot wounds in fights with bandit gangs. But few bad men dared go up against him alone, for his reputation and deadly skill with the Winchester and forty-five cowed them. He slept on the prairies night after night until his strong body was racked with rheumatism, and ate skimpy meals washed down with water from a running stream. Despite the hardships and the constant threat of death, he never lost sight of the fact that he was a representative of the Federal Government. He lived and acted as was expected of him.

In all his public career, with opportunities always present, he never profited by ill-gotten gain, nor did he dig into the public crib. He died a man of moderate finances. His reward was the satisfaction of having served his Government well. He contributed as much as any man to the building of a great state. His record as a fearless officer is without parallel in the history of the West.

GLENN SHIRLEY

Stillwater, Oklahoma

1

A Fighting Georgian
Goes West

The first train robbery in America occurred on October 6, 1866. It was committed by the Reno brothers, who made their headquarters at Seymour, Indiana, and established a pattern for all the train robberies that were to disgrace the whole country through the years. The James-Younger gang of Missouri perfected the method in its first train holdup on July 21, 1873.

From this date, the deeds of Jack Sheppard and others, who used to entrap unwary travelers upon the King's highway, seem utterly tame and insignificant when compared to these high-handed artists who coolly stepped upon the steel rails, stopped the snorting iron horse of commerce, and plundered express and mail cars while the officers of the same stood powerless and the terrified passengers sat shivering and helpless before the muzzles of their cocked rifles and revolvers.

By 1878, the audacious, deliberate proceedings spread into Texas. The first sign of trouble on that date of February 22, Washington's birthday, came in late afternoon when a stranger on a gray racing pony rode into Allen Station, a little prairie village eight miles south of McKinney and twenty-four miles north of Dallas, on the Houston and Texas Central Railroad.

No one paid any attention to the tall rider as he hitched his mount to the rail in front of Tom Newman's saloon. He paused a minute, rolling a cigaret, his hat pulled low, covering and

1

shading his eyes as he surveyed the half-dozen other buildings, including the little depot at the end of the street, before he strode inside. He told the saloonkeeper he was a sporting man and inquired if there was any gaming in town.

"Only stud and draw poker," the bald, pudgy Newman replied.

He observed that the stranger was about thirty-five years old and weighed about 170 pounds. His grayish-blue eyes were set deep in his head, the right one giving the curious appearance of being larger than the left. His skin was light, his brown hair long, and his short, thick beard was trimmed Vandyke. In the course of their conversation, he also asked casually, "What time does the southbound train arrive in the evening?"

"Eight o'clock," Newman told him, "and it's usually on time."

Disregarding a couple of poker games that were in session, the stranger returned to the hitching rail, mounted his gray pony, and left town. After dark, four men rode in from the west without being noticed and tied their horses in a clump of trees near the depot. Then they loitered nearby, until they heard the shrill whistle of Train No. 4, and saw it's headlight glow in the north.

Putting on bandanna masks, they hastened up to the little station. The agent stood on the platform under the oil lamps, and they quickly took him in custody. In a few minutes, the train rattled up to the station, spraying soot and ashes over the group as it ground to a sighing halt beyond, so that the express and baggage car was opposite the platform.

Before the wheels stopped turning, two of the masked men leaped upon the engine steps, pointed their pistols at the astonished fireman and engineer, and cut the bell rope. The second pair rushed the express and baggage car, where the Texas Express Company's messenger, Jim Thomas, had just rolled back the heavy door to discharge mail pouches and odd pieces of freight.

"Throw up your hands," shouted the leader, "or we'll blow out your brains!"

For a split second Thomas thought it was a joke. Then he saw their masks. He whipped out his revolver, fired one shot at the bandits, and leaped back inside the car, entrenching himself behind some boxes and keeping his gun aimed at the door, which he couldn't close without exposing himself.

2

"Come outa there, damn you!" Pistols ready, the robbers jumped into the doorway. A fusillade met them. The tall bandit went tumbling backward as a slug tore off his hat. The leader stepped all over him as he scrambled for the opening. Both men threw themselves beneath the car.

"I ain't comin'!" It was the young, anxious voice of the messenger. But the masked men were prepared to change his mind.

They crawled from under the train and sprinted to the shelter of the platform. From there, they laid several shots through the windows and doorway. The other two bandits, meanwhile, brought up the engineer, fireman, and station agent and took shelter at the end of the car. When the firing stopped, they could hear the messenger yell again: "I ain't comin' out, and I'll kill the next man who comes through that door!"

"Let's rush the dirty—" the tall bandit muttered.

"No, wait," the leader cautioned. "No sense gettin' shot up if we don't have to." He nudged the engineer with his pistol. "See what you can do," he said.

The engineer pleaded with the messenger to come out and surrender, but the answer was still a shaky, but emphatic "No!"

"We don't want to kill nobody," shouted the leader, "but we want the money in that car!"

The next move, executed in the classic style invented by the Reno brothers, showed more verve. They forced the engineer back into his cab, ordered him to back the engine to loosen the coupling pin, and separated the express and baggage car from the rest of the train, then had him pull it over the switch sixty feet ahead.

"Now, your oil can," the leader said.

The engineer produced his oil can. The bandit splashed the fuel over the wooden side of the express car and touched a match to it.

As it burst into flames, the engineer again pleaded with the messenger to surrender, and this time Thomas replied: "All right, if they promise not to kill me." The promise was quickly made, the fire put out. Thomas appeared in the opening and turned over his revolver, and the two robbers sprang into the car.

"Now, open the safe," snapped the leader.

3

Thomas opened it, while the tall bandit held a cocked pistol in his face. Thomas noted his long hair, the heavy beard bulging from under his mask, and the peculiarity of his deep-set eyes. *I'll know this smart bastard when I see him again,* the messenger thought to himself. *He'll be caught.* This was the first robbery in the territory for the company. *Our detectives will be swarming over the county in no time. And I'll help them, too.* With that pleasant expectation in mind, the messenger passed over the parcels from the safe containing nearly $2,000.

Squatting beside the tracks, the robbers tore open two packages containing silver. This seemed to satisfy them, and they mounted their horses and rode off to the west without molesting the train's nearly two hundred passengers. No resistance had been offered by the frightened occupants of the coaches and sleepers.

"The whole business took less than five minutes," Thomas told express company officials in Dallas at midnight.

"If I had been in your shoes, they wouldn't have got the money!"

The men in the room turned to stare at the rangy youth who spoke. He had been in the employ of the Texas Express as a messenger only a few weeks. He was Jim's cousin, "Heck" Thomas, a nickname given him by his schoolmates years before in Georgia. Now he was twenty-eight, all gristle and muscle, dark-haired and handsome, and quick for a joke.

Jim's blood stirred at his remark. "Just what do you mean by that?" he asked.

"Why, Jim, them scoundrels had no intention of burning the car with all that money inside!" There was a youngster's bravado in Heck's voice.

The officials nodded, and Heck grinned.

"Just what would you have done?" Jim challenged. "Suppose they hit your car next?"

"I don't intend to throw my life away, I have a family," Heck replied, thoughtfully. "But I think I can fool these robbers if they tackle me."

"How?" The men in the room were serious.

4

"I'll think of something." Heck grinned again. But behind his grin was a daring and brave spirit that made the officials uneasy.

The Texas Express Company's new messenger may not have looked like a tough one to handle, but, according to what they had learned of his reputation in the ante-bellum South, he already had acquitted himself on numerous occasions in a manner worthy of a man of more mature years. Henry Andrew Thomas was born January 6, 1850, at Oxford, near Atlanta. He was the youngest of twelve children of Martha Ann Fullwood Bedell of Virginia and Colonel Lovick Pierce Thomas, an old Georgian who had attained distinction long before the "Gate City" had thrown away its swaddling clothes.

Heck was nothing less than loyal to the scene upon which he first looked. His ancestors had come to America in 1632 and were prominent in the nation's early history. Edmond Howard, second son of the Duke of Norfolk, had been disinherited because he forsook the Catholic Faith and became a Protestant. Sir Thomas Holliday was Lord Mayor of London in 1605. The Honorable Francis Thomas was Governor of Maryland. Several other relatives had served as Congressmen, and General Leonard Covington had fought in the Revolutionary War. His brother, Ed P. Thomas, was the first sheriff of Fulton County. He was a nephew of General Edward Lloyd Thomas of Confederate fame. So no one was surprised when Heck showed an inclination to martial life.

Marbles, kites, leapfrog, and stilts had no appeal to him. Reared amidst uniforms, sabers, guns, and cannon, pranks of his boyhood had been with these elements of warfare, and even before he entered his teens these accouterments had come into his hands for deadly work.

In the six-day battle around Richmond, Heck's father was badly wounded in the right lung. When Colonel Thomas returned to Uncle Ed's brigade in General Robert E. Lee's army the summer of 1862, he took 12-year-old Heck with him as a courier.

Heck took great pride in writing his address: Henry A. Thomas, Thirty-Fifth regiment Georgia volunteers, Thomas brigade, A. P.

5

Hill's division, Stonewall Jackson's corps. And if he could find a soldier's envelope with something like "Stand firmly by your cannon, Let ball and grapeshot fly, Trust in God and Davis, And keep your powder dry" printed on it, he was happier than wise.

The day after Heck reached Lee's army, the second battle of Manassas was fought, and he was assigned a duty that contributed his first paragraph to history. The one-armed Mexican War hero, Major General Phil Kearny, of the Federal Army, was killed by a member of Uncle Ed's brigade, and his horse, saddle, and sword turned over to Heck for safekeeping.

Then Lee's army started its big raid down the valley of the Virginia, capturing Harpers Ferry and 14,000 prisoners. Uncle Ed's brigade was detailed to hold these prisoners while the rest of the command went on to fight the battles of Chantilly and Fredericksburg. While they were guarding the prisoners, General Lee ordered Kearny's horse and gear sent through the lines under a flag of truce to his widow.

Heck took them through. Kearny's mount was a big black, very "showy" horse and Heck hated to give him up. But it was the proudest moment of his life.

In the winter of 1863, Heck came down with typhoid and was sent home in a dying condition. By the time he recovered, General Sherman had begun his campaign from Chattanooga. Atlanta, a supply depot and rallying point for recruits, was one of the most important cities in the Confederacy. In Sherman's march through Georgia, it was totally destroyed and more than 30,000 Federal and Confederate troops killed, wounded, or taken prisoner. Heck walked over dead men, in some places two and three feet deep, shot through the face, neck, and head.

These scenes he never forgot as his family was reunited during the Reconstruction.

In 1865, the whole South was struggling for existence. Fifteen now and hungry at all times, Heck was sitting in front of his father's little store, its grocery shelves almost bare, when two drunken soldiers passed. One snatched the rabbit fur cap from his head and ripped it to shreds.

6

Heck leaped from the bench. "Nobody 'cept Yankee scum would do a trick like that!" he cried.

The soldier flung down the scraps with a roar. He came at Heck with fists swinging.

Heck tore into him in full fury, with the soldier getting the worst of it. Then Heck landed a left that cracked his chin and laid him out cold.

The other soldier aimed his pistol at Heck's head. Heck's father jumped to the doorway with a hatchet in his hand, and the soldier swung the pistol toward his breast.

Heck sprang at the soldier, knees first, from behind, and knocked him sprawling in the street. He was on him like a cat. Grabbing him by the hair, he shoved his face into the dust. Colonel Thomas rushed up to pull Heck off after taking the soldier's weapon. When the soldier looked up and saw the colonel standing there, with the hatchet in one hand and the pistol in the other, he screamed in terror, leaped to his feet, and fled.

Heck's early schooling was considerably higher than the three R's considered sufficient by most people of the day. The district superintendent for the churches around Atlanta was a close friend of the family. Mrs. Thomas wanted her youngest son to become a minister. For a time he attended Emory University, but his studies soon terminated. Colonel Thomas was appointed city marshal of Atlanta, and at age eighteen Heck became a policeman.

These were stormy times. Negroes, excited by the agitations of the period, were easily aroused to violence. The intense racial feeling culminated in the Bush Arbor Riot of 1868.

Andrew Whittaker, a Negro Democrat, started cursing a group of two hundred other Negroes having a torchlight parade. Heck and his partner, Jack Smith, arrested Whittaker and started with him for the station house. They ran into a second torchlight procession that was ignorant of the reason for Whittaker's arrest.

"Turn him loose!" yelled the leaders. They knocked Smith down, walked over his body, and began beating Heck with their sticks and clubs.

7

Heck kept his feet, blowing his whistle for help. Three more policemen responded. Under an old-fashioned gas lamp in Decatur Street, Captain Ed Murphy, Lieutenant John Johnson, Smith, Sid Holland, and Heck took on the mob.

A big colored man swung at Holland's head with an ax. Shifting his pistol from right to left hand, Heck laid out the Negro with a blow across the temple. Pistols roared from the mob, and Heck went down with balls through his left arm and thigh. Propped on an elbow, he fired into the advancing rioters until they turned into a rout.

Two other outbreaks occurred in Atlanta during the early '70's. In both, Heck was very much in evidence with his nerve, discretion, and good judgment. He established a reputation as a man of peace, as well as a fearless one, and his word carried much weight.

In 1871, he married Isabelle Gray, daughter of Reverend Albert Gray, a prominent Oxford minister. To them were born a son and daughter, in 1872 and 1875, named Henry Gray and Belle Fullwood. During these years, Atlanta was rid of its ugly element. With added responsibilities, Heck resigned from the police force to engage in the wholesale grocery business with two friends, A. C. and B. F. Wyley.

But life was no longer strenuous enough for his adventurous spirit and love of the outdoors. He took his wife and children and headed for Texas. By the time they got off the boat at Galveston, Cousin Jim had found a job for him with the Texas Express, and Heck moved his family to Dallas. The southern point of his route was Galveston; the end of his run north was Denison.

The Allen Station express robbery caused great excitement in the towns along the Houston and Texas Central. As recently as 1872, Dallas citizens had subscribed $5,000 for a diminutive station on the prairie and brought the railroad north from Houston. In 1873, with some maneuvering in the legislature and a $100,000 bond issue, they had supplied a broad right-of-way that brought the Texas and Pacific through the city. Dallas had boomed to dizzying proportions, and other promoters were building railroads in every direction. For a decade Texas had been notorious

8

for desperate characters who sought refuge on its sparsely settled frontier, and the railroads brought a new force of riffraff. But the civic-minded were fighting for a decent way of life. Already they had suffered from the robbery of stagecoaches and did not care to see train robbery inaugurated. Governor R. B. Hubbard offered a $500 reward for the arrest and conviction of each member of the gang, and the Texas Express and the Houston and Texas Central Railroad matched this offer, making each bandit worth $1,500.

While posses scoured the country without picking up the trail of the robbers, and Captain Lee Hall and his Texas Rangers, who were having some excellent, well-publicized success at the time, rode out to look for clues and returned empty-handed, the express company detectives were having a little more success. Chief Agent W. K. Cornish got to Dallas within forty-eight hours. Jim Thomas described the tall bandit with the long hair, generous beard, and large right eye. Taking Heck with them, Jim and Cornish rode immediately to Allen Station to pick up the case from the beginning.

The witnesses and hostages could furnish only meager descriptions of the masked quartet. But Tom Newman, the saloonkeeper, remembered the man who had inquired about the time the train arrived from the north. He also told the officers he thought the man was Tom Spotswood, a farmer who lived on Little Elm Creek in Denton County, fifteen miles northeast of Allen. He wore a thick beard, his right eye was glass, giving it a somewhat larger appearance, and he owned a gray racing pony.

"I think we'd better pay this Spotswood a visit," Heck suggested.

Cornish said, "We'll contact the officers at Denton."

They proceeded to Denton and talked to Deputy Sheriff George Drennan. Drennan shoved his big hat back on his high forehead, bit a fresh chew from a plug of Horseshoe, and nodded.

"Yeah, I know Spotswood. He's a bad one from Missouri. Came here from Sedalia three-four year ago. Killed a man up there named Jones in a quarrel over a cheap girl both were escortin' home one night from a circus."

Spotswood, they learned, had hid out in a hayloft several days

9

before he was captured and locked up in an old log house that was being used as a county prison.

"Before his trial came up, he escaped," Drennan said. "They say he had it in for a merchant at Calhoun named Edmonson, too, and that late one night as Edmonson was entering his store where he slept, Tom shot him from ambush."

Spotswood had left the country then, coming to Texas and settling near McKinney. In 1874, he had been arrested on a requisition from Missouri and returned there for trial. But most of the important witnesses for the state had left the country by that time, and he was acquitted. He had lost no time getting back to Texas, as relatives of the murdered merchant at Calhoun planned to swear out a warrant for his re-arrest.

"He's been livin' here ever since, and ain't never give us no trouble," Drennan concluded.

He agreed to accompany the detectives to Spotswood's place in the cross-timbers. They surrounded the house at night. At daybreak, they rushed in and searched the place. But Spotswood wasn't at home. His wife said he had gone to a farm he owned in Cooke County, nine miles north of Pilot Point.

"We'll need fresh horses," Heck said.

"We can pick some up at Pilot Point," replied Cornish.

As the officers were walking across the Pilot Point square to the livery stable, Drennan sighted Spotswood entering town in a wagon.

Cornish whipped out his pistol and commanded: "Throw up your hands!"

Spotswood surrendered. He was unarmed. Heck and Jim searched him. They found only twelve dollars in his pockets.

Spotswood denied any knowledge of the robbery. Jim, however, identified him, except for his whiskers, which had been freshly shaved.

They took Spotswood to the Collin County jail at McKinney. Here, Tom Newman and others identified him as the man they had seen in the saloon at Allen. He was given a preliminary examination and held for trial under $2,500 bond.

Heck, Jim, and Cornish continued their search for the other members of the gang. They had plenty of suspects. A list of

10

fugitives in Texas just published by the Adjutant General gave descriptions of 4,402 criminals. This included only three-fourths of the counties, and some of the most populous had failed to report.

Heck didn't believe Spotswood was the leader. "I think he was sent to Allen to get information, and I think the gang intended to rob the Central pay train that passed the station nine hours ahead of the express."

Cornish agreed. The spot chosen for the robbery narrowed the list of suspects considerably. Allen lay only a dozen miles from the hide-outs in Elm Bottoms in the cross-timbers of eastern Denton County. Denton had no railroad, though the Dallas and Wichita had been built to the county line near Lewisville. By far the handiest was the Houston and Texas Central, which passed through Collin County just east of the Denton County line, with express and sleeper connections with the Katy in St. Louis. The robbers had fled into Elm Bottoms, where it would be almost impossible to locate them, and there was no assurance they had not merely gone into hiding and would not strike again.

Heck realized that his express car was a likely target. Back of the office in Denison was a room in which off-duty messengers slept and passed away their time at the end of the run. Quietly he secured some old newspapers and a pair of scissors. He cut the newspapers into strips the size of greenbacks and stuffed them into express envelopes of different thickness. On the outside he wrote fictitious addresses and amounts of money and sealed them with wax.

Weeks passed with no further attempts to molest the trains. Agent Cornish was optimistic enough to think that Spotswood was the leader of the gang after all.

"The rest probably got scared and left the country," he said.

"I'm taking no chances," asserted Heck.

On each run he carried his bogus money packages.

The evening of March 18, he left Denison aboard the through express to Galveston. At 10 o'clock, the train pulled into the station at Hutchins, a little hamlet ten miles south of Dallas. At that time of night the population had gone to bed. Dark clouds obscured the moon and stars.

11

The passengers had gone to bed in the sleeping car. Up in the coaches, others were smoking, talking, or trying to read by the struggling lights. In the express car, Heck got his Hutchins freight ready. In the adjoining compartment, the mail clerk was making up pouches for wayside delivery.

A few minutes before, three men wearing bandanna masks had overpowered both the agent and his porter and forced them to the station platform. When the train stopped, they captured the engineer and fireman and two tramp printers from Dallas who were taking a free ride on the pilot. Marching the captives before them, they approached the express car.

The mail clerk stepped to the door to throw out the mail bag. Quickly he leaped back, slammed the door and yelled, "Robbers on the platform!"

Heck blew out the lights with a sweep of his hat. He leveled his revolver through the window at the bandit standing on the platform with a rifle.

The station agent screamed, "For God's sake, don't shoot; you'll hit one of us!"

Heck held his fire and barricaded the door.

"Open up!" yelled the leader.

"Go to hell!" Heck yelled back.

A volley of lead ripped through the sides and door. Heck ducked on the floor among the boxes of freight.

Voices and the sound of feet; the clash of steel as they cut the car from the train and ran it down the tracks. Heck heard someone climbing on the roof. The next instant, bullets came flying through the ventilators.

He wormed his way to the safe. Removing packages containing $22,000, he substituted the envelopes filled with newspaper. He left a small sack containing $89 in silver, and closed the safe. Then he crawled to the rusty red stove, unused during the warm months, and secreted the money packages among the dead coals and ashes.

The clamor outside was deafening. Someone was chopping the door with an ax. Heck sent a couple of slugs tearing through the panel, and the chopping ceased.

Some oil-soaked waste was brought from the engine and a fire

12

started under the end of the car. Heat and black smoke poured through the cracks inside.

A savage voice shouted, "Open up in there, or we'll roast you alive!"

Sudden nausea swept over Heck and stunned his nerves. The smoke was so thick now he hardly could breathe. The atmosphere was scorching.

"What will you do if I open the door?" he yelled.

"We'll let you live. If you don't, you die!"

Heck slid back the door and tossed out his revolver. The leader leaped through the smoke into the car, covering him with a forty-five. He coughed a little, then demanded, gruffly, "How much on board tonight?"

"Enough to ruin my company," Heck replied. "Over twenty thousand!"

The robber's eyes shone like a starved wolf's, and Heck realized what would happen if the man discovered his ruse. "Quick now! Open the safe."

Coolly Heck tossed the keys at his feet. "Open it yourself."

The cocked forty-five almost exploded, and Heck could almost see the devilish ferocity that crossed the face beneath the bandanna mask. "Open it, or I'll blow you to hell!"

Heck opened the safe door. The bandit threw down a sack. "Put the money in there."

Heck tossed in the bag of silver first. The clink of the coins made the man's eyes glisten. Quickly Heck threw in the bogus, wax-sealed envelopes.

The bandit jerked the sack shut with a grunt and ordered him outside. He marched Heck to where the others were being guarded by the robber with the rifle. Then he and the third bandit entered the mail car.

Meanwhile, the brakeman and conductor had slipped off the train and run to the hotel for assistance. They found no help, and the only weapon available was a shotgun. Returning to the train, they opened fire on the guard from the darkness.

The captives ducked beneath the platform. Heck, seeing a chance for a fight and possibly to capture the bandits, dashed for the engine where the fireman and engineer kept revolvers.

The guard's rifle cracked. A bullet cut Heck's cheek to the bone just below his left eye and ripped through the base of his neck. He leaped back under the platform beside the engineer.

The rest of the train crew and passengers in the coaches, with guns and the courage to use them, began shooting from the end of the train. The robbers in the mail car leaped outside, carrying the sack of loot and some packages, unopened. Unable to determine the size of the attacking forces, they ran to their horses.

Heck whispered to the engineer, "Let's get out of here—I've saved the money!"

Quickly the engineer backed up, coupled on the coaches, and the train was on its way. Heck was bleeding badly. He tore a sleeve from his shirt and bandaged his wounds the best he could and insisted that he continue on his route. At Corsicana, however, he was compelled to stop and was taken to a physician.

He told no one that the stove contained the real treasure until they reached Houston and the run was placed in charge of Superintendent C. T. Campbell.

The robbers had fled northwest toward the Trinity. As the alarm went up the line, Sheriff Marion Moon left Dallas with a posse to intercept them. City Marshal W. F. Morton, with several members of his force, rode to Hutchins, gathered all information there, and set out in direct pursuit. They found no trace of the bandits, and active search soon ended.

But Heck's daring and ingenuity became the talk of northern Texas. So did his description of the leader of the gang, whom he had studied closely in the express car.

"He is older than I—about five and a half feet tall and muscular —walked with a stoop. His black hair and eyes made me think he was Indian. He spoke through his nose like a Yankee, very different from the drawl of us Southerners."

This description, given to Agent Cornish, together with information being collected by Sheriff W. F. Eagan and Deputy Drennan, of Denton, caused the officers to take cognizance of rumors that linked the name of Eagan's former hired man, *Sam Bass.*

2

Trailing Sam Bass

Bass already was widely known in Texas as a young man who had gambled his money on a famous racer called "the Denton mare." He had run away from home in Indiana as a boy and had come to Denton, where he worked in the stables of the Lacy House. As a handy man for Sheriff Eagan, he made many trips with Eagan's freight wagons to Dallas and Fort Worth before he began racing horses. He had become involved in so much fighting, litigation, and bad company that Eagan fired him, and he had gone to south Texas. In San Antonio, he sold the Denton mare, invested the proceeds in a herd of cattle with a saloonkeeper named Joel Collins, and drove them to Deadwood, Dakota Territory.

What Heck and Agent Cornish didn't know was that Bass and Collins had lost their cattle money in the gambling halls of Deadwood and turned to robbing stagecoaches in the Black Hills. The pair soon became disgusted with small profits, however. The death of one of their companions from a charge of buckshot dampened their spirits further. Big shipments of gold were coming east from California on the Union Pacific. Sam, remembering the holdups of the Reno brothers in Indiana, decided one big haul would make them rich for life. In September, 1877, he and Collins, with cronies Jack Davis, Jim Berry, Tom Nixon, and

Bill Heffridge, took $60,000 from the Union Pacific Express near Ogallala, Nebraska.

Collins and Heffridge had been killed by U. S. troops as they fled south. Berry was shot later by a deputy sheriff in Missouri; Davis had left the country, never to be seen again; Nixon was still at large. Sam had reached Texas with $20,000 and had contacted an old crony of his days with the Denton mare, Henry Underwood. Underwood had rustled cattle and killed two men on the Concho, so was easily persuaded to take up residence with Sam at a hide-out forty miles from Denton in a wilderness known as Cove Hollow.

Another of Sam's associates was Jim Murphy, who lived in a shack between Cove Hollow and Denton. Murphy visited at the hide-out, and Sam spent considerable time at Murphy's. Murphy introduced him to another Denton ruffian named Frank Jackson.

All wondered at Sam's prosperity. He told them he had struck it rich in the Black Hills. He bought horses from Murphy for Jackson and Underwood, and the three of them rode to San Antonio to celebrate. While on this spree, a prostitute told Sam that a Pinkerton detective, Sheriff William Everhart, of Grayson County, and Deputy Tom Gerren were in town to arrest him as one of the Nebraska train robbers and thought Underwood was Nixon.

Sam and his pals galloped out of San Antonio, but soon lost their fright. On December 21, they held up the stage at Cleburne, nine miles west of Fort Worth. Sam and Jackson returned to Cove Hollow, but Underwood wanted to be with his family on Christmas Eve. On Christmas day, Sheriff Everhart and a posse arrested him at home. He was taken to jail in Nebraska, at Kearny.

This caused Sam to move camp to the brakes of Hickory Creek. Jackson wanted to leave Texas, but Sam insisted that they were safer in the cross-timbers among friends. They stayed there two weeks, then held up the Fort Worth stage at Weatherford and returned to their old hide-out in Cove Hollow. Next, Sam decided to rob a train. Jackson thought it too risky for two men, so Sam had recruited Tom Spotswood and a desperado named Seab Barnes, who had served time for murder.

16

So, for three months before the Allen Station robbery, Sheriffs Everhart and Eagan knew that Bass was one of the Nebraska train bandits. They knew about the stagecoach holdups at Cleburne and Weatherford, and knew Bass was in the country. But neither suspected Sam. Heck's description of the Hutchins bandit awakened them.

The newspapers began to harp on their inefficiency and demanded to know how passenger trains could be robbed and the United States mails rifled with impunity in Texas' two most populous counties. Federal authorities entered the investigation, and the Texas Express hired guards to accompany its messengers on both the Houston and Texas Central and Pacific roads.

When Heck recovered from his wounds and returned to Dallas, he was assigned with Detectives Sam Finley and James Curry to investigate the Bass gang. A second team, headed by Cornish, consisted of June Peak and Jim McGinley. Peak was recorder for the city of Dallas. He had been city marshal and established a reputation as a daring, resourceful officer. Cornish induced him to resign his office and work for the Texas Express.

First, Cornish sent Peak and McGinley into Denton County to get information. While they stopped for a drink at the home of Green Hill, Bass and Underwood rode past on their way to Murphy's. Peak sent Tommy Stout, a 16-year-old boy he'd hired as a guide, to Murphy's to see what he could learn there. Bass and Underwood captured the boy and held him all night. Sam asked him what Peak and McGinley were doing in the timbers. The boy told him, and he warned: "If you're seen ridin' through the woods with them detectives tomorrow, you'll be killed with them." Peak and McGinley returned to Dallas, satisfied that Bass and his party were the express robbers and that the Murphys, Green Hill, and others in the timber harbored and supplied them.

The middle of March, Underwood escaped from the Nebraska jail with a killer named Arkansas Johnson. Arkansas Johnson was a heavy man with shaggy hair, blue eyes, and a face pitted with smallpox scars. They reached Bass's camp together on March 31. On the night of Aprl 5, the gang held up the Texas and Pacific train six miles west of Dallas at Eagle Ford, looted the express safe, and escaped. Posses scoured trails to Hickory bottoms, finding fresh tracks but no bandits, while indignation reached a higher pitch. The towns might be raided next! Frantic appeals were sent to the Governor. Street-corner gossip berated the authorities, and officers in Denton County became subjects for jeers and disparaging remarks.

Heck, Finley, and Curry picked up a trail leading into Denton County. They followed it north during the day and lost it at dark in the cross-timbers.

The next morning they started toward Denton, scouting for a fresh sign. They sighted two horses tied in the woods, and their riders napping beside a creek.

As the detectives attempted to surround them, the two men sprang to their feet. One whipped up his rifle and sent a bullet whistling over Finley's head. Finley leaped from his saddle. Heck and Curry took shelter behind trees.

"How about it, Heck?" whispered Finley. "Do you recognize them?"

Heck peered carefully through the branches. He caught only brief glimpses of the rifleman and his shaggy-haired companion with the pox scars on his face. Later, he learned that they were Underwood and Johnson, but Heck had never seen them before.

He shook his head. Neither of the pair had entered his car at Hutchins.

Not certain that they were members of the Bass gang, Finley called to them to hold their fire. "Why are you shooting at us?" he asked.

"Hells-fire!" yelled Underwood. "I shot at a rabbit!"

"Then come out and identify yourselves," Finley challenged.

"We don't know you either," Underwood shouted back. "Just stay where you are."

He kept his rifle leveled, while Johnson brought up their mounts. When both were in the saddle, they let out a whoop and dashed off through the woods.

Heck and his companions followed cautiously. They lost the trail on the outskirts of Denton, rode into town to rest their horses, searched the woods for two more days without sighting the bandits, and returned to Dallas on April 10.

On that date, Texas railroad officials were in Austin beseeching Governor Hubbard to protect their trains against these assaults.

18

The Governor agreed to double the reward on Bass. And at 11 o'clock that night, Bass, Barnes, Johnson, and Underwood, with two Dallas County farm youths, Sam Pipes and Albert Herndon, who now joined the gang, held up the Texas and Pacific twelve miles east of Dallas at Mesquite!

This time the robbers got a hot reception. They captured Jake Zurn, the station agent, and when the train stopped, lined up the engineer and fireman. Conductor Julius Alvord was just stepping off the train. He snuffed his lantern, whipped a double derringer from his pocket, and began firing. Messenger J. S. Kerley emptied his revolver at the robbers from the half-opened door of the express car, then closed and bolted it and put out the light. The baggagemaster emptied a shotgun at the robbers from the other end of the car. The express guards, Jack Allen and J. C. Lynch, using a shotgun and two six-shooters, drove the bandits under the platform.

Oil was brought from the engine and splashed over the side of the express car. Bass yelled: "Set fire to the whole shebang, and kill the sons-of-bitches as they run out!"

At that instant, some Mesquite merchants, aroused by the shooting, arrived at the train and joined the fight. A slug tore at Pipes's left side. Barnes was limping from wounds in both legs. With lead flying thick and fast, Bass called retreat, and the gang fled north toward Duck Creek.

Heck, Finley, and Curry began a fresh search for the outlaws. They found a rifle dropped by the roadside. A farmer, who had seen the band pass in the night, heard one of the wounded men wailing: "Oh, my God, what shall I do!"

With four train robberies in two months, people refused to ride the trains or send valuables by express or through the mail. Businessmen loaded their shotguns and rifles and placed them behind counters and doors. Some withdrew their money from the banks, preferring to bury it rather than take a chance on Bass. Newspapermen swarmed into Dallas and Denton counties. They filled their columns with sensational stories of the holdups, labeling the area "Sam Bass country," his gang as "Sam Bass and Company." Their stories furnished the state with more exciting news than it had known since the surrender of General Lee at Appomattox.

19

Governor Hubbard now ordered Major John B. Jones of the Frontier Battalion of the Texas Rangers to Dallas to take charge of the investigation. The city became headquarters for no less than 150 bandit hunters from all over the country, including a dozen or more self-appointed detectives ambitious for the large rewards. Almost every day an expedition was made into Denton County, but there was no organized head to the operation, and Bass's spies kept him advised of every movement.

There was no Ranger company near Dallas. Major Jones organized a detachment as part of Company B, and asked June Peak to command it. Peak was made lieutenant and furnished with thirty men.

Peak arrested Pipes and Herndon. Pipes claimed the wound in his side was a boil. When a doctor probed it, he admitted it was a bullet wound but claimed a friend had shot him accidentally. He and Herndon were lodged in the Federal jail at Tyler.

From there the plan was simple. Major Jones ordered the arrest of everyone suspected of aiding the gang and pumped them for information. He questioned Spotswood at McKinney, arrested Green Hill, Jim Murphy, and Jim's old dad, Henderson Murphy, who was on particularly good terms with the outlaws. They were indicted at Tyler and bonded as accessories. The Murphys could not make bond and remained in jail.

On April 18, Peak and his Rangers rode into Denton with warrants for Bass, Barnes, Jackson, Underwood, and Johnson. On April 24, he led his men into the cross-timbers below Bass's headquarters; Sheriff Everhart and a posse came in from above; and Sheriff Eagan and his men advanced on the front of the robber stronghold.

Eagan was first to flush them. Only a few miles from Denton, he "met in battle array" with his former handy man and trusted teamster. It was a brief skirmish, but the rifle shots echoed throughout Texas. Railroad officials smiled, Heck and the other messengers of the Texas Express rejoiced, United States postal agents breathed easier, and the traveling public again boarded the trains.

The hundred-day campaign conducted by Major Jones is a matter of history. With the co-operation of Federal and local authorities, he and his gun-fighting Rangers ran Bass and Company from the Elm and Hickory bottoms, west of Stephens County, and south to the finale of gunfire on July 19 in the street of Round Rock, north of Austin. In that time, two of the gang had been sentenced to prison, Bass, Barnes, and Johnson had died from Ranger bullets, Jim Murphy had gained immunity for himself and his father by betraying his companions, only to commit suicide afterward, and Underwood and Jackson had left Texas forever.

Of those who trailed Bass, many were to hold high public office. June Peak became Captain of Company B and remained in the Ranger service for years. He and his detachment received the rewards for capturing Pipes and Herndon. The Texas Express and the Houston and Texas Central Railroad sent Major Jones a thousand dollars to be divided among his men, and Heck, Jim Thomas, and Messenger Kerley were presented gold watches for their resistance against the bandits.

Heck also received the following letter:

Henry A. Thomas, Esq., Messenger H. & T. C. Route

Dear Sir:—Inclosed please find the sum of $200 which I hand you in the name of the Texas Express Company and beg your acceptance thereof as a slight recognition of the zeal and fidelity displayed by you in the robbery of this company at Hutchins on the night of March 18.

The officials of this company realize the fact that your coolness, foresight and thoughtfulness were instruments in thwarting the designs of the robbers and reducing to a minimum the amount of booty secured by them, and were it not for the extreme depression of business and the serious losses lately sustained they would testify in a more substantial manner to their high appreciation of your conduct, which has stamped you in the estimation of the officers of this company as in all respects a first class messenger.

> I am respectfully,
> C. T. Campbell
> Superintendent.

A few weeks later, Heck was again pleasantly surprised. He was promoted to chief agent at Fort Worth.

3

Longhair Jim Courtright

When Heck Thomas saw Fort Worth in 1879, it had
grown from a "dirty, mean little place of three hundred souls" into a thriving city of six thousand. For
years it had been the major stop on the cattle trails
to Northern markets. The main trail from southern
Texas split just north of San Antonio, the Western Trail going
to the feeder ranges of Colorado and Wyoming. The Eastern
Trail, with the sale herds, passed through Fort Worth to Red
River and connected with the Chisholm Trail that snaked through
Indian Territory across the Canadian and Cimarron. In 1873,
when the Katy Railroad building through Indian Territory
crossed Red River to Denison, cattle could be shipped from this
point to Baxter Springs, Kansas, at a hundred dollars a carload.

But to reach Denison, the trail herds still had to come through
Fort Worth. It was the last place where trail hands could re-
provision, whoop off their money on dice, cards, and women,
and take their last drink before beginning the lonely, dangerous
trek north. They ran their bawling, rangy longhorns down Commerce Street, raced their horses full speed, and fired six-shooters
in the air, and nobody cared. The cowboy was royalty.

The thousands of Plains Indians herded into the western half
of Indian Territory by the Federal Government had to be clothed
and fed. Across the plains beyond Fort Worth stretched a line
of military posts garrisoned against the still untamed tribes.

22

Hundreds of miles further west another line of forts stretched down the Pecos in New Mexico. Scattered over the intervening region were the trading posts of the ranchers and buffalo hunters. In 1876, when the Texas and Pacific Railroad arrived from Dallas, a giant wholesale trade had developed. Fort Worth was now the supply point for this vast empire.

Heck watched the freight caravans rumble off into the setting sun and head across the Trinity for the Territory. He saw wagons loaded with skins of buffalo creak in from the west, acres of hides piled fifteen feet high along the Texas and Pacific tracks, and as many more acres covered with horns, hoofs, and bones to be shipped east to carbon factories. He counted a hundred wagons parked on the big commons north of the Trinity at one time, and a dozen more bogged in the mud of Main Street on their way to the cotton market in the square.

And he saw the inevitable riffraff come to reap the golden harvest—gamblers, thugs and gunmen; black-bearded freighters and buffalo hunters handy with fists and knives; sweating, cursing railroaders; and beefy chorus girls who jostled in the narrow streets and saloons; dance halls and brothels that stayed open day and night to accommodate their carousals while the air throbbed with the discordant din of banging pianos, shrill, coarse laughter, yahooing and guffawing and the clink of chips. It reminded him of Atlanta during Reconstruction.

For the most part, Heck discovered, the Fort Worth bench was occupied by scalawags and carpetbaggers. Citizens who hoped to stay had organized a city government and elected its first slate of officers in 1873. They had imposed regulations on gambling, restricted the carrying of weapons, and outlawed mobs. But the first city marshal had lasted only eight months. In the next two and a half years, they had four chiefs of police. The fourth had served only three months in 1876. Crime had gone virtually unchecked, and the city government had become a vehicle for personal gain of unscrupulous politicians and certain professional people who found an easygoing administration to their advantage. The forces of good and evil had fought it out in the election of 1877.

Into this rough and tumble, vice-ridden picture had stepped

23

Marshal T. I. "Longhair Jim" Courtright, a tall, ice-nerved gunman with a slightly crippled right hand, who let his hair grow to his shoulders after the fashion of the Indian scouts of the period. He wore two guns, butts forward, and used the cross-body draw. He could produce the guns in the twinkling of an eye, and was an accurate shot.

Heck had first met Courtright with a posse near Denton while looking for Sam Bass. The marshal had made several trips out of Fort Worth after the Cleburne and Weatherford stagecoach robbers. More recently, he had won favor with the Texas and Pacific Railroad for his sensational capture of Lee Witt, who had murdered their ticket agent at Corsicana. Witt fled to Fort Worth. Courtright, learning of his whereabouts in the city, started after him with a squad of men. Witt mounted his horse and made a mad dash for the Trinity, but before he could cross it, Courtright was peppering the air about his head with buckshot, and he surrendered.

Heck saw Longhair Jim in action many more times while the latter was chief of police through 1879. They were often seen on the streets and in the saloons together, and from him Heck learned much about the science of frontier law enforcement. Gunmen respected Longhair Jim. He dealt firmly with flagrant violators, horse thieves, and murderers. Unruly cowboys were more reckless than dangerous and responded to discipline if treated fairly. A log structure at Commerce and Second streets served as a jail. On Saturday nights, twenty to thirty guests crowded its two cells and dungeon. The marshal had four assistants. Two patrolled the city by day and two at night in blue uniforms and black slouch hats.

But Longhair Jim's greatest difficulty was with the district, county, and mayor's courts.

"They have their own ideas about what constitutes law and order," he told Heck one night while they were having a drink together. "They think I should do nothing more than protect women against insults and arrest drunks who shoot off their pistols in the streets, gambling dens, and whore houses. They actually believe this town would die if regulations were enforced to shut down or hamper the tavern proprietor."

Left alone, Heck thought, Jim could have done much to clean up Fort Worth.

At the end of 1879, he told Heck: "It's a thankless job. I'm not going to run for another term."

He showed Heck a telegram he had received from Colonel A. J. Fountain of the New Mexico Militia to come to Lake Valley, in old Dona Ana county. By 1882, Courtright had established a Boot Hill for this end of the track mining center and tamed the dance hall girls, Indians, and desperadoes. In 1883, he was employed by the Sierra Mining Company to protect its interests against the depredations of roving bands of cutthroats and thieves. He was back in Fort Worth in 1884, operating his own detective agency.

Fort Worth, in that year, was as riotous as ever. A political quarrel was raging between City Marshal Sam Farmer and James Maddox, who served repeatedly in later years as chief of police. Heck had just finished checking his freight one morning when he saw the pair meet on the sidewalk in front of his office.

Both men stopped, facing each other stiffly. The flashing glance of absolute hate that passed between them seemed almost to cut the humid air of the street like a giant saber. And then, as if the tension was too much and had passed the bounds of human feeling, Farmer snarled:

"Goddam you, Maddox, you've lied about me for the last time. I'm going to kill you!" His shoulder hunched forward, his right hand swung loosely past the butt of his six-shooter.

Maddox' face paled, but was otherwise expressionless. "Sam," he replied, "you can't kill me now. I'm not carrying a gun."

"Then, damn you, get one!"

"You got no business carrying one—I'll take yours!" In a flash, Maddox' right hand shot downward, snatching the revolver from Farmer's holster.

Leaping past him, Maddox whirled, facing the officer from ten feet away, the weapon leveled at his chest. "You," he said coolly, "are the one who's going to die!"

By that time Heck had reached the doorway. Maddox stood on the sidewalk so close that Heck could have reached out and touched him. Heck suddenly raised his arm and brought it down with a sharp, heavy slap across Maddox' wrist. The revolver flew from his fingers and went skittering into the street.

Then Heck leaped, scooping the gun from the dust only a second before Farmer reached it. Dumbly he stared at Heck for a moment, wheeled away, then walked off. He carried his anger down the street, and then was ashamed of it. When Heck returned his revolver to him at his office a few minutes later, Farmer thanked him for saving his life.

Heck had his reasons for seeing Fort Worth a civilized, peaceful community. He was now the father of another son, Albert, who had been born just before he had left Dallas, and a daughter, Mary Jo, born in 1883. His wife Isabelle constantly objected to rearing and educating their children on this wild, unsettled frontier.

Heck organized a citizens' group, urging Courtright to run for his old office. But there were rumors that Jim was involved in the murder of some Mexicans during an attempted silver train robbery in New Mexico. Two prominent ranchmen had been arrested in connection with the affair. They had been slain, allegedly on the pretense that they had attempted to escape. Jim was a fugitive with a $1,000 price on his head.

Nobody in Fort Worth seemed interested in collecting it.

Heck assured him, "Half the population are your friends."

And Jim confided, "I'd rather die here than go back and be killed by Mexicans."

Heck was locking up his office the night of October 18 when he saw three men get off the train. He recognized Lieutenant Grimes and Corporal Hayes of the Texas Rangers. Later, he observed them in friendly conversation with Courtright and heard them introduce the third man as Sheriff Harry Richmond of Albuquerque. The next morning they invited Courtright to their rooms in the Ginnochio Hotel to look over some photographs of suspects believed to be hiding in Fort Worth. As Courtright finished thumbing through the pictures, he looked up into the muzzles of three revolvers.

Aware of Courtright's popularity and realizing his friends might mob the jail and free him, the officers decided to keep him hidden in the hotel room until the 9 P.M. train left for the west.

But when Courtright failed to appear at his office, a hurried check by his friends revealed what had happened.

The news swept town: "Longhair Jim's under arrest on the second floor of the hotel!" Within a few minutes an angry mob had filled the street between the hotel and railway station and jammed the lobby where police guarded the stairs.

They demanded that Courtright be placed in the Fort Worth jail in custody of local officers so that he would not be harmed while his friends fought his extradition before Governor John Ireland. Lieutenant Grimes appealed to the crowd to disperse. He promised that the prisoner would be protected as long as he was in the charge of the Rangers. But the mob shouted: "Let Jim speak for himself!"

When Jim appeared at the window in handcuffs and chains, they yelled: "Let's turn him loose and give him a gun!"

The crowd increased until the officers in the hotel faced two thousand guns. Any attempt to remove their prisoner now meant bloodshed, and they couldn't hold off the mob until train time.

Heck moved through the crowd, a strange feeling of fear gripping his stomach as he passed each angry man. The policeman on the stairs acceded to his request to talk to the Rangers. A few minutes later, Grimes had agreed to his plan to get Courtright to the county jail.

There was a space in the alley behind the hotel wide enough for a carriage to be driven under the stairs. Heck hired a fast team of bays, then got Bill Capps, a well-known lawyer friend of Courtright's, to mount a shed over the window of the railroad ticket office across Front Street and address the crowd. While the lawyer held their attention, pointing out that Courtright was guarded by a half-dozen local policemen besides the Rangers, the officers slipped their prisoner into the carriage and galloped away.

Someone spied them, and shouted: "There he goes!"

The mob dashed after them, yelling, "Turn him loose!" But before they could catch up with the carriage, the officers had Courtright in the county jail.

Longhair Jim was no ordinary prisoner. He was allowed the freedom of the sheriff's office, and was taken to the Merchants

27

Restaurant near the jail for the noonday meal. Heck and his friends lined the street to watch him pass. In the evening, Jim was taken to the restaurant again for supper. While eating, he dropped his napkin.

"Want to pick it up?" he asked one of his guards.

"Pick it up yourself," the guard said, suspecting a trick.

Jim stooped to recover the napkin from under the table. The cloth drooped halfway to the floor. When Jim's hand reappeared from beneath it, his guards looked into the muzzle of a six-shooter.

"It's my turn now," Jim said.

The guards did not argue the point. As Courtright backed from the restaurant, Heck and his friends crowded between them. Jim dashed up the street to a horse, vaulted into the saddle, and raced off into the twilight.

Nobody ever knew who fastened that six-shooter beneath the table, but Heck always smiled to himself when the affair came up for discussion in his presence.

He heard later that Jim had caught a train to Galveston and a ship to New York, then had gone to Canada. Courtright finally went back to New Mexico, where he was cleared of the charges against him. He returned to Fort Worth and was killed by the king of the gamblers, Luke Short.

Heck moved on with the frontier. The Texas Express had been the only such company operating in the state. It was soon opposed by Wells Fargo and Company and the Pacific Express, Jay Gould's outfit. With such competitors, it didn't last long. Heck was thirty-five when he left the company.

He was six feet tall, an outstanding figure in any crowd, and his soft drawl and gentlemanly manners had won him many friends in Fort Worth. He could size a man up at a glance, and found his judgment seldom at fault. People still talked of his exploit with Sam Bass, and his experience as a policeman in Atlanta qualified him for a career in law enforcement. If society was to gain the upper hand in Fort Worth, crime had to be suppressed. In 1885, he ran for city marshal.

Elections were stirring affairs during the "reform years." Voters carried firearms and bowie knives. Guards had to be stationed a half mile from polling booths to collect their weapons. Disarmed, they generally were mouthy and boisterous.

A fight broke out in front of one of the polling places. The judges became frightened and closed the polls nine minutes before time, when Heck had forty-one of his own men standing in line. He was defeated by twenty-two votes.

With four hungry mouths to feed, Heck followed in the footsteps of his idol Courtright. In May, he began his first operations as a member of the Fort Worth Detective Association.

4

Heck Thomas Collects

A few days later, Heck looked up from his desk as a tall, grizzled figure filled the doorway. He introduced himself as Alva Roff, a wealthy Texas cattleman.

"I have been told you are a reliable man to do business with," he said.

Heck invited him to have a seat. "I appreciate that, sir—and how can I be of service to you?"

The cattleman settled into a chair beside his desk. "Let's put it a little differently," he said, "and say—shall we?—that you can be of service to yourself. I have offered a reward of $2,500 each for the capture of Pink and Jim Lee for the murder of two members of my family in the Chickasaw Nation. I have just come from the Governor's office in Austin, and the state has added $1,000 reward for the capture of the Lees as the leaders of the gang that has been terrorizing the northern counties of Texas around Gainesville." Roff laid a copy of the notice on the desk. "My offer, of course, is open to anyone who can collect it."

Heck studied the descriptions of the two brothers on the poster. Jim Lee was in his thirties, five and a half feet tall, slender. Pink was taller, just past twenty. Both wore long hair, short, sandy whiskers, and mustaches, rough clothing, and carried Winchesters and a brace of six-shooters.

"It won't be easy," Roff added. "The Lees are two of the worst outlaws who ever crossed Red River to rob and pillage."

Heck had heard all about the Indian Territory outlaws who crossed Red River to rob and pillage. This vast country between Texas and Kansas and No Man's Land and Arkansas had become a refuge for the most debased characters on earth. Fort Worth newspapers had been full of reports of bloody atrocities committed against lone travelers and raids upon freight caravans and Texas trail herds.

The Territory was attached to the Western District of Arkansas for judicial purposes and to protect the Indian against the criminal intruder. In the eastern half and along the Texas border lay the Nations of the Five Civilized Tribes. The railroads had brought an influx of whites who had intermarried with the Indians and were little disposed to law and order. Texas cattlemen leased large grazing areas. Alva Roff's brothers, Jim and Andy, had operated a ranch between Caddo Creek and the Arbuckle Mountains in the Chickasaw Nation. Others had moved onto the two million acres of free range in the heart of the Territory, called the Unassigned Lands (still held by the Government and not assigned to any Plains tribe), and, since 1880, colonies of boomers from Texas, Kansas, and Arkansas had claimed this area subject to pre-emption and settlement under the homestead laws.

The Indian Nations had their own laws and courts and policed themselves with mounted troops called Light Horse. But tribal laws did not apply to the white man. The Federal Court was the only protection from the criminal refugees. Isaac Charles Parker, a former district attorney and Congressman from Missouri, had been appointed judge of the court in 1875. His executions on the gallows had attracted the attention of the world. Working out of Fort Smith, a force of two hundred Federal marshals policed the trackless region in wagons and on horseback with rifles and six-shooters. But two hundred officers were only a handful in so large an area. In the far reaches of the Chickasaw Nation, three hundred miles from the Fort Smith court, there was no safety for white men doing business under tribal permits; they had to protect themselves. The Roff brothers' ranch was the only

31

sign of habitation and the first residence north of the Delaware Bend country on Red River.

Delaware Bend formed the northern boundary of Cooke County, Texas. It had been overrun with outlaws, who fattened themselves off the thrifty stockmen and farmers and found shelter in the uninhabited jungles across the river. The Lee gang was the most notorious. Its principal members consisted of Pink and Jim, their brother-in-law, Ed Stein, and Frank Pierce.

Heck knew Pierce. His real name was Frank Pierce Roberts when Courtright had run him out of Fort Worth in 1879. Pierce lived at Johnsonville, Chickasaw Nation, and peddled whisky to the Indians. Stein operated a store at Delaware Bend on the Texas side and suppled Pierce with whisky. Jim Lee had married a squaw, which gave him a "right" in the Nation. He had built a cabin and fenced a large pasture fifteen miles northwest of Delaware Bend on Cold Branch, a tributary of Caddo Creek. Pink lived with him, and the place was a "hold" for most of the badmen passing through the country.

Heck had read about the murder of Jim and Andy Roff in the papers. He listened carefully as Alva Roff filled him in with the details:

In April, the Lees had stolen some cattle from his brothers and two settlers named Estes and McColgin. Jim and Andy were up in the mountains rounding up some strays, so Estes and McColgin had picked up the trail of the rustled stock. It led to Stein's store at Delaware Bend. The Lees, Pierce, and Stein met them on the porch with rifles.

Outnumbered two to one, the settlers didn't mention their cattle. "We're looking for a span of black mules," Estes said.

"We ain't seen no mules," Jim Lee grinned, showing his dirty teeth. Beside him, Pink impatiently fingered the lever of his saddle gun.

Estes and McColgin thanked them and rode back across the river. They told the Roffs what they had seen. Jim called on Sheriff Hill at Gainesville.

"I've got a posse above the river. We'll meet you any place you say and wipe out these rustlers."

32

Hill was more cautious. "My deputy, Pat Ware, and me ain't known by the Lee boys and Pierce. We'll go to the store on the pretext of buying supplies, and if our men are there, try to get the drop on them. Wait on the Territory side till you hear from me."

Neither Hill nor Deputy Ware had gotten inside the store. Pierce met them on the porch with his rifle cocked. His black, shoe-button eyes gleamed suspiciously. His heavy torso swelled, and his stubby legs spread apart as if bracing himself for a shot.

"What in hell do you fellows want?"

Sheriff Hill, taken by surprise, mumbled something about being on their way to Dexter and wanted to know what road to take. Pierce pointed to the road with his rifle.

"Hit it," he growled, "and don't look back."

With no word from Hill, the posse across the river grew restless. Roff sent Jim Shattles, who lived in the neighborhood and traded at Stein's store, to investigate, believing that he wouldn't arouse suspicion among people acquainted with him. When he arrived at the store, Pierce ordered him to get inside and stay there.

When Shattles didn't return, the posse crossed the river to investigate for themselves. As they approached the store, a member of the party, John Washington, dismounted and took position behind a rail fence. He saw Pierce dart from the back door and start across the lot.

"Hold up there!" he called.

"Hold up yourself!" Pierce yelled. His rifle cracked. The bullet struck the top rail, scattering splinters in Washington's face.

Pierce leaped onto his horse and started across the river. The posse unlimbered their weapons. The outlaw fell from his saddle on a sand bar, literally shot to pieces.

The Roffs had found their cattle in a brushy pasture down the river. Shattles told them that the rest of the gang had gone to the Lee ranch on Cold Branch.

Warrants were issued for the arrest of Jim and Pink Lee and placed in the hands of Sergeant James Guy, of the Indian police, and a deputy United States Marshal. Guy also carried a writ for Della Humby, a Negro charged with wife murder, and known to be hiding at the Lees. A Chickasaw law prohibited Indian citizens fencing more than 640 acres of land and provided for the removal of all fences enclosing excess holdings. The Lees had refused to take down their fences, and Governor Wolf had ordered that their pasture be cut.

On the morning of May 1, Guy had marshalled his forces at Henderson's store on the Washita, ten miles from the ranch. Besides Guy and the Roff brothers, there were two regular possemen, Windy Johnson and Emerson Folsom, and a Roff cowboy named Billy Kirksley. They left before dawn, arriving at the Lee ranch at sunup.

The house was a two-room log affair with a breezeway through the center. There was a small window on the north side of the east room with a board shutter and a stick-and-dirt chimney on the end. The structure had been carefully arranged to resist attack, with portholes in the chimney and one on each side of the east room.

Two hundred yards east of the house ran Cold Branch. When Guy's forces reached it, they found the stream so boggy from recent rains that only Jim Roff's horse succeeded in crossing. They agreed to leave their mounts in Johnson's care and walk to the house. Guy said, "If the Lees refuse to surrender, we'll not stage a fight, but withdraw and send for more men."

As the posse approached the northeast corner of the house, Stein lifted the board shutter and asked what they wanted.

"I hold writs for Della Humby and Jim and Pink Lee and an order to cut their fence," replied Guy. "If they will come out and surrender, I'll see that they are protected."

"Come around in front, and we'll talk about it," Stein said, and closed the shutter.

Guy and Folsom had walked to the front of the house. They stopped at a large oak tree near the end of the breezeway, and Guy set down his rifle. Della Humby fired from the west room of the cabin, killing him instantly.

Folsom sped back to the posse as a volley burst from the portholes. Jim Roff and Kirksley died in their tracks with two bullets through their bodies. Andy, badly wounded, tried to reach Jim's horse, but died before he crawled a dozen yards.

Only Folsom reached Cold Branch with a whole skin. He and Johnson rode to spread the news of the brutal slaughter. Armed settlers and cowboys went to the ranch to capture the gang and recover the bodies. Finding the place deserted, they burned it to the ground.

Stein had been arrested at Denison on May 6, committed without bail by the United States Commissioner at Sherman and transferred to Fort Smith. Della Humby had vanished. But Pink and Jim Lee had been seen frequently in the country between Delaware Bend and the Canadian River.

Alva Roff finished his story: "They've threatened death to anyone giving aid to those seeking to capture them and vowed not to be taken alive."

Heck finished scanning the poster. The rewards, he noted, called for their capture, dead or alive, and "delivery to the jail door."

Heck thanked the cattleman for coming. "I just might give it a try," he said.

Heck didn't do anything about it at the moment. He put the notice in his desk. For another couple of weeks he went about the matter of organizing his new business and handling a minor case or two that came to his attention.

He read in the papers that officers and detectives from Dallas and other Texas points had gone to Gainesville to join the hunt. Jack Duncan, the famous detective who had captured the notorious John Wesley Hardin, went up to look for the Lees and came back empty-handed.

Finally, the rewards were an inducement that Heck couldn't resist. One night he told Isabelle, "I'm going to see what I can do."

His wife pleaded, "You may be gone for months—and your expedition will end up like all the rest."

"Honey," Heck said, "I have to try."

He left Fort Worth on June 5. A few days later, the papers noted, "he passed through Whitesboro on his way to Delaware Bend and the Yellow Hills country." He had a friend there named Jim Taylor.

Taylor was a veteran officer. Heck had made his acquaintance while killing time at the end of express runs when Taylor was a constable and deputy sheriff of Dexter precinct. Now he was a deputy United States Marshal in the Chickasaw Nation, working for the Fort Smith court. Among other qualifications, he was extremely handy with a gun.

Heck said grimly: "I'm looking for the Lees." He gave Taylor a hopeful glance. "I'd like you to help."

"What is your plan?" Taylor inquired.

"To stalk them until they cross Red River onto Texas soil, where they have neither kinfolk nor friends," Heck replied.

Taylor agreed. "If we capture them in the Territory, we'd never get them to Gainesville to claim the reward."

A two months' investigation failed to unearth even the slightest lead as to where the two killers were hiding. Every inch of the Delaware Bend lagoons and jungles was scoured. The valleys and slopes of the Chickasaw Nation were inspected carefully for any sign of a trail. Doc Lee, another brother, and two sisters lived near Delaware Bend, but Pink and Jim had not been seen at their homes.

Heck voiced a growing realization to Taylor: "They've left the country, and I don't think they'll return until the heat dies down."

"Then we should go into hiding ourselves and give them a chance to show," Taylor suggested.

"Yes, I suppose that is the most sensible thing to do," Heck agreed.

They established headquarters on a hill on the Strother Brown farm, between Dexter and Delaware Bend, across the river from the Lee clan. Another week passed, without any significant revelations, and they were thoroughly downcast.

One night Heck arose from a cold supper they had eaten without a fire and announced quietly: "I'm going over to see Strother Brown."

"You have some sort of lead?" Taylor asked, searching his face.

"Just an idea," he replied, cryptically.

Heck insisted that Taylor remain in camp. Alone, he would have a better chance of making the trip without attracting attention.

At sunup, he was back. The perplexed, frustrated lines had

left his face, his eyes were bright and calm. "I had a chat with Jim Shattles."

Taylor looked at Heck, surprised. "You mean the Roff spy? The Lees have been after him for months. I thought he'd left the country to keep them from killing him."

"He's back," Heck said. "We're spreading the word that he's hiding at Strother Brown's."

August faded into September, with still no news of the killers, and Heck and Jim Taylor began to grumble about the futile quest.

Then, the night of September 6, Pink and Jim Lee crossed the river, headed for Brown's pasture. At sunup, Heck and Taylor saw them approach on the knoll of open prairie and dismount to cut the fence.

A long branch ran through the prairie near where the outlaws stood. The officers, entirely concealed from view, traveled up it to a point where it forked near the crest of the hill. They peeped over the top. The Lees were seventy-five yards away, gazing toward Brown's house.

"If they show fight," Heck whispered, "you take the short one and I'll take the tall one."

They arose with Winchesters, and Heck called out: "Hands up—we're officers!"

The Lees dropped their nippers and seized their rifles. Heck and Taylor fired almost simultaneously. Pink spun and fell, blood gushing from his head and ears. Jim knelt on the grass, pumping three wild shots before he pitched forward, blood running from his neck.

While Taylor rounded up their horses, Heck gathered up their weapons. They borrowed Strother Brown's team and wagon, loaded the bodies into it, and headed for Gainesville.

Pat Ware was sitting in the sheriff's office when he glanced out the window and saw the fast-moving team and wagon swing to a half turn in front of the jail and back up to the small front porch. He saw the two men climb down from the spring seat, unhitch the traces, and wrap the brake handle with the reins, then walk to the rear of the wagon. They removed the endgate, pulled out a dead man, and laid him on the porch.

Ware hurried into the hallway entrance. When he opened the

front door, he saw two dead men on the porch, covered with blood.

He recognized Jim Taylor, then looked up at the striking figure beside him wearing a Stetson, corduroy trousers tucked in top boots, flannel shirt open at the neck, six-shooters in holsters hung to a filled cartridge belt, and Winchester in his hand. His keen eyes were like black diamonds. With his well-kept, rather long mustache shading a firm-set mouth, and a small goatee, he looked like a carved thing of bronze.

"Are you the sheriff of Cooke County?" he asked, slowly and in a low tone.

Ware told him he was his deputy.

"I'm Heck Thomas," Heck said. "Taylor and I have just returned from a hunting trip. Them," he added, pointing with his rifle to the bodies on the porch, "are what's left of Pink and Jim Lee. The reward calls for their delivery at the jail door, and I want a receipt."

Ware looked doubtful. "Sheriff Hill is out of town, and I've never seen Pink and Jim Lee. But I'll give you a receipt for two dead men."

Heck asked for a sheet of paper. He wrote a claim for the rewards and tacked it to the jail wall with a butt of a six-shooter.

By this time a curious group had gathered. A hack driver inspected the bodies and said, "Them's Pink and Jim Lee!"

The bartender from a saloon on the square exclaimed: "Damned if they ain't!"

The blacksmith and liveryman identified the dead men.

Finally, Ware invited Heck inside. He wrote him a receipt, and Heck returned to the wagon.

He put in the endgate and screwed up the rod while Taylor hitched the traces. Then they climbed to the spring seat, and with a "Giddap!" left town with the team in a long lope, leaving the crowd staring at the bodies.

5

Riding for Judge Parker

The bodies were removed to the courthouse, stripped, washed, and clothed in new shirts and trousers. No relatives appeared to claim the remains, and they were buried in the Gainesville cemetery at county expense. Governor John Ireland declared the feat "one of the most remarkable in the history of Texas law enforcement!" There was a "general feeling of relief" that the Lees were dead, and the citizens of Delaware Bend "went back to their vocations without fear of molestation."

Heck and Jim Taylor shared the reward paid by Alva Roff, and Heck returned to Fort Worth.

He found the local citizens "unstinted in their praise for him." Those who had followed his banner to defeat as candidate for city marshal "felt a thrill of exultation which amply recompensed their bitter disappointment."

"He will get there yet," they predicted.

City Marshal W. M. Rea's term would not expire until 1887. But a new election was approaching in Tarrant County. Within the week, leaders of the Democratic Association visited Heck at his detective agency.

"We would like to put you on our ticket as the next sheriff for Tarrant County," a spokesman said.

Heck thanked them and asked for time to mull it over. After the delegation had departed, he found himself torn by indecision.

It revolved around Isabelle, who was so sensitive to conditions on the frontier. She wanted to return to Georgia.

"Stay in Texas," Governor Ireland told Heck, when he paid a visit to Austin to collect the state reward for the Lee brothers. "I want you in the Rangers. In no time you could become a lieutenant."

Heck declined the commission.

As the story of his killing of the Lees spread over the Southwest, he received strong offers from tough towns in Arizona and New Mexico. But his thoughts were to the north, across Red River, where the handful of deputy United States Marshals from Fort Smith were making a desperate effort to exterminate the outlaw bands in the Indian Territory.

Finally, he told Isabelle: "There is a real need for Federal officers in the Territory, and they say Fort Smith is a modern city, with churches and schools for our children. . . ."

Isabelle agreed. More than anything she wanted to leave Texas. A change, thought Heck, was all she needed.

But there was more to the motive that moved him. Somewhere up in the Territory, with a $400 price on his head, was the last of the Lee gang, Della Humby.

That night, he mailed an application to Colonel John Carroll, a Virginian and Confederate veteran, whom President Cleveland had appointed United States Marshal for the Western District of Arkansas, asking to join his force.

Within two weeks he had a reply signed by Chief Deputy Marshal Alexander Vandeventer. The letter asked him to come to Fort Smith for an interview and bring written recommendations from Texas peace officers.

Heck sent his family to visit Cousin Jim in Galveston and caught the first train to Arkansas. He was in Fort Smith the next day. He was a bit nervous as Chief Deputy Vandeventer checked his credentials and admitted him to see Carroll.

Physically the marshal was a big man even for the frontier. Though less than six feet in height, he weighed nearly two hundred pounds, and it was not fat that bulged his massive shoulders. He still wore his hair longer than the current fashion, just as his drooping mustaches and heavy sideburns trailing down his cheeks into a sweeping, gray beard were the heritage of another day. He wore a fine business suit with the trousers tight and unwrinkled on long legs; his boots were made by hand and stitched with a fanciful design; around his waist was a strongly made cartridge belt with a beaten silver buckle, and in a slick, worn leather holster was a ridiculously long-barreled Colt.

They tell a lot of stories about John Carroll in Arkansas—how he spent his early years with the Cherokees east of the Mississippi and married a fullblood Cherokee woman at Fort Gibson; of the numerous battles he fought throughout the Civil War, and his hell-raising crusades as a member of the Arkansas Legislature and the Constitutional Convention of 1874, before becoming United States Marshal. Certainly, he never won a reputation for having an amicable disposition, but he soon put his prospective recruit at ease. Heck found that the ground had been unexpectedly smoothed for him.

"Thomas," the marshal said, "I've already talked to one of my deputies who speaks highly of you—Jim Taylor, out in the Chickasaw Nation."

Heck relaxed. "Jim's a right good officer. He helped me bring in the Lee boys."

Carroll studied Heck carefully. "They say you went after them for the reward."

Heck nodded. "That—and because nobody believed they could be brought in."

"It took guts," the marshal commented. "We don't like to get complaints from people out in the Territory telling us that our deputies didn't have the guts to go after somebody. You know there is no salary—that you will have to depend on fees and mileage?"

"Yes, sir," Heck replied.

"You will receive six cents a mile when on official business, fifty cents for serving papers, two dollars for an arrest, and a dollar a day expense money while chasing criminals—if you present receipts and vouchers in order. Out in the Territory, you'll be lucky to get one in the English language."

Heck made no protest about the fees and mileage, and the

41

marshal continued: "You will be allowed seventy-five cents a day to feed each prisoner, but you make your own arrangements for yourself and guards. Expenses like buying information and splits with volunteer posse come out of your pocket. If you bring in your man, you can claim ten cents for you and your prisoner; if you kill him, you get nothing—and you forfeit the dollar a day expense money for chasing him before the gun fight."

"A man could come out in such cases if he picked up a reward," Heck suggested.

The marshal's laugh grated on him. "Don't count on rewards, Thomas. The Government sometimes offers them for mail robbery and the murder of Federal employees, but you can't collect them because you're already being paid by the United States to catch these criminals." Then, irritably, he added: "Usually we can't even get the rewards offered by express companies and private parties."

The profit was in fees and mileage. A trip paid well when an officer brought in a large batch of prisoners.

This was the financial side of the ledger. The other concerned Heck's personal welfare.

A deputy could be sent to any part of the Territory. Not only must he hunt down his quarry in remote places, but he had to live with his prisoners, often for months, camping under the stars with his rifle across his knees, until he could return with them to Fort Smith.

This required alertness at every moment. Often a whisky peddler was more dangerous than a murderer.

Willard Ayers was a rough-and-ready deputy, who, for nine years, had demonstrated his skill and resourcefulness as an officer of the court. Then he went to arrest Emmanuel Patterson on a charge of larceny.

"Open up!" he ordered, pounding on the door of the shack where the Negro had taken refuge. "I'm a Federal officer!"

It was routine. He had spoken the words a hundred times. But Patterson was nervous and frightened. Firing through the door, he shot the deputy. The Government had offered a reward for the killer. So had Columbus Ayers, a local clothing merchant and Willard's brother. But Patterson was still at large.

Again, in 1883, popular Addison Beck, a peaceful, gentle man

42

with a wife and three children, had gone after two thieves and come back dead. One of his killers had been wounded by a posse and died before his trial, but the other had escaped. So Beck's death was only partially avenged.

Eleven other deputies had been badly wounded and crippled for life while making arrests for minor offenses.

And there was always the possibility of attack.

The criminal classes who had fled to the Territory for the protection of its wild prairies and mountain fastness looked upon the marshals as intruders and often connived together to prevent them from performing their duties. In 1885, Dave Layman, one of the oldest officers in point of service, had been ambushed while bringing in a load of prisoners.

As Marshal Carroll put it: "We're the most hated humans and the most hunted by the badmen."

The current topic of conversation was the cold-blooded murder of Deputy William Irwin. A few weeks before, he had started from Webbers Falls with Felix Griffin, a member of the Starr gang, whom he had arrested for robbery. Griffin's pals had concealed themselves at Pheasant Bluff, on the Arkansas River, and shot Irwin in the back as he rode past.

"Like Beck, he left a family. But the Government makes no provisions for their families," the marshal told Heck. "There is no medical fee, nothing for disability or burial. They were just ordinary mortals, who took their jobs to feed their wives and children."

Still Heck made no objection and answered "yes" when Carroll asked him if he still wanted a commission. He wanted to tell the marshal just how he felt about the glories of serving the cause of justice on this wildest frontier. Instead, he said, simply: "I have a wife and children to feed too."

The marshal told him he would do; the next day, Heck appeared for his formal appointment, and was handed his first territorial assignment.

Rist McDonald and Cab Bruce owned the stage on the mail route between Fort Smith and Muskogee, a distance of one hundred miles. They received a salary from the Government for carrying the mail and ten dollars per passenger.

"There've been several holdups and a lot of whisky peddling

43

along this route," Marshal Carroll said. "See what you can do about putting an end to this situation."

Heck was assigned to work with Orrington "Red" Lucas. Lucas was a lanky, sandy-haired deputy who had served as a detective on the Muncie, Indiana, police department before coming to Fort Smith in 1883. Although it was his case, Heck was willing to listen to an experienced officer's suggestions. Lucas was a good friend of McDonald and Bruce. On the next run, Red hired out as stage driver, and Heck became his passenger.

There was a stage stand north of Sallisaw where they picked up fresh horses. Heck and Red reached the stand at midnight. They crossed the Big and Little Vian and the Big and Little Sallisaw by ford to the Arkansas, crossed the Arkansas a mile below the Illinois and, a couple miles farther, reached the next stand at Webbers Falls. The route cut northwest, then across Dirty Creek to the top of Brushy Mountain. From there it was twelve miles to Muskogee.

Most of the holdups had occurred on this last leg of the journey. In the moonlight, Heck spotted, at the bottom of the mountain between two hills, a lonesome-looking cabin with a couple of sheds.

"A likely hide-out," he remarked to Lucas.

On their return trip, they stopped near the cabin. While Lucas pretended to repair a piece of harness, Heck stepped to the front door.

He knocked and a voice said, "Come in."

As he entered, a big man with a heavy beard and a mouth like a steel trap sat facing him with a six-shooter. A second man, with thin gray hair and little button eyes, entered the back door, carrying a rifle.

"It's only the stage driver and his passenger," said the man with the rifle.

"The driver was fixin' the harness; I didn't think anybody lived here," Heck explained.

They looked at him steadily from under their hat brims and inquired about deputy marshals.

"Haven't seen one the whole trip," Heck lied.

The pair seemed to relax. In another moment, Lucas signaled

that he was ready; Heck returned to the stage, and they continued toward Fort Smith.

The next day, they led a posse across Brushy Mountain and swooped down on the cabin. But the suspects had fled. Heck was unable to identify either man and never saw them again. But the holdups stopped.

The whisky peddling flourished. Heck was amazed at some of the methods used. Men carried bottles in the tops of their boots. Some rolled bottles in the curtains of the stagecoach. Sometimes they used drums covered with leather and shaped like traveling bags. Or the goods would be hidden in the regular luggage, or the false bottoms of suitcases. The entire population along the route appeared to be bootleggers or outlaws.

Heck consulted with Marshal Carroll. "Better make a swing around and clean up," the marshal said.

Heck rented a hotel suite for his family and sent train tickets to Isabelle and the children in Galveston. Then, armed with a score of capiases, he headed for the Territory, hoping to return before his family reached Fort Smith.

He took Lucas and Deputies George Williams and L. P. Isbell, a half-dozen good riding horses, a chuck wagon loaded with provisions and extra ammunition, and two wagons with drivers for prisoners. They rolled westward over Indian trails through the Cherokee Nation, crossing the Arkansas into Creek country, then cut south over the Canadian into the San Bois Mountains and the land of the Choctaws. Deep in hostile territory, with a main camp established, the prison wagons began roving the region in the wake of the deputies on horseback.

Heck paid little attention to the names on the warrants he carried. They could be changed easily. He went by a face or characteristic—a habit he had developed as a policeman in Atlanta. By observing a person a few moments, he could remember what he needed to know about him.

Each arrest he made he took possession of the prisoner's property and issued a receipt. The property would be turned over to the jailer at Fort Smith. The prisoner was shackled and placed in the bottom of one of the wagons. The drivers rode on high spring seats, unarmed lest the prisoners got any foolish ideas about escaping, and armed guards rode comfortably on horseback a short distance away.

Unlike a posse, which must register at the marshal's office before starting a trip, guards were picked up as needed along the way. A guard's only duty was to see that the prisoners did not break custody. Sometimes Heck rode alongside them, studying the captives as an essential to his life and work. By watching a man's actions a couple of days, he could tell whether he should be trusted or kept in chains. Heck took no chances with recalcitrants. But he never abused one, nor allowed his posse to do so.

In camp at night he saw that the prisoners made themselves useful. They peeled potatoes, chopped firewood, and washed the tinware. If they grumbled, they didn't eat. At bedtime, he fastened a chain to a tree or through the wheels of the wagons, and shackled them to it like fish on a string. He slept nearby.

It was an eerie expedition that set the blood tingling—a daredevil crew in which the coward and the shirker had no place. The smoke of battle was always imminent . . .

The second week out, Heck and Lucas were in one of the wagons, scouting a thinly settled section on San Bois Creek. Having been without sleep until it seemed they could stay awake no longer, they pitched camp early in a patch of timber near a grass-grown trail.

Supper was cooked and the fire extinguished before sundown. As the long twilight deepened across the wide prairies, they spread their blankets about sixty feet from the wagon. With always the chance of assassination, they knew that the enemy would first examine the ground where the wagon stood.

It was an indefinable gray night with a moon banked behind clouds. Objects could be seen moving at a distance. About 2 A.M., a half-dozen riders passed along the trail within twenty feet of them.

Heck nudged Lucas awake. As they listened, the hoofbeats entered a little draw to the south and ceased. In this lonely place at this hour, the riders could be up to no good. Having sighted the marshals' horses and wagon in the timber, they were creeping back to shoot them while they slept.

"Let's get out of here!" Heck said.

46

Their rifles were under their blankets. They agreed that Heck would suddenly seize his Winchester and sit upright, ready to return any fire, while Lucas rolled into the brush and, in turn, covered Heck's escape.

"Now!" Heck whispered, and jerked erect. Lucas went rolling into the brush, and Heck rolled after him.

At the same instant a half-dozen guns blazed at the wagon, cutting spokes from the wheels. Heck wormed out into some high grass, but he was unable to recognize the attackers as they dashed off into the night.

Afterward, he could always sense when anyone was approaching. It was like electricity in the air. He could be sound asleep, and if something moved noiselessly toward him, its presence would awaken him.

The prairie dog and rattlesnake became his closest neighbors. Sometimes he would ride alone all day and not see a person. Maybe the next day he would see one or two Indians.

He always watched for the smoke of a campfire. Sooner or later, the man he was trailing would make fire for food. Usually it wouldn't be the right man at all. Occasionally it was someone who would give information.

But Heck never expected assistance from anybody. Fear made most natives hesitant. Many a wanton, unpunished murder had shown that there was a real basis for this fear. There were whole communities that practiced a sort of asylum in exchange for immunity.

The arrival of the prison wagons in the settlements was a social event. People gathered around to see who the marshals had picked up this time. If they held a warrant for some member of the populace, he had been added to their cargo when the wagons rolled on.

More often, the moment the wagons were sighted in the neighborhood, those wanted were hidden, or fled. There was always a border class who gave assistance and warning to the criminal.

The Indians talked very little. They made signs and grunted. Most were friendly. If one told a marshal anything, it was the truth. If he promised anything, he kept his word. If he liked an officer, he would die for him. But if he shook his head and threw his arm away from his place, the marshal had better leave.

Heck stopped at an Indian's cabin to get directions. The door opened, a gun was stuck in his face, and he was told to "fill the saddle."

As Heck explained to his companions later: "There was plenty room in my saddle and other ways of finding out where I was."

If he sighted a lone tree, he rode to it, for he could always find a trail. Everyone used lone trees as landmarks. He rode to a huge oak on Mill's Prairie at the head of San Bois Creek, where a trail crossed the Winding Stair Mountains toward Texas.

A sign, printed with black paint and nailed to the tree, read: "Mr. Deputy Marshal, this is the dead line. When you cross it, you take your life in your own hands."

Heck disregarded the warning. When his wagons rolled back to Fort Smith, he had in custody four men wanted since December, 1878, for the slaying of Matthew Fletcher on a farm near Jimtown. He had four other prisoners—two men charged with killing a boy at Burneyville, a horse thief, and a whisky peddler.

Lucas had two whites charged with robbing Turk's store at Oklahoma. Deputy Williams had a pair of cattle thieves, and Isbell had five prisoners in tow—a bigamist, two thieves, a man who had shot and killed a Creek Negro in the brush, mistaking him for a turkey, and the burly mulatto, John Stephens, who had murdered Annie Kerr, a widow, and her 16-year-old son for testifying against him in a larceny case. Stephens had entered their home at night, while they slept, and chopped off their heads.

A huge crowd gathered at the docks to see the wagons ferried across the river. The Little Rock and Fort Smith Railroad extended through the Indian Territory across the Arkansas, but ferryboats and skiffs were the only means of conveying merchandise and passengers to the city. It would be another three years before Jay Gould (whose Pacific Express Company had squeezed Heck's outfit out of Texas) promoted the construction of a combination railroad and wagon bridge that would connect the depot and the town.

All Fort Smith, accustomed to such arrivals as it was, rushed from store doorways, offices, and kitchens to gawk as the caravan

48

rolled into Garrison Avenue. A score or more strung out behind the wagons and followed them to the entrance gates in the grim stone walls of the abandoned fort at the end of the street.

The wagons stopped before the two-story brick barracks building that had been partitioned for a court room, jury room, and offices for clerks, attorneys, and the United States Marshal. Its basement, eight feet deep and divided by solid stone walls, served as a jail. The jail prisoners shoved their faces against the barred, small basement windows and hooted and yelled while the deputies discharged their cargo. Then the jail guards took over, the crowd broke up as the new prisoners were marched into the damp, foul-smelling dungeon, and the main gate closed.

Heck filed his claims and turned in his reports at the marshal's office. For the past week he had been dreaming of getting back to Fort Smith again, thinking of a soft bed, hot grub, and the fee and mileage money he'd collect—but none of these mattered now. . . . When you rode for Judge Parker, you rode for the most remarkable court in the annals of jurisprudence. You rode for the greatest distinctive tribunal in the world—no other existed with jurisdiction over so great an area—and there was a vast amount of work to be done.

The end of an expedition was the time to relax. His drivers and guards headed for the nearest saloon to celebrate. Marshal Carroll told him that Isabelle and the children had arrived from Galveston. Heck hurried to the hotel for a long-awaited visit with his family.

6

Winter Campaign

Heck found little time to spend with his family in the months that followed. Arresting criminals was only a part of his work; he had to be present throughout the long court trials and ready, at a moment's notice, to mount and ride posthaste to bring in some much-needed witness.

Witnesses often failed to report, and made themselves scarce. If he summoned one without a subpoena, he was held responsible for the fees. And when he signed an information, he must have seen the witnesses by whom he expected to sustain the charge before he was allowed the writ.

This rule was strictly observed by Judge Parker as a protection to the citizens from unnecessary arrest, protection to the Government against useless expense, and protection to the deputy marshals, whose accounts were disallowed if the prosecution was shown to have been frivolous. He commented often on Heck's loyal assistance to the bench and the careful manner in which he obtained evidence.

But criticism arose in the Territory. A petition was sent to the court asking for Heck's removal because he swore out too many warrants.

Heck was out in the Nations at the time. When he returned, Parker summoned him to his quarters in the old stone commissary building.

The judge was a bigger man than Heck, over six feet tall, with broader shoulders, a square-set jaw, piercing blue eyes and tawny mustache and goatee. When he spoke, his deep basso voice filled the room:

"What do you know about this?"

Heck scanned the petition, then smiled. "Your Honor," he said, "I brought in sixteen prisoners this trip. Four of them have signed this paper, all arrested on writs sworn out by the district attorney himself."

The judge turned to the window, keen eyes staring into the jail yard. Three hundred feet away, on the site formerly occupied by the fort's powder magazine and within his clear view, stood the famous gallows which already had launched more than two-score souls to eternity. It was a strong structure, with a twelve-by-twelve I beam supported by heavy timbers, and four traps furnishing room for twelve men to drop to their deaths simultaneously. Suddenly he faced Heck, thanked him for coming, and dismissed him without another word.

When the four prisoners were arraigned, they pleaded guilty. Judge Parker sentenced them to long terms in prison.

As Heck noted later, "I firmly believe, had their crimes warranted it, that they would have died on the rope."

One thing Heck learned early was that the criminal class and their relatives never tired of telling lies about the deputy marshals, even on the witness stand and at the risk of a charge of perjury. One of their stock tales, told with many variations about different officers, was how they put whisky in wagons and buggies of their victims and then arrested them for introducing it.

Something like that may have happened, but Heck never knew of an actual case. Anyway, why should an officer go to all the expense and trouble of buying whisky and putting it in a man's wagon or buggy when he could find plenty of them already supplied with the stuff?

"The trouble is," Judge Parker explained, "you don't have to cater to this class for votes. You get your commission from the marshal, and he got his from the President; so there are only three things they can do—jab you, lie on you, or kill you."

Heck said, "They've tried all three."

The criminal in the Territory had felt the brunt of his activity. During his first six months with the court there were few issues of the weekly Fort Smith *Elevator* that did not contain the customary phrase: "Deputy Thomas came in since our last with the following prisoners . . ."

His exploits were the talk of Fort Smith, and his children listened in wide-eyed fascination to his stories of adventure, until Isabelle would protest.

"I just won't have their lives shaped by such tales. I should think you could talk to them about something besides robbers and murderers and those thieving Indians."

"The ones who gave up their lands to the whites in Georgia?" Heck asked.

"What?"

"Oh—nothing."

She tried to adjust to the routine, the new discomforts. But the abandon and brutality of this more primitive frontier stunned her. With all the employment opportunities back East for a peace officer of her husband's caliber, why did he have to take the risks of a foot-loose lawman?

Heck tried to explain. "It's the beginning of a new empire, Belle." His voice was sympathetic, almost melodious. "Out there" —he waved a hand to the west— "one day there will be a great civilization. And we'll know that we had a big hand in building it."

"Oh, bosh!" she said.

But often their brief periods together were pleasant. She was amazed at the knowledge he had acquired of the country and its people. Heck loved this wide land where the sky and evening stars were the only visible limits, and the bluestem touched his saddle skirts. She had never seen him so happy.

Once he rented a fancy rig and took her for a sight-seeing trip into the Nations. To relieve her tension and fears, he joked and roared snatches of songs handed down through generations of his people from England:

> O, Nannie, wilt thou gang wi' me, Nor sigh to
> leave the flaunting town?

52

Can silent glens have charms for thee, The lowly
cot, and russet gown?

A few minutes later she saw him shoot and badly wound a
half-breed trying to steal their horses, which they had unhitched
and left to water in a stream while they climbed to the top of
a rocky knoll to survey the countryside. The cursing, foul-smelling
prisoner rode handcuffed in the seat between them as they drove
back to Fort Smith.

The experience left her shaken. But not nearly so as a few
nights later when there was another killing in one of the west-
side saloons, and a stray bullet crashed through their hotel
window, shattering glass across the sleeping children.

"Henry," she cried—she always called him by his given name—
"it's even worse than Texas!"

Heck shook his head gently. "Simmer down, Belle. Fort Smith
will. Why, in two years its population has jumped to 11,000.
Already it's a city of the first class, with sidewalks, gasworks,
electric lights, and one of the best waterworks in the South. Its
cotton market handles nearly 50,000 bales each season. There
are two gristmills, three big sawmills, two furniture and a half-
dozen wagon factories, and the great United States Court is
disbursing over $200,000 a year. Three big schools are being
built for whites and one for Negro children.

"We'll move out of this hotel—buy a home here. Most folk
are Southerners like ourselves, and respect a deputy marshal's
wife."

Isabelle flared up at his reasoning. "I don't want to rear our
children behind a gun. We both came from refined religious
families, and you seem to forget it with all your new glory. Well,
I haven't forgot—for either of us!"

This little set-to jarred Heck. But he smiled sweetly, and took
her in his arms. "Somewhere out there," he said, "I'll find Della
Humby."

Then he was off again to the Nations, while her life progressed
into one of homesickness and loneliness and sleepless nights.

In August, when their fifth child, a son named Lovick, was
born, Heck was still away. Isabelle bore the burden with the help
of the older children.

She was quite serene. Vaguely she wondered why he had not returned. Of course nothing had happened. He had always come in unscathed.

And in another part of her mind she imagined a dozen dreadful things. Indians. Why not? Many a white had died in the Territory at the hands of these wily red men who called themselves civilized. Perhaps there had been a moment of carelessness with one of his prisoners. He might have been shot from ambush. She could almost see his body lying out there, chewed by some wild thing, waiting to be discovered by some lone traveler. . . .

In sudden panic she arose from her bed, tossed a robe about her shoulders, and rushed to the marshal's office. There was no word from Heck. But Marshal Carroll was kindly and reassuring. No use worrying like that. He took her home.

The rest of the night she sat alone, waiting, ashen-faced, her eyes fixed in a kind of horror. She would never see her husband alive again. . . .

Then Heck returned from the Choctaw country with another load of prisoners, and she felt sheepish, looked very wan in her prim gray dress, with tears streaming down her cheeks, running down the street to meet him. And Heck smiled more sweetly than ever, and his posse looked at him, an enigmatic glint of humor in their weather-beaten faces.

Heck was pleased with their new son. He was at home for some time. But he soon grew restless, anxious to be off on another expedition. At Christmas, he was away again. His winter campaign took him far west into the Chickasaw Nation.

On Christmas Day, he and his posse made camp on the Washita, between Erin Springs and Whitebead Hill. They had fourteen prisoners for the court and were scouting the country for more. Heck ordered his camp cook to give them a turkey dinner, having provided two fine birds for the occasion.

About 11 A.M., a big Dutchman, pale and breathless, dashed into camp.

"Iss der Fort Smith deputy marshal here? Der cowboys at Whitebead iss drunk und iss shooting my house down und iss scaring mine vife to death!" he cried.

Satisfied that it was only a Christmas frolic and the cowboys would do no real damage, Heck persuaded him to put up his horse and eat.

A moment later, a second man came crashing through the brush, a bloody scarf about his head and covered with gore to his feet. He reported that he had been shot in an argument with the cowboys the night before, the bullet plowing around his scalp without penetrating the skull. Regaining consciousness after several hours, he had fled to the marshals' camp for protection.

Heck cleaned and dressed his wound, and invited him to dinner. As they were sitting down to eat, a tall, gaunt Negro in a soldier's overcoat galloped up on a lathered mule and flung himself down before the fire.

"Is Heck Thomas, de U. S. Marshal, here?"

Heck answered, "I am Heck Thomas."

"Please den, for God's sake, Mista' Thomas, help me! Mah name's Robin Grayson. Out here close to Johnsonville at Unc' Isaac Carolina's, dey tried to kill me, an' dey shots dese holes in mah coat. If you help me, I stay with you 'til we git dese niggers, for if you don't ketch dem, dey gwine ketch me. Dey is Tom Ike and Della Humby."

Heck's pulses leaped. It was the first word he'd had of Humby since the Roff murders.

"I want Humby bad," Heck replied, "and I hold warrants for Tom Ike for larceny, whisky selling, and assault with intent to kill."

Grayson's tremulous jowls relaxed as his big lips spread in a smile that showed blue gums and long, fanglike teeth. *Black outside but a good heart inside,* Heck thought. *You'll make a good scout.*

After dinner, he sent one of his posse to Whitebead Hill with the Dutchman. The Dutchman's house hadn't been shot down, but the cowboys had shot away its chimney and left town, whooping and yelling.

Meanwhile, Heck took Grayson and John Swain, another deputy, and started for Johnsonville. Christmas night they camped in the South Canadian bottoms where the down timber was plentiful. They remained there until the following afternoon while Grayson did some scouting among his kin.

About 3 P.M., he returned with good news. "Dey's gwine to be a double weddin' at Quash Carolina's at 4 o'clock. Tom Ike and Humby will be dere."

The place was four miles from their camp. The marshals hurried through the timber, getting as close to the double log building as possible without showing themselves.

Heck instructed Swain: "You charge the west side of the house and a little beyond. I'll make my run to the east and a little beyond, so nobody can get away to the north, and I can watch the south side too."

They ran at breakneck speed across the clearing. Della Humby wasn't there, but Tom Ike was. He grabbed his rifle and backed to a tree, facing them. But his nerve failed when Heck threatened to blow him in two.

Heck found two others on the ground that he wanted—John Davis, a huge, fine-looking Negro, who had killed a white boy at Brownswood, Texas, and Emmanuel Patterson, who had murdered Deputy Ayers six years before. He arrested them and returned to camp. When Grayson saw that he didn't have Humby, he became frantic.

"Why, Mista' Heck, soon as you leave, dat nigger will git me shore!"

It snowed hard during the night and turned cold. The next morning, Tom Ike told them that Humby was headed for the wilds of the Seminole country, where he had a number of friends and relatives.

Heck ordered Swain to take the prisoners back to their camp on the Washita. "I'll take blue-gum for a guide and go after Humby."

The temperature dropped toward zero during the day. They reached Grayson's shack down the river at nightfall. Grayson's wife cooked them a big pan of spare ribs with brown gravy, hot corn bread, yam potatoes, and black coffee. Heck remembered it as one of the best meals of his life. He slept warm, but "not too dry." Before daylight, they were riding again.

It was so cold now that their quarry couldn't stay in the woods. Humby began showing up at houses along the edge of the settlements to get something to eat and warm.

In mid-afternoon, they arrived at the home of a widow, Lizzie Harris, a Chickasaw woman who lived on Sand Creek. She had a fire roaring in the fireplace and coffee boiling in a can.

As they sipped at their cups, she told them Humby had visited her only hours before, half frozen and in an ugly temper. He had inquired about the ford across the Canadian and the best trail to Sasakwa.

"I let him thaw and gave him some coffee," Lizzie said.

Then he had tried to make love to the widow, cursed her when she resisted, and stalked out, boasting that he would fight if the whole United States came after him.

Heck and Grayson took a short cut over the river. The water was only half side deep to a horse and the ice about half strong enough to support a horse and rider. Heck rode in with a club and broke their way through.

On December 29, they reached Sasakwa where John Brown, wealthy Seminole chief, had built his mansion and operated a trading post and store. Chief Brown summoned an Indian policeman to assist them. Just before dark, they located Humby in the abandoned cabin of an old trader named Manual Beunes.

Now came the ticklish part. Humby was inside, seated in the chimney corner by the fire and armed with a rifle and six-shooter.

"Robin," Heck whispered, "that door looks weak. I want you to hit it. Turn the knob quick and strong and throw it open the first flirt you make. If it's fastened inside, you must break it down, or Humby will kill both of us."

Luckily, the door wasn't locked. As Grayson burst it open, Heck sprang into the room, Winchester breast high, and shouting:

"Hands up!"

Humby raised his left hand, but his right grasped his rifle.

"Both hands up," snapped Heck, "or you're a dead man!"

Then Grayson was in the room beside him, yelling: "Yes—bofe of 'em, bofe of 'em!"

Heck seized Humby's weapons. It was dark now. He had

57

Grayson to saddle Humby's pony. He started to handcuff the prisoner to the saddle, but decided it was too cold. He thought about shackling his feet under the pony's belly, but decided against that also.

The moon came up, shining as bright as day on the snow. Heck handed Humby's bridle reins to Grayson, and said, "Della, you sit straight and look between that pony's ears. If you make a wrong move, I'll kill you before you hit the ground."

It took them two days to get back to camp on the Washita, and in the middle of January, Heck reached Fort Smith with his prisoners.

Emmanuel Patterson got life for killing Deputy Ayers, and died in prison. Davis was prosecuted in Texas. Tom Ike received a stiff sentence for his crime.

Humby was ably defended by Fort Smith attorneys, who fought his case through two terms of court. In the first trial, he was found guilty; in the second, acquitted. And when Heck went to collect the $400 reward, he learned that it had been withdrawn.

In concluding his sketch of the campaign, he wrote: "I only received my mileage and fees, and felt I earned them. . . . I took Grayson to Columbus Ayers' store and bought him a black suit, a black hat and black shoes, then took him to see Marshal Carroll. When I told the colonel how he had helped me capture Humby, the old Negro looked at one of us then the other and tears like pearls and big as the end of my thumb fell from his eyes."

7

Law of the Forty-Five

After capturing Della Humby, Heck had planned
to be in Fort Smith long enough to buy a house and
settle his family. But the unpredictable luck of deputy marshals who rode for the Federal Court willed
otherwise; a young man and his wife named Marriot
had been murdered in the Kiamichi Mountains, southeast of
Talihina.

The Marriots were from southern Kansas. They had been
married only two weeks and en route to Texas on a honeymoon,
traveling on one horse, which the wife rode, and carrying a small
suitcase of personal belongings.

In this sparsely settled section of the Choctaw Nation, they
had stopped at the home of Wa-har-key Son, who had two wives
and several children, to ask directions. As they started on, Wa-
har-key Son and his old father followed stealthily. They ambushed Marriot, pursued his wife as she fled in terror to the
top of a high bluff overlooking a stony creek, and shot her. Her
body fell down the embankment and lodged in the stream. They
piled rocks on it, leaving it where it had fallen, then buried the
husband in a shallow grave nearby. They burned the suitcase, but
kept the horse and the saddle. Later, one of Wa-har-key Son's
wives became jealous of the other, and reported the murders.

By the time Heck reached the cabin, Wa-har-key Son and his
father had fled. Heck knew the other wife would tell him noth-

ing, and the jealous one could not give evidence against her husband. So he made friends with the children.

One was a boy of twelve. Heck took him hunting. When they were alone in the woods, he asked him about the white man and woman.

The boy was reluctant. "My father will kill me if I tell."

But Heck promised that no harm would come to him.

Finally, the boy said, "Father is angry because so many whites come into the country."

He showed Heck the shallow grave and the creek where the victims lay buried. The stream had shifted the woman under the rocks. One hand and arm protruded from the water. Heck removed the stones and cut some curiously shaped red buttons and a piece of dress from the decomposed body for identification. Then the boy led him to the hide-out of the two Indians on the Kiamichi River, where Heck arrested them and recovered the horse and the saddle.

He took the boy to Fort Smith and placed him under the protection of the court. At the trial, the little fellow wouldn't talk or answer questions. Then Heck noticed the father watching him with an evil eye. He called this to the court's attention. When the boy was placed where the baleful look would not be encountered, he told the whole story. The boy was sent to a Government school for Indian children. The men were convicted and sentenced to life terms in prison.

Within a week, Heck was working on another tough case. He had started to Red River to bring in a bright mulatto woman named Cherry Scott, who arose one morning, dressed herself, picked up her stepfather's pistol, and deliberately shot her mother through the head while she slept. Heck stopped at Limestone Gap to pick up a few provisions at the general store when he heard that a young farm hand named Ed Davis had been found murdered on the outskirts of town.

The only officers in the vicinity were marshals traveling through, so he went to the scene and began an investigation. Davis had been missing several days after attending a dance in the neighborhood, and some boys passing through a cornfield had discovered his body.

The dance had been held at the house of George Morris, whose father made his home with young Morris and his wife. The old man had played the fiddle at the dance.

The evening passed merrily, enhanced by several bottles of whisky. Young Davis left to go home, and as the crowd prepared to leave, old man Morris called:

"Don't go yet, let's have another dance!"

He stood in the doorway, playing his fiddle. His son had been gone from the house nearly half an hour.

It had rained the day before the body was discovered, and Heck was afraid clues would be scarce. But he found a corner of thin paper with a wavery brown stripe that had been used for wadding in a shotgun shell. A single charge had been fired into the body. He found footprints in the field made by cowboy boots with "run-over" heels. The sole of the left boot was loose at the toe, leaving a "dragged" impression.

Heck inquired about enemies and female associates. He learned that George Morris and his father had been suspected of cattle thefts in the area, and Davis was supposed to have some knowledge of this—also that Morris' wife was an old sweetheart of Davis', and there was jealousy between the two men.

Upon searching the Morris home, he found paper lining a dresser drawer in an upstairs bedroom that matched the paper used as wadding in the shotgun shell. The paper was a corner torn from the dresser drawer lining. He searched for the cowboy boots and finally located them stuffed far back under the house. The "run-over" heels and torn sole fit the prints he had found near the body.

When he arrested Morris and his father, they confessed the murder. Young Morris had waited beside the road and shot Davis as he left the dance, then carried his body into the cornfield.

Heck picked up Cherry Scott on Red River, and returned with his three prisoners to Fort Smith. When Morris and his father were arraigned, they pleaded guilty. Morris was sentenced to life imprisonment; his father drew a long prison term as an accessory. Cherry Scott was acquitted by reason of insanity.

This was only the beginning of one of the busiest years in

the history of the court. Quoting the Muskogee *Indian Journal* of January 26, 1887: "The thirteenth shooting affray in the Territory since January 1st took place at Atoka last Saturday night. . . ." A Negro named Busby got into a quarrel with Cash Ellis, a Choctaw, over a razor the latter claimed Busby had stolen from him. Cash shot Busby through the back and lungs and fled to Savannah, he was captured by Marshal Will Fields, though not until both his legs were broken by a shot from the officer.

On the same date, Charley Narcomey, a rowdy, young full blood, left Muskogee, slightly intoxicated. A mile and a half east of town, near Fisher's sawmill, he met Tuck Thornberry, with a log on his wagon. Dashing up in front of Tuck's team, he exclaimed: "Tuck, God damn you, I am a man!" and whipped out his Colt revolver. Thornberry jerked his horses around just in time for one of them to catch the bullet in the center of the forehead, killing it instantly. "Tuck rolled off on the other side, and Charley, after firing two more shots, whipped up his mount and fled. . . ."

Deputy Marshal Bud Kell, searching for Narcomey, ran into Robert Young, a Cherokee for whom he had a warrant on another charge, and killed him while attempting to arrest him. At his examination before U. S. Commissioner Tufts, there was "so much lying by witnesses" that the case was continued "until more truth can be got at," and it was thought "safe to turn Bud loose." When the case reached the Fort Smith court, it was proved that Major Vann, who had testified that he was present during the affair, had been in his house a half mile away. Judge Parker sentenced him to two and a half years in the penitentiary. "Perjury," he said, "is the vilest and most dangerous of crimes, because it destroys the temple of justice, and conspires to defeat the ends of all laws."

"The judge," Heck wryly commented in his memoirs, "was determined, as far as possible, to put an end to false swearing by special efforts to punish liars."

On February 7, Deputy Marshal Ed Wingo and his posse saw two Indians entering a shack on the Canadian, twenty miles west of Eufaula. Believing one of them to be Narcomey, they approached to investigate, when the Indians opened on them with

Winchesters. The officers returned their fire, but the Indians succeeded in standing them off, and they rode away as if leaving the neighborhood. Instead, they hid in the woods nearby. Within a few minutes, the Indians dashed from the shack for their horses. A pitched battle ensued. One bullet splintered a tree in front of Wingo's eyes, nearly blinding him. He killed one of the Indians and shot his companion in the leg. But the Indian succeeded in reaching his pony and escaped.

Heck, coming through Eufaula with another load of prisoners, heard about the killing. From Policeman Alf McCay he learned that the dead man was a half-Seminole and half-Mexican outlaw called "Long Jim." His companion who had escaped was "Mesquite Joe," wanted for introducing and selling whisky in the Territory. Heck scouted the area, struck his trail, and arrested him in the river bottoms near Hillabee. The Indian's wound was too severe to permit his traveling by wagon with the other prisoners, so Heck secured a hack and came in ahead of his outfit, which arrived the following day.

On this trip, he brought in seven men charged with lynching a couple of horse thieves and a 14-year-old boy named Moore, who happened to come upon them while the thieves were in custody. The *Elevator* reported: "They hanged the boy to keep him from being a witness against them, notwithstanding he begged for his life. . . ."

The records of the court do not reveal that Narcomey was ever arrested. One unverified report extant was that he fled to the Chickasaw Nation, where he was killed at Mount Summit by John Swain, who had helped Heck bring in Ike, Humby, and Patterson.

Two more of Heck's comrades, Isbell and Williams, also enjoyed profitable hunting during the spring of '87. Both had been assigned to the Cherokee Nation. In a three-month period, from February to May, they were responsible for lodging more than a score of criminals within the walls of the Federal jail.

Heck remembered one case he worked with Williams: "A white man named Thomas Jefferson was charged with threatening to kill a man named Dotson after seducing his [Dotson's] wife. . . ." Jefferson had accomplished the act by giving her doctored candy, then ran Dotson off, taking full possession of his property. Dotson came to Fort Smith and swore out a warrant, but when Heck arrived at his home near San Bois, Jefferson had left with the woman.

Heck learned they were headed north into the Cherokee country and wired ahead to Williams. Shortly after midnight, Williams located them in the Starr neighborhood on the Canadian, "occupying the same bed." Said the *Elevator:* "He restored the woman to her husband and brought Jefferson in on the charge stated."

It was the other way around for Deputy Marshal John Phillips' posse when he arrested a young Creek named Seaborn Kalijah on a whisky charge. En route to Fort Smith, Phillips was summoned on another investigation to Eufaula, and left Kalijah in camp in custody of the cook, William Kelly, and two guards, Henry Smith and Mark Kuykendall.

When he returned the next day, he found his prisoner gone and his posse dead. Smith and Kuykendall had been brained with an ax, their beds set afire, and their bodies burned from the waists down. Kelly lay only a few yards away, his throat cut and his face horribly mutilated.

Phillips recaptured Kalijah at the home of two relatives, Doc Walker and John Ohoola, both Creek full bloods. At first, Kalijah denied that he had committed the crimes:

"After dark, the guards laid down to sleep in the tent. The cook and I sat outside. Becoming sleepy, we started into the tent to lie down. Just as we stood up, the cook exclaimed, 'Look out!' and at that moment a shot was fired and the cook fell. I fled into the timber, and just kept running. . . ."

When Walker and Ohoola were charged with complicity in the murders, he repudiated his confession and claimed that he alone had slain the three officers.

Marshal Carroll wasn't satisfied. He told Heck: "Two six-shooters and rifles were stolen from the dead men. These haven't been recovered."

Heck nodded and was off to the Creek Nation. The next day he searched Walker's home, and found the weapons hidden under the kitchen floor.

When the three men were arraigned, Kaijah pleaded guilty,

64

exonerating his codefendants. Judge Parker declined to accept the plea and appointed him counsel.

The evidence at the trial was circumstantial, stronger against Walker and Ohoola, Kalijah being in custody at the time the officers were slain. But Walker and Ohoola went free, and Kalijah went to the gallows.

The jury that indicted the trio was in session twenty-two days, returning 109 true bills, and the Federal Court convened with one of the most crimson dockets in its history. The grand jury docket showed twelve murder cases with fifteen defendants, and the court docket showed twenty-four charged with murder, besides sixty-two others charged with manslaughter, rape, mail robbery, larceny, embezzlement, perjury, bigamy, and assault with intent to kill.

"Our sole object," reported the grand jury, "has been to fearlessly and conscientiously perform our duty as citizens in assisting this honorable court in the enforcement of law, knowing the great difficulties the officials of this district labor under in performance of their duties. . . . While we are aware of the diligence and ability of our worthy U. S. Marshal and his determined and efficient force of deputies, we believe the herculean duties devolving upon him and his staff required for the suppression of crime too hazardous and inadequate to cope with the powerful odds against them. The sacrifice of good and brave men is too great. . . ."

The law provided for the arrest of an Indian only for revenue and whisky violations, counterfeiting, larceny of Government property, and violations of postal laws. Congress helped this year by including such crimes as "assault with intent to kill or maim, or murder, upon an Indian Agent, Indian policeman, Indian United States deputy marshal or guard, or any person at any time while in the discharge of his duty," with the provision that he be "tried in the same courts and subject to the same penalties as a citizen of the United States."

The Indian newspapers declared this "a great safeguard to our Indian officers" and "a great step toward the suppression of crime in the Territory."

Heck relied on his Winchester and Colt forty-fives.

8

Dangerous Quarry

His hips shaped a bit from much riding. He habitually wore knee-length, shop-made boots, corduroy trousers, and open-necked flannel shirt, with a broad-rimmed white hat, which he had a kindly, gallant way of doffing with a sweeping bow when he met someone he respected.

His mustache hung below his chin, his imperial touched the diamond in his shirt front, and he wore his long, heavy brown hair brushed straight back over his head. Dumas would have beheld him with ecstasy.

He was mounted on the best horses and equipped with the finest arms of the day. With a bristling cartridge belt supporting his two ivory-handled Colts, and a decorated .44-40 saddle gun to match, he looked the part of the range-riding marshal who epitomized the coming of law to the Southwest.

Deputies who had ridden for the court since its beginning admired him because he rode and fought well and had an uncanny way at guessing where to find a wanted man, and his undaunted courage attracted the most daredevil young men of the country as his posse. One of these was Frank Dalton, eldest of the notorious Dalton brothers.

Dalton was twenty-eight years old and unmarried, his home being with his mother at Chelsea, Cherokee Nation. Heck described him as "an honest, upright young man, highly esteemed by all who knew him for his many good qualities of head and heart." He had jumped into prominence in December, 1886, by his vigorous pursuit and capture of the drunken assassins of Captain Sam Sixkiller, Chief of the United States Indian Police at Muskogee, who had been ambushed on Christmas Eve.

Heck and Dalton worked their first case together the spring of 1887.

Albert Jones, a white man residing at the home of George Johnson, another white citizen, in the Saline District, Cherokee Nation, had disappeared mysteriously. Johnson claimed that Jones had "just ridden away in the night."

Dalton wasn't convinced. Through a relative, he learned that Jones allegedly had seduced Johnson's daughter; there was the matter of $32 received for a pony and "considerable other cash" known to have been on his person a few days before; and on the night of his disappearance, Johnson had been observed returning from a bluff near his home, carrying a shovel.

"It's my guess," Dalton told Heck, "that Jones lies buried in the side of that hill."

"We'll see," Heck said.

They took turns watching the house and working the hillside with pick and shovel. Within a short time they unearthed the skeleton. When they faced Johnson with this evidence, the farmer confessed.

On their return to Fort Smith with their prisoner, Heck and Dalton "served several whisky warrants" and "registered eight more in the federal jail."

The following week, they left for the Chickasaw Nation with extra saddles horses and two wagons. The *Elevator* noted their departure: "They expect to be out forty or fifty days this time. Criminals in that locality had better begin hunting their holes."

On May 6, the *Elevator* reported: "Deputy Thomas and his posse arrived this week with ten prisoners. . . . On the trip Thomas arrested, near Stonewall, one S. Fletcher Hargrove, for whom there is a reward of $200 in Tennessee, where he is wanted for murder committed several years ago."

Heck hardly gave his saddle time to cool. On May 16, he started for the Cherokee Nation in search of the slayer of Deputy

Marshal Daniel Maples. Commented the *Indian Journal:* "Should he get the right man, he would make a very profitable haul—there is a $500 reward for the murderer."

Maples had been a likable officer. A native of Bentonville, Arkansas, he had worked mostly in the Cherokee country, being familiar with the tribe and its language. Marshal Carroll praised him as "part of the cream" of his staff.

Heck mulled over the details of the killing as he rode northwest: Maples carried a whisky warrant for an Indian named John Parris. On May 4, he had camped on Spring Branch near Tahlequah. A woman named Nancy Shell dispensed liquor in a log house on the west side of the creek, and he thought Parris might be there. Shortly after dark, he started across the stream on a foot log, when he sighted Parris and a companion approaching on the opposite bank.

Maples commanded them to halt.

"It's that damned marshal!" Parris yelled.

A revolver blazed from the darkness, Maples tumbled from the log into the stream, and the men vanished in the timber.

Citizens rushing from the shanty hill town had discovered Maples' body in the water. Deputy John Curtis, who made the preliminary investigation, arrested Parris and Nancy Shell. Parris denied he had fired the shot, but refused to identify his companion. The woman admitted that Parris had left her place a few minutes before the slaying, but "thought he had been alone." She pleaded guilty to selling whisky in the Nations, was fined $100, and sentenced to thirty days in jail.

Heck's business was with a young Indian named Charley Bobtail. Bobtail was an old offender. In 1884, he had been sentenced to eighteen months at Detroit for introducing and selling whisky in the Indian country, and served a one-year term in 1886 for horse thievery. Since his return to the Going Snake District in March, he and Parris had been constant companions. Heck arrested him at home the night of May 20, and took him to Fort Smith.

Bobtail denied any knowledge of the crime.

"I was at another place at the time," he said.

Heck told the district attorney: "He has no witnesses—nothing to prove his alibi."

Bobtail was arraigned on a charge of murder and his bond fixed at $5,000.

Then Parris confessed. "Bobtail wasn't there. The man who killed Maples is Ned Christie."

Christie was a native of Rabbit Trap Hollow, a wild and almost inaccessible wilderness of scrub brush and forest, fifteen miles southeast of Tahlequah. A fine specimen of his race, he stood six feet, four inches, wore his long black hair down over his shoulders, and had eyes like a cat. He was a gunsmith by trade and an excellent shot. He came from a prominent fullblood family and, like many Cherokee youths of the day, had grown up without a formal education. But he had learned to speak English. In 1885, Chief Dennis W. Bushyhead had appointed him to the national council.

The national council corresponded to the United States Cabinet. Its members advised the Chief concerning matters of executive administration. Christie's judgment was considered sane and his opinion much sought after by those who did business with his department.

But he liked his whisky. He was in the habit of acquiring a bottle at the end of each week before starting home.

"He had been drinking and was carrying a bottle in his pocket when we left Nancy Shell's," Parris said. "After the shooting, we ran back to his boardinghouse and talked to a close friend on the council. . . ."

Christie claimed he had drawn his gun on the spur of the moment, that he had only fired to frighten the deputy.

". . . The friend said, 'Go about your business, keep your mouth shut, and see what happens.'"

Next morning, he had attended the council session as usual. He kept quiet when they arrested Parris. Like most Indians he lived in mortal fear of the gallows trap at Fort Smith. When word of Parris' confession reached Tahlequah, he went on to scout near his home.

Deputy Joe Bowers rode into Rabbit Trap to serve the murder

warrant. Christie fired from the underbrush, the ball struck Bowers in the leg as the deputy escaped, and a charge of assaulting a Federal officer was filed against the outlaw.

Afterward, Christie stayed close to his cabin. "I no give up," he told friends and relatives. "I die here fighting!"

Deputy John Fields, who understood the conflict between the Indian's conception of right and justice and the white man's idea of law and order, thought he could talk Christie into surrendering. He reached the cabin before breakfast.

Christie's wife nudged him. Catlike, he sprang from his bunk, seized his rifle, and kicked open the door. At sight of the outlaw, Fields changed his mind about talking and, like Bowers, wheeled his horse to escape. This time Christie aimed a bit higher and shot Fields in the neck. Fields kept riding, and Christie held his fire.

He sent word from the hills: "No want to kill another marshal —just want them stop sneaking around."

A third charge was filed against the outlaw. Marshal Carroll admonished his deputies: "Quit trying to take him alive."

Christie purchased a new .44 Winchester from one of his neighbors. "With new rifle," he said, "I live longer."

From that day, officers were unable to ride into Rabbit Trap without Christie being warned. The whole neighborhood became his signal system. He knew when strangers were in the vicinity an hour before they arrived. While his wife brought in drinking water, Christie and his hired boy examined their weapons, hung pouches filled with ammunition about their bodies, and settled down for a siege before the portholes.

Once a whole posse approached. Christie wounded three of them, then held his fire while the others carried away the injured. When they had gone, the neighbor children ran down to see the battleground and pick up empty cartridge cases, delighted that Ned had come through safely again.

Christie laughed heartily. He played marbles with the children in the yard, while his hired boy lay hidden in the house, ready to fight should the posse return.

The reward for Christie increased to $1,000. Heck left Fort

Smith for Tahlequah. His old friend Isbell, with Deputies Dave Rusk and Salmon, came down from Vinita to meet him.

They left their horses in the hills, moving into Rabbit Trap on foot, and hid in the woods three days without being discovered. Carefully, sometimes crawling, they worked their way up the hollow without disturbing Christie's private alarm system. The quail whistled and the doves called. In the trees, the birds sang and the squirrels chattered fiercely.

The morning of the fourth day, in the quiet hour before dawn while life in the woods still slept, they moved in to surround Christie's cabin. But Christie's dogs scented them and began barking.

Heck yelled: "Make a rush for it!"

The posse moved with speed, reaching good positions in the yard next to the cabin before Christie got into action. Heck told Christie who they were and demanded his surrender, but the outlaw made no reply. He took refuge in the loft, knocking a plank off the gable end, and opened fire on the officers, which they returned.

Again Heck demanded his surrender. "If you intend to fight, send out your woman."

Christie replied with another blast from his rifle.

Heck was behind a small building adjoining the cabin that Christie used for a gun shop. He set it on fire and retired to a large hickory tree where Isbell had taken refuge.

As the structure burst into flames, the posse held its fire and waited.

"That ought to smoke him out," Heck said.

Isbell, turning to get a better view, accidentally exposed himself. Christie's rifle roared from the gable. The deputy went down with a groan, his left shoulder shattered. Heck leaped out, grabbed his legs and drew him back behind the tree. The same instant, Christie's wife ran from the house into the woods.

The blazing outbuilding set the cabin on fire. As new flames shot into the morning sky, Christie's hired boy leaped from the doorway. Mistaking him for the outlaw, Rusk and Salmon cut down on him as he fled into the underbrush.

71

Christie took advantage of this interlude to make his bid for freedom. He leaped from the gable and hit the ground running. Heck fired at him through the dazzling light. He saw the outlaw grab his forehead and fall at the edge of the timber.

Isbell's shoulder was bleeding badly. Heck left Salmon with him, took Rusk, and scoured the woods. They found the boy, shot through both hips and the lung. But Christie and his wife had vanished.

The officers improvised a litter and carried Isbell to their horses. By this time, the deputy had lost so much blood Heck had to rush him to Tahlequah. He remained with Isbell several days before he could remove him to Vinita and safety from Christie's five brothers and other relatives.

Isbell remained a cripple for life. But Christie also carried the scars of one of his toughest fights. Heck's bullet had split the bridge of his nose, knocking out his left eye. His people had found him unconscious in the hills and carried him to a doctor. His wound healed, but he remained an unsightly object, which constantly fed his hatred for the white man.

He returned to Rabbit Trap and constructed a "fort" of huge logs on a high hill where he had a view of a hundred yards in any direction. Although it took five more years and a posse of seventeen marshals armed with a three-pound cannon and a half-dozen sticks of dynamite to blast his body from the fort and haul it to Fort Smith for official identification, this was Heck's only brush with the Territory's most dangerous outlaw.

9

Whitebead Hill

While Christie was convalescing in the hills, Heck was being transferred from Fort Smith to Smith Paul's Valley, in old Pickens County, the far western portion of the Chickasaw Nation.

This part of the Chickasaw County had been set aside for the Chickasaws in a treaty at Doaksville in 1837 and organized for their benefit under the Choctaw constitution and laws. The Treaty of 1855 at Washington separated the two tribes, and in 1859, the Chickasaw Legislature divided the nation into four counties: Panola, Pontotoc, Tishomingo, and Pickens. Pickens covered the widest area, lying between the Washita and Red rivers to the 98th meridian, now included in nine counties and parts of counties in southwestern Oklahoma.

The fertility of the soil was attested by miles of bluestem high enough to hide a man on horseback, but the Chickasaws did not use it because of the hostile pressure from the Plains Indians. When Fort Arbuckle was established on Wild Horse Creek south of the Canadian in 1851, the section fell under the protection of the United States Cavalry, and Smith Paul settled in the Washita Valley. Due to his leadership and vision and limitless energy, his family became widely known and the place where they lived was looked upon by his people much as ancient Israel looked upon Egypt and the Nile.

With Fort Sill and Fort Reno to the west and north, Fort

Arbuckle and Fort Washita to the east and south, long wagon trains came from all sides to buy and haul away corn, hogs, and other produce from this land of plenty. Pauls Valley was merely a stage stop on the Butterfield line, consisting of a store and a few log houses in a clearing.

White men had been drifting into the country since its establishment as an independent nation. Mostly they had been Texas ranchers who had long viewed the prized land from the other side of Red River, paying an annual fee of $1 and a tax of 25 cents per head on their cattle. Their number was comparatively small and the permit system in force proved satisfactory. In 1876, the legislature passed an act by which white men were permitted to rent land or be otherwise employed in the nation, provided they entered into contract with an Indian citizen and paid a fee of $5 per year.

Whites came to the land in droves. The permit taxes they paid constituted an important part of the revenue needed to operate the Chickasaw government, and the Indians welcomed the business activity they brought. Traders and merchants were required to pay an *ad valorem* tax on their stocks of goods in addition to their license. They purchased the Indians' surplus cattle and farm products and supplied manufactured goods from the states in exchange. Mechanics and farm laborers desiring to remain in the nation for a shorter time than one year paid fifty cents per month. Physicians and hotel men were obliged to rent houses from citizens, or they might rent land from a Chickasaw occupant and make their own improvements upon it. Thus several small communities grew composed entirely of whites in improvements they had erected.

Then, in 1887, the Santa Fe Railroad was completed through the nation. The 172 miles of rail from Fort Worth north to Walnut Creek (later Purcell), on the Canadian, and the proposed terminus of a road south from Arkansas City through the Indian Territory were joined, and towns sprang up everywhere. With the sudden increase in population, business, and disorder, the Chickasaw governor had petitioned the Federal Court for a resident marshal.

Much of Heck's activity had been in this area. "You know the country already, and you are respected out there," said Marshal Carroll.

Heck nodded soberly. "I don't know how my wife is going to take it, Colonel. But if those people need protection . . ."

He left the rest unsaid. He remembered the promise he had made Isabelle about building a home. But all his plans for the future were dependent on commitments made when he pinned on the badge for the great Federal Court. Heck knew that this time the consequences of his act might be serious. But he was more disturbed by the possible consequences of his refusal to accept the assignment. He didn't mention the matter to Isabelle right then. Facing her, with her baffling opinions, was a more grueling experience than cross-examination by some of Fort Smith's best criminal lawyers.

However, it was inevitable that he face her before making this change. She demanded an explanation after reading the announcement in the newspaper. Meantime, Marshal Carroll had done what he could to help Heck. Exactly what his conversation was with Isabelle, Heck never knew, except that she had commented bitterly on the foot-loose propensities and irrelevant heroisms of men.

But she believed what Heck told her: "I know it means breaking my promise. But I feel it my duty to help those people."

Whitebead Hill, five miles west of Pauls Valley, was the largest settlement in Pickens County. A boarding school for children, two stores, and several other enterprises made it the mecca of travelers and the center of culture in a new world wrested from its primeval state. Heck moved his family there by wagon late in the summer of '87.

Pierce Institute, the boarding school, one of the largest of its kind in the Territory, was the creation of John C. Powell, a Virginia minister, who had been among the first educators in the valley. Whites were permitted to attend by paying tuition, but like most of the early Indian schools, its supervision was lax under the superintendent of public instruction for the whole Chickasaw Nation, and the qualifications of the teachers were considered poor. The only other school was for Negro children of former slaves of the Indians.

A few white families hired private tutors. Others, who couldn't afford this, banded together and shared the costs, maintaining subscription schools with classes in lodge halls and other buildings. But the greater part of the citizenry were illiterate and felt no need for education.

Religion was a hit-and-miss affair. Several denominations had sent ministers into the valley. A Methodist circuit included Cherokee Town, Erin Springs, Randolph, Beef Creek, Florence, and Silver City. A Cumberland Presbyterian preacher served a circuit that originated in Wynnewood and ended at Marlow. But no real effort had been made to establish permanent churches.

If Isabelle was stunned by the raw frontier to which she already had been subjected, she was now utterly bewildered—frightened. She did her washing on a washboard, her ironing with a sadiron, swept her house with a broom (after she was able to obtain one), and cleaned her lamps at night after the rest of the family had retired. Until Heck had a stove shipped in from Texas, she cooked their meals in a pot in the back yard. There were no sewers, no scavengers, except the herds of hogs that ran through the streets, alleys, and yards that were not fenced, no water except from individual wells and cisterns.

Things she found plenty of were fleas, lice, bedbugs and malaria, typhoid, smallpox and diphtheria. Over half the funerals were for children.

These were the days of high infant mortality and equally high death rate in the second summer after weaning. Scores of stones in the Old Cemetery still mark the graves of children who never reached their third year. Burials were made helter-skelter, and processions often were without a hearse. The father of the dead child carried the casket on his saddle or simply took it in his arms and walked behind the preacher the short distance to the newly dug grave.

Bereavement and poor living, educational, and religious facilities became only a part of Isabelle's life. Yelling, cursing cowboys from the nearby ranches rode in and out of town at a dead run. "Dirt soldiers" in from the long drives to the forts with faces and clothes caked with dust "whooped it up." The tough railroad gangs swaggered in the streets, and the influx of lawless elements made handy by the Santa Fe did little or nothing to foster good will and improve the community. Several killings took place in a short period. Whisky and beer, notwithstanding both were prohibited, were doled out in large quantities, and "shooting up the town" was a common sport.

Trains whistled eerily in the night. Freight caravans rumbled and clattered, hoofs pounded the dry, parched streets and sloshed when mud took over, and the shouts of drivers with their "giddaps" and "whoas" and foul oaths echoed as mules and oxen strained under heavy loads of cotton, hay, and corn. Every day more weather-beaten wagons arrived loaded with household effects of new families and children sticking their heads from under dirty, torn canvas.

The din. The stench of manure piles and outhouses and burned powder from roaring firearms. A population about equally divided between Indians and whites. And Heck spending day and night in the saddle.

Long before the end of that first nightmarish month at Whitebead Hill, Isabelle confronted him with eyes blazing. "I won't bring up my children in a place like this!"

"All it needs is a little taming," he said. "Be patient, honey. It'll take some time for that."

"It's horrible! It's—those dreadful people."

"Without fellows like them our civilization might have died on Plymouth Rock." Heck struck his old attitude.

Isabelle stared dully. "Plymouth Rock? Fellows like them?"

"Empire builders, honey." He kissed her, and was gone, strapping on his twin six-shooters with their menacing ivory handles protruding just above the holsters. They had become symbols for everything she hated and despised. She heard his light step creaking down the rickety stairway, his deep, vibrant voice lifting above the raucous speech of the posse outside. . . .

There was an area along the Washita known as Wildcat Thicket where search for bootleggers and fugitives from justice had been virtually impossible. That night, Heck and his possemen, Ed Stokley and Bill Moody, swooped down on a river saloon. There was a wild race into the thicket with a wagon loaded with barrels of beer, and when the chase ended, the wagon was empty and half the town stayed drunk all night.

It was daylight when Heck came in. Isabelle sat on the bed in her high-necked, long-sleeved nightgown, her eyes like black holes in her ashen, tear-streaked face and her forehead still cold and wet.

"Why, honey, you've been crying. And I bet you haven't slept a wink!"

"That shooting. And screaming. Men hollering. What was it?"

"Shooting—hollering—? Oh—" Heck threw back his head and laughed "—that was Ed and Bill and me, rounding up some more prisoners for Fort Smith. We're taking in seventeen this trip—first thing tomorrow morning."

He came over, put a hand on her shoulders. She shrugged away from him, furious that he viewed her plight so callously. Her fear and bewilderment fused and hardened in unreasoning rebellion. "I'm going home, Henry." She began trembling a little. "I'm going back to Georgia."

"All right, honey," he said, and put his arms around her.

Her voice rose in hysteria. "You don't understand . . . I'm taking the children—I'm—" She broke down in racking sobs and cried like a child.

"Now, now, Belle. The trip will do you good. You can go by rail all the way to Galveston. Give my regards to Cousin Jim. You can take a boat from there."

Heck put his family on the train, then sent a wire to Marshal Carroll. On November 20, he rolled out of Pauls Valley with three wagonloads of prisoners and six guards, including Moody and Ed Stokley.

Stokley was twenty-seven years old and lived with his father near Marietta. For more than a year he had served as a posse in the Chickasaw Nation, was well-liked and respected. He planned to be married in January.

"I'm recommending you for a regular commission when we reach Fort Smith," Heck promised. With luck and good weather, they could make the 260-mile haul in a couple of weeks.

Their luck held, but the weather turned bad. For three days

78

it rained continuously. Their wagons bogged to the axles. High water made streams almost impossible to cross. On November 29, they reached McAlester.

Heck had a telegram waiting for him from Marshal Carroll: "Deputy Frank Dalton murdered the 27th inst. His killer believed heading for the Choctaw country. . . ."

The details were the same Heck had read a dozen times: Dalton had reached Fort Smith on Friday, the 25th, with six prisoners, the fruits of a hard trip through the Creek country, turned them over to the U. S. jailer and struck camp on the opposite side of the Arkansas in the Cherokee Nation until ready to start out again. He had a writ charging horse stealing for Dave Smith, onetime member of the Starr gang and companion of Felix Griffin, and Deputy James Cole had a writ for Smith for introducing whisky in the Indian country. Learning that he was hiding at a wood chopper's camp four miles away in the river bottom, the two officers set out early Sunday morning to arrest him. They had found Smith in a tent, armed and waiting, with his brother-in-law Lee Dixon, Dixon's wife, and a boy horse thief named William Towerly.

"We want only Smith!" yelled Dalton. "No call for the rest of you mixing in his trouble."

Smith fired, and Dalton fell with a bullet in his breast. As he lay on the ground, helpless and moaning that he was dying, young Towerly ran forward.

"Oh! You son-of-a-bitch . . ." he snarled, and fired his Winchester into Dalton's mouth. He reloaded and blew out Dalton's brains.

Meanwhile, Smith, Dixon, and his wife were shooting at Cole. But Cole was no amateur in combat at close quarters. In 1886, he had killed a drunken bully in a ferryboat brawl, and, shortly before starting out with Dalton, had been winner in an attempted ambush of his posse by a Cherokee desperado, Big Chewee. Dixon wounded Cole in the side with his rifle, but firing fast from the hip, Cole killed Smith and the woman and crippled Dixon in the left shoulder and back, claiming him as a prisoner.

Dixon died of his wounds in the jail hospital. Towerly had escaped. His home was in the Choctaw Nation, where he resided with his parents and sister on Boggy River, five miles from Atoka.

Recalling the fate of Deputy John Phillips' posse during his absence, Heck decided to stay with his prisoners. He sent Stokley and Moody in search of Towerly.

"We'll bring him in alive, if possible," Stokley said. "The Government still don't pay for dead men."

Stokley and Moody boarded the southbound Katy train to Atoka. Here they rented a couple of horses, crossed the Boggy before daybreak, and set up watch on the house.

William arrived home late in the night. While he slept the sleep of exhaustion in blankets in the open by the porch, old man Towerly stood watch.

The little killer clutched his revolver as he slept. The old man didn't hear Stokley and Moody slipping through the brush. They were within clear striking distance then, but decided to wait until dawn to take him.

At daybreak, William's mother brought a sack of food and awakened him. She pleaded with him to stay with her.

"I have to get a long way gone," he said.

"Aren't you afraid, Will?" she asked.

"Ain't afraid of nothin'!" He shrugged and started for his horse, the words trailing after him.

The officers sprang from the brush. "Hands up!" shouted Stokley.

The youth whipped out his six-shooter. Stokley shot him through the leg, and Moody shot him in the right shoulder, hoping to take him alive.

He fell to the ground, dropping his revolver. But he grasped it quickly in his left hand. Stokley leaped in to disarm him. But before Stokley could reach him, he shot the officer twice in the heart and right groin.

He kept firing until the gun was empty, then flung it toward his father, yelling: "Reload it and throw it back, so I can kill that other damned marshal!"

Moody was being prevented from doing any effective shooting. The mother and sister had sprung upon him with the fury of two wildcats. They seized him, clawing the skin off his hands and dragging him backward, finally shoving him inside the house

80

and locking the door. Moody leaped to the window. He smashed out the glass with his Winchester, and killed the cursing outlaw.

Stokley's body was put on the train that afternoon. Moody accompanied it to Gainesville, then north on the Gulf-Colorado and Santa Fe to Marietta.

While Dalton's murder affected Heck deeply, he was greatly shaken over the death of Stokley. It was exceedingly difficult to find dependable, first-rate possemen in the Territory. When he reached Fort Smith with his wagons, he told Marshal Carroll:

"Ed could have killed Towerly on sight. By trying to save the life of a brute, he lost his own. I should have handed him the responsibility of seventeen prisoners and gone after the killer myself."

The *Elevator* noted: "This makes fifteen marshals killed in the Territory in two years. Most of their difficulties arise from having to bring prisoners to the U. S. jail in wagons. . . ."

Heck kept thinking about this after he returned to Whitebead Hill. Railroads were being used in the Territory where practicable. The Katy ran from the Kansas border south and southwest across the Cherokee, Creek, and Choctaw Nations through Vinita, Muskogee, McAlester, and Atoka, across Red River to Denison and Sherman. The Atlantic and Pacific had built a line across the Shawnee and Wyandotte reservations into the Cherokee Nation and connected with the Katy at Vinita in 1872. In 1883 it had extended its line southwest to Tulsa and Red Fork in the Creek country. In 1886, the Frisco had extended its Fort Smith line southwest across the Choctaw Nation to Paris, Texas. The Iron Mountain and Southern was completing a line up the valley of the Arkansas from Van Buren to Fort Gibson, thence to Coffeyville, Kansas.

For Heck's part, the railroad through the Chickasaw country to Gainesville provided direct connections on the Texas Pacific east to Sherman and Paris, thence northeast on the Frisco through the Choctaw Nation.

"If you can get the Department of Justice to allow me the railroad mileage," he wrote Marshal Carroll on February 10, 1888, "I can show plainly that this route will be cheaper for the Government and better for me."

How he explained it is told best in his letter forwarded to Washington, February 21:

Take, for instance, my last trip. After starting from Pauls Valley, I. T., on the 20th day of Nov., 1887 . . . it took me until the 12th of December '87 to reach Fort Smith. Had I started on the railroad, I would have reached there the 22nd of November '87, just two days after starting instead of 22 days which it took to come by wagon. It will be seen at a glance that there would have been a saving of twenty days board on each prisoner in favor of the rail route.

The total board on the seventeen prisoners, by wagon, was $279, and the trip was made as speedily as possible under the circumstances. By rail the total board on seventeen prisoners would have amounted to but $35, a saving of $244.50

Besides this, I could have made the trip with three less guards than was possible by wagon, obliged as I am to come through a thinly settled and dangerous country. Three guards at $26 each amounts to a saving of $78.

I am free to confess that the rail route would be of great advantage to me also, for it would enable me to make several more trips each year, as I could save nearly a month's time on each trip.

Besides the above, there would be less danger of prisoners escaping and less danger of all kinds. . . .

Marshal Carroll gave the letter official endorsement, and Judge Parker added this cryptic note: "I concur with the within request and recommendation . . ."

The judge had fought constantly to improve the working conditions of the marshals since coming to the bench. "Without these men," he said time and again, "I could not hold court a single day." In 1884, he had presented to Congress a bill to pay deputies salaries "to attract good men who will know just what they can make, and prevent trumped up cases and the wholesale subpoena of witnesses for fees . . ." but it was defeated on the grounds of "inequality of service to be performed" by the officers themselves. There had been little change as the years passed.

Despite Heck's showing, Washington felt that such a circuitous route was not feasible. He pursued the course no further. He became involved in more personal problems in the spring of '88.

He had received a brief note from Isabelle at Christmas time.

She had placed the children in school in Georgia, and was not returning to the Indian Nations.

"You still want to build a reputation, Henry; it has become as much a part of you as your heart and brain. I want to build a home."

Heck tried to be tactful. "I am sure that you are doing what you think best for the children. But you must return at once."

A few weeks later there came a one-line reply from Isabelle: "Never unless you resign."

Heck had no intention of resigning. But he never blamed her. After they were divorced, he was always first to admit it was because man hunting had got in his blood.

10

A Lesson in Hanging

An unusually busy season helped to shove his regrets, losses, and disappointments into the back of his mind.

Owing to the failure of Congress to appropriate sufficient funds to defray the expenses of the court in the trial of criminal cases, all witnesses summoned to appear before the grand jury in February were freed until the May term. There were fifty-seven prisoners in jail awaiting trial at the time, twenty-seven of them charged with murder. In two of these cases, Heck was chief witness for the prosecution.

When he finally came in from the Chickasaw Nation again in April, he surprised Judge Parker with the largest number of prisoners ever brought to Fort Smith in a single group. "He had thirty-two in tow," one contemporary report claimed, "representing every violation in the book, nine of whom were found guilty of crimes punishable by death."

Parker sentenced three men to die on the gallows at 2 P.M. on April 27, and Heck stayed around for his first lesson in hanging.

On April 23, 1886, shortly after Heck had gone to work for the court, two men had been hanged together. Two more died on July 23, and one hanged August 6. On January 11, 1887, the morbidly curious who gathered in the jail yard saw four murderers drop through the trap at the same time. Two were hanged

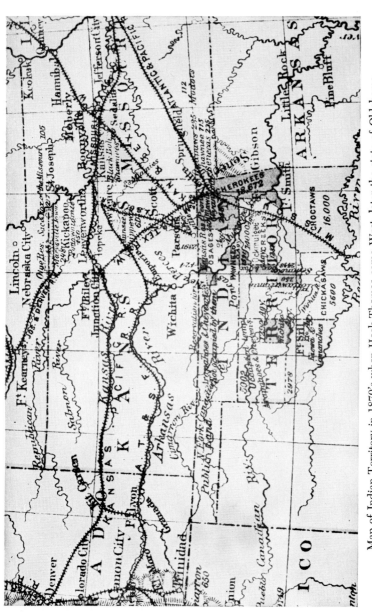

Map of Indian Territory in 1870's when Heck Thomas came West, later the state of Oklahoma. *From Author's Collection.*

Heck Thomas (seated center) and group of Texas Express officials in 1878, who trailed Sam Bass. Detective Sam Finley (standing, left). *Courtesy Colin S. Monteith, Jr., Columbia, South Carolina.*

Heck Thomas as Deputy United States Marshal at Fort Smith, Arkansas, 1886. *From Author's Collection.*

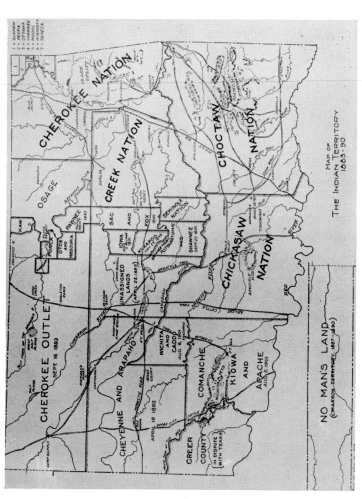

Indian Territory, 1889, before opening of Unassigned Lands for white settlement. *From Author's Collection.*

Isaac Charles Parker, the "Hanging Judge" at Fort Smith, Arkansas, who commented often on Heck's loyal assistance to the bench and the careful manner in which he obtained evidence. *From Author's Collection.*

Ned Christie, the Territory's most dangerous outlaw, who fought the United States marshals and Indian police for years before he was killed and captured. In his one clash with Heck Thomas, Heck shot away the bridge of his nose and shot out his left eye. *Courtesy C. H. McKennon, Tulsa, Oklahoma.*

First photograph of Tulsa, Creek Nation, as it appeared when Heck Thomas arrived there after being wounded in battle with Purdy gang in 1888. *From Author's Collection.*

Matie Mowbray, daughter of Reverend George W. and Hannah Mowbray, whom Heck Thomas met in Tulsa while recovering from his wounds in 1888. *Courtesy Beth Thomas Meeks, Tulsa, Oklahoma.*

Heck Thomas as Deputy United States Marshal taken at Arkansas City,
Kansas, while working with Chief of Detectives Fred Dodge of Wells Fargo
and Company, trailing the Dalton gang in 1892. *From Author's Collection.*

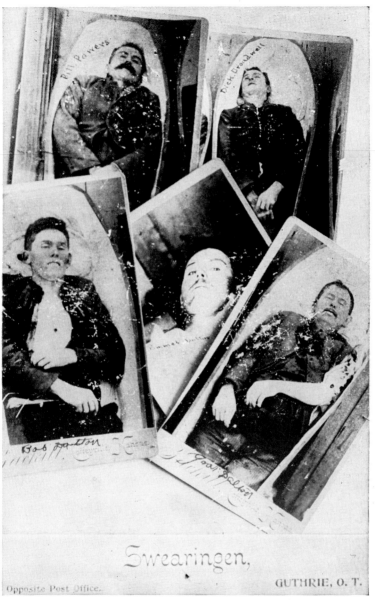

Dalton gang after Coffeyville raid October 5, 1892. Bill Powers (upper left); Dick Broadwell (upper right); Bob Dalton (lower left); Grat Dalton (lower right); Emmett Dalton, wounded (center). *From Author's Collection.*

Hell's Half Acre (Perry, Oklahoma Territory) September, 1893. *From Author's Collection.*

Perry six months after Cherokee Outlet opening, after being tamed by Heck Thomas and Bill Tilghman. *From Author's Collection.*

Crowds in line at Perry land office, September 28, 1893, after opening of Cherokee Outlet. *From Author's Collection.*

Land Office clerical force and Deputy U. S. Marshals at Perry, October 13, 1893. Heck Thomas (at far right, standing, with muzzle of Winchester on porch); Chief of Police Bill Tilghman (sixth from left, standing, in white hat and light coat and tie, with muzzle of Winchester near toe of right boot). *Courtesy Division of Manuscripts, University of Oklahoma.*

Pawnee Gallery,

MISS NORA HANSON,   Pawnee, O. T.

(3), Heck Thomas; (2), Deputy U. S. Marshal Morris Robacker; and (1), Spotted Dog Eater and (4), Howling Wolf, Osage Indian scouts. Taken in 1894 while trailing Doolin gang after bank robbery at Pawnee, Oklahoma Territory. *From Author's Collection.*

Bill Raidler, member of Doolin gang, shot and captured by Heck Thomas and Bill Tilghman in the Osage Nation in September, 1895. *From Author's Collection.*

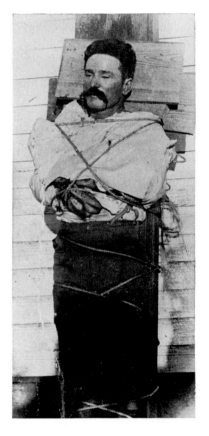

George "Red Buck" Waightman (dead on slab) after slain by posse near Arapaho, Oklahoma Territory, in March, 1896, the most vicious member of the Doolin gang. Heck first arrested him in the Cherokee Nation for horse-thievery and sent him to prison in 1890. *From Author's Collection.*

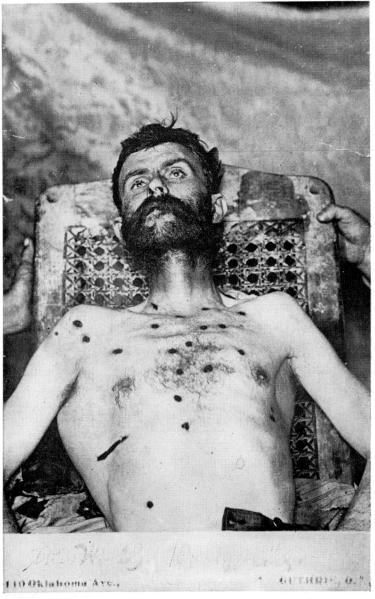

Bill Doolin (dead in Guthrie morgue), shot and killed by Heck Thomas at Lawson (now Quay), in Payne county, Oklahoma Territory, in August, 1896. *From Author's Collection.*

Little Dick West, member of the Doolin gang, shot and killed by Heck Thomas, Bill Tilghman and posse on Thompson Creek near Guthrie, in April, 1898. *From Author's Collection.*

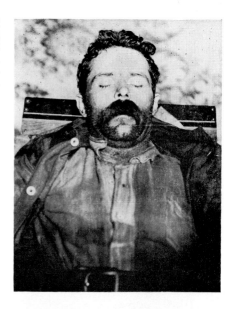

Heck Thomas, Chief of Police, and his first police force at Lawton, Oklahoma Territory, following the Kiowa, Comanche and Apache opening in 1901. (Left to right) Heck Thomas, Leka Hammon, Harry Foster, Bill Bruce, and Colonel Hawkins. *From Author's Collection.*

Heck Thomas, Chief of Police, and police force at Lawton about 1905. (Heck seated second from left, with hat on ground). *Courtesy Colin S. Monteith, Jr., Columbia, South Carolina.*

Heck Thomas (seated), son Henry G. (standing). *From Author's Collection.*

the same year on October 7. On each of these occasions, Heck had been on an expedition in the Territory. This portion of the court's functions was repulsive to him. But he felt obliged to learn as much about it as possible. Sometime in the future it might become his duty to carry out such an edict of the law, and he wanted to be able to do it properly.

The trio scheduled to die on the gallows were George Moss and Owens D. Hill, both Negroes, and an Indian desperado named Jackson Crow.

Crow had sent more than one man to the "happy hunting grounds" during his life in the wilds of the Territory. His father was a Creek full blood and his mother a Negro woman. He had been reared in the Choctaw country, and enjoyed the reputation of being a hard citizen. Early in 1880, a white man named Uriah Henderson, who had a store on the line between the Territory and Arkansas, left with Crow and was never seen afterward. Other men reported to have visited Crow's section to buy cattle had disappeared completely. On August 7, 1884, the body of Charles Wilson, a Choctaw merchant who stood high in commercial circles in Fort Smith, was found on the road a few miles from Kulla Chaha.

Investigation proved he had been assassinated while returning from an election, and the murder was charged to Crow, Robert Benton, Peter Coinson, Ned McCaslin, John Allen, Dixon Perry, Charles Fisher, Jim Franklin, Cornellus McCurtain, Joe Jackson, and John Slaughter, all Indian citizens, except Crow, who up to this time had failed to take advantage of the Choctaw Freedman's registration law. His companions, all prominent men, were freed by the Indian courts. Crow took to the woods and remained at large until December, 1886, when Deputy Charles Barnhill and posse brought him to bay in a log house in the Poteau Mountains. A revolver belonging to Wilson was found in his possession.

Jackson and Slaughter became Government witnesses at his trial. They testified the party had met Wilson on the road, that Benton had a few words with him over the election, and as Wilson grappled with Benton, Crow shot him in the back with a Winchester. After he fell, the murderer beat out his brains with his pistol.

Owens D. Hill's crime was an even more revolting instance of human brutality. He resided with his wife near Gibson Station, Cherokee Nation. They did not get along very peaceably together, and his wife left him to live with her mother, a short distance from their home. On the night of June 25, 1887, Hill appeared at the house of his mother-in-law with a shotgun. After beating her over the head with the weapon until he thought she was dead, he threw the gun aside and sprang at his wife with a razor. She tried to escape, but he caught her in the yard and cut her throat, almost severing her head from her body. He fled to Kansas City, where he had been arrested in August after writing to a friend inquiring if his wife had died of her wounds.

Heck remembered Moss as "the last of four men who took part in one of the most diabolical murders I ever investigated." On November 26, 1886, Moss, Sandy Smith, Factor Jones, and Dick Butler had conspired to steal a beef on the range in Red River County, Choctaw Nation. They proceeded to Red River bottom and shot a fine steer belonging to George Taff, a prominent farmer. Unfortunately Taff happened to be in the bottom looking after his stock and appeared on the scene immediately upon hearing the shot. Moss promptly killed him. During the exchange of fire, the murderers separated, the beef was abandoned, and Moss's horse got away from him. Unable to catch it, he had gone home on foot. Taff's absence overnight alarmed his family, and the following day a searching party discovered his body. They also found Moss's horse in the bottom, saddled and bridled, and arrested Moss. In his anxiety he named his three companions.

Moss and Sandy Smith had been turned over to Heck, who happened to be in the vicinity with a load of prisoners. En route to Fort Smith, Smith attempted to escape and was badly wounded by Heck's posse. Since Jones and Butler were citizens of the Nation, the Federal Court had no jurisdiction. The infuriated citizens, doubting that the two men ever would be punished by the tribal courts, took them to the spot where Taff had been murdered. After hearing their confessions, they "riddled them with bullets and left their bodies on the spot where their victim fell." Smith had died in jail just before the case came to trial, leaving Moss alone to pay the penalty for their crime by due course of law.

Doing the honors was George Maledon, the veteran hangman. A wispy, black-bearded Bavarian with a tight lip and a brooding eye, he had drifted into the Southwest as a young man, settling down in Fort Smith where he served as a deputy sheriff and policeman. He had little education, but was as quick as a cat, an excellent shot with the two pistols he carried, and liked prison work. These qualifications and his record in the First Arkansas Federal Battery during the Civil War had won him a job at the United States jail in 1871. It was the marshal's duty to spring the trap or have one of his deputies do so, but after the first few hangings, none of them wanted the job, so, at five dollars a head, Maledon had volunteered for the lethal chore.

From that day he become a man set apart from his fellows by his macabre trade. Merchants, saloonkeepers, even the town loafers shunned his vain quest for a friendly glance, and mothers sought obedience of recalcitrant children with the threat that "old Maledon will get you." Journalists called him the "Prince of Hangmen" and the scaffold on which he performed "The Gates of Hell."

But Heck talked to him often, and was strangely attracted by the natural pride he took in his work. On one occasion Maledon showed him a tintype of each notorious desperado with whom he had dealt, numerous mementos, and leg irons, straps, ropes, and other gruesome instruments of his office.

With one of these ropes he already had hanged eleven men.

"It is made of the best hemp fiber, hand-woven in St. Louis and treated to keep it from slipping," he said. He treated all his ropes with a pitchy, oil substance, stretched them on the gibbet with 200-pound bags of sand, and oiled them again.

Heck could see that the rope was of the best quality. Originally one and one quarter inch in diameter, it had shrunk to a tight one inch—perfect for knotting and oily enough so that it gave no squeak when jerked. Maledon showed him how the noose was tied.

87

"Why do you use such a big knot?" Heck asked.

Maledon smiled, something he seldom did any more. Heck's observation seemed to please him.

"You are the first man who ever asked me that. A big knot is the secret of a good execution. The humane way to hang a man is to break his neck, not strangle him to death. If you strangle a man, it isn't a pretty sight. He kicks and twists a lot. If you break his neck, it is a painless death and instantaneous. Not even a quiver. He just sways and twirls a little. Let me show you . . ."

He dropped the noose around Heck's neck and tightened it over the larynx until it touched the skin all around.

"Now we place the knot right under the left ear, this way."

Heck felt the knot in the hollow back of his jawbone.

"Now, here is the secret most of them don't know," said Maledon. He brought the rope upward and over the top of Heck's head, and let it hang down in a curve on the other side.

"That holds the knot steady under the ear. When I spring the trap and the man drops through, the rope snaps taut; the big knot throws the head sideways and fractures the spine. It always works that way for me."

"I see." Heck removed the rope, then asked cautiously: "I've heard many stories about the gallows being haunted and how strange beings have been seen coming over the walls at night— do you have any qualms of conscience or fear of the spirits of the men you've hanged?"

Maledon's reaction startled him. He actually threw back his head and laughed.

"Such stories are largely believed by Negroes and superstitious whites. No ghosts have ever haunted me. I reckon I hanged them too. As to my conscience, I can say I've only done my duty. I've never hanged a man who didn't deserve it."

The morning before the execution, Maledon chose three of his best ropes and dropped them from the great crossbeam of the old gallows. He inspected the steps and platform, tested the trap doors, and got out his oil can and oiled the hinges. Then he picked six special guards, issued them uniforms and weapons, and gave them their instructions to make sure that everything went smoothly and none of the condemned men had a chance to escape.

Next he provided new suits and coffins for the prisoners and arranged to have any unclaimed corpses carted to the cemetery. Finally, he supervised the issuance of passes to persons who wished to attend the ceremony.

Early hangings had been witnessed by thousands, many of whom traveled hundreds of miles and remained in the city for days, camping on the ground and sleeping at the foot of the scaffold the night before to have ringside places. By 1882, these spectacles had taken on such "aspects of a carnival" that Washington had ordered them closed to the public. A stockade had been built around the gallows, and the number of official witnesses cut down to forty. Maledon allowed Heck the privilege of checking in the official witnesses.

Meanwhile, the condemned prepared themselves to die. They were urged to pray and talk to the ministers who came to their cells to "save their souls for eternity." "No matter how many stains of blood there may be on the hands," Parker had said in sentencing them, "lift those hands in supplication to the judge of the quick and the dead . . . and let the heart speak out contrition and sorrow."

Moss and Crow had jeered at his words. But Hill had asked permission to be taken from the jail and baptized. Interviewed by an *Elevator* reporter, he exclaimed: "Thank God! Thank God! I am ready to die. In a few more hours I will be free from prison walls and my soul will be in heaven."

He had just completed writing a number of farewell letters to his relatives and friends, and handed them to the reporter unsealed, requesting him to mail them after he was dead. One was addressed to his mother-in-law.

"She brought my death upon me," he said, "but I have forgiven her from my heart . . ."

Moss and Crow were morose and gloomy, refused to talk, but appeared unnerved at the thought of their impending fate.

At 12:30 P.M., Marshal Carroll entered the jail and read the death warrants, and the sad march to the gallows began. The prisoners walked with a steady step, Hill singing and praying alternately. On his breast he wore a large card with the letters "M. B. S.," made from the hair of his mother, brother, and sister, which he had braided himself.

After reaching the gallows, short religious ceremonies were held by the attendant clergymen. Then the culprits took their stand on the trap.

Maledon came to his post, dressed in a modest black suit and wearing his big pistols under his coat. Heck watched him fasten his straps, adjust the nooses, and slip the black caps in place. Then he released the bolt.

There was a thudding noise as the cumbrous doors fell apart. The three men shot down to the ends of the ropes, their heads tilted curiously to one side, and "all that was left of the wretches dangled between heaven and earth."

After hanging half an hour the bodies were lowered. Hill was turned over to his sister, who had visited him in his cell that morning. She had accompanied him to the gallows, standing upon the platform until the fatal plunge was made, and arranging his hands and closing his eyes after his body was placed in its coffin. Moss and Crow were taken to potter's field.

Heck could see that the necks of all three were broken. Death had been instantaneous. As Maledon had told him, "It always works that way for me."

11

Moonshiners and Train Robbers

After this experience, Heck determined that if ever he was called upon to perform this task he would obtain the services of a professional. He had never batted an eye at the toll of battle, but he had no stomach for pulling the gallows trigger. For his part, his service as a deputy marshal always would be to bring them in for trial. Hunting a man was the most interesting part of the business. After catching him, everything else was routine.

On June 1, Marshal Carroll, with several guards, left Fort Smith by train with twenty convicts for the Federal prison at Little Rock. Heck had wanted to accompany him on the trip to learn something of this phase of the duties of the office, but a new threat had thrust itself into the Territory situation.

For more than a decade, trains had rattled north through the Nations with huge loads of Texas cattle, sheep, hides, grain, coal, and cotton. They came back loaded with farm machinery, boots and shoes and furniture—all kinds of goods manufactured in the East for the counters of the stores in the settlements and bigger towns. Worse than that, they brought back more settlers to exploit the resources of the Nations.

Slowly the Indians were beginning to realize that they faced the prospect of being permanently deprived of their property, even their way of life. In the Chickasaw country alone, the white population of noncitizens was approaching 50,000. The some 4,000

Chickasaw citizens could not hope to hold their own under such circumstances. In the Choctaw country, thousands of acres of coal lands were being developed, and hundreds of whites had been imported as laborers in mines, paying the annual fee for each man. Many had married Indian women, acquiring citizenship rights, and had become a power in the affairs of the Nation. Hundreds more were developing the timber resources, building sawmills, and turning the forests into merchantable lumber.

The Indians hated the railroads from the beginning. They had fought the right-of-way concessions in the Federal courts and lost. Their permit systems had brought the white man more than anything, but they blamed the railroads for the dreaded "civilizing" influence that befell them in the eighties.

Despite stiff Federal penalties, trains were derailed, installations were sabotaged, and at least one organized band of 'breeds terrorized travelers and local citizens alike in an effort to discourage all attempts at orderly use of the lines.

Even the law-abiding Indian saw little wrong in making the operations of the railroads as difficult as possible. Tandy Walker, the well-to-do nephew of a former chief of the Choctaws, who lived in a fine log house overlooking the Katy tracks south of the Canadian, would post himself behind a convenient rock to wait for the morning passenger train and see how many windows he could shoot out of the coaches before the snorting monster passed!

Such actions brought death and severe injuries to many. The gang of terrorists had been arrested and sentenced to long jail terms by Judge Parker.

The criminal class took advantage of the Indian's utter repugnance to the railroad. Since the middle of March, systematic thefts from freights on the Katy had occurred between McAlester and Muskogee. The thieves would board the train on a long pull up a steep hill or mountain and toss out the plunder, then jump off as it arrived at the grade beyond. Captain Charles LeFlore, of the United States Indian police, had either been notified too late to catch them or unable to pick up a trail.

Another theft consisting of a large quantity of sugar had occurred south of Muskogee. In throwing it off the car, one of the sacks was broken, and the sugar leaked out as the thieves carried it off to a wagon.

Heck and Captain LeFlore examined the stretch of track the next day. Following the trail of sugar, they found the wagon tracks and followed them into the Creek Nation to a cabin on Cane Creek, where they found the plunder—thirty-five sacks of sugar, four gallons of ether, sixty pounds of lard, a box of tobacco, and a surveyor's compass.

"There was only a woman at the cabin," Heck said in describing the event later. "We arrested her and took the stolen freight to Muskogee, where I learned she was the widow of Sam Brewer, a Cherokee bootlegger with no hands or feet, whom I had arrested the year before and sent to the Little Rock penitentiary."

Brewer had died in prison, and his widow had been living with a moonshiner named Joe Campbell. Campbell had two partners, Aaron Purdy and Ed Howell. Purdy headed the gang, and was operating a wildcat still on Snake Creek south of Red Fork.

"Taking three possemen, Burrell Cox, Hank Childers and Jim Wallace, I started for Snake Creek the night of June 15th, when I received word that five men had just held up the passenger train on the Katy at Verdigris river tank six miles north of Muskogee and killed a prominent cattleman. . . ."

Heck had heard nothing like it since his early days in Texas and the exploits of Sam Bass.

At 10:30 P.M., when the train stopped at the tank for water, a man who called himself "Captain Jack" and had his face blackened with mud, crawled over the tender and covered the fireman and engineer with a six-shooter. At the same moment, four other men appeared, wearing bandanna masks and carrying Winchesters. They seized mail agent W. S. Colton and forced him to lead the way to the express car, where they surprised Messenger A. B. Codding and looted the safe of $8,000.

While they were looting the safe, Colton attempted to escape through the door, and one of the robbers, who had been left on the ground, shot him through the left forearm. The train boy, Harry Ryan, ran out on the steps of the smoker to see what was happening, and the same robber shot his left arm to splinters. The bullet, passing through the open door, struck B. F. Tarver under the left jaw and broke his neck. Tarver, a Marlin, Texas, cowman who was returning from Chicago, fell forward on the steps in front of Ryan.

The robbers and messenger then jumped out of the express car and came back to the engine. The messenger stopped in the glow of the headlight, and Captain Jack yelled, "Get out of that light, or a bullet will punch hell out of you!" Codding moved out of the light quickly. One robber ran across the tracks into the darkness and returned with their horses. After firing several more shots to frighten the train crew and passengers, they mounted and fled north toward the Cherokee Nation.

The wounded and dead were brought to Muskogee, and the Indian police notified. Captain LeFlore and his men left in direct pursuit of the bandits. On a hunch that the gang might cross the Verdigris and double back through the Creek country, Heck rode west with his posse on the north side of the Arkansas.

He "didn't know if they had any connection with Purdy's moonshiners and freight thieves," but "it was the first train robbery of its kind in the Nation," and his "avowed purpose was to show them it was no place to ply their vocation."

Heck never recorded in his memoirs to what extent he was successful. The Eufaula *Indian Journal,* under a June 19 date line, reported:

News has just reached here of the capture of three of the robbers (near Mingo) in a house occupied by Harry Sisson, who was sentenced to be hanged once by the courts of this nation for murder but was saved by the interference of Judge Parker . . . and has since served a two year term at Detroit, Mich. Two of the parties captured were brothers named Phipps, applicants for citizenship in this nation, and one colored man named "One-Eyed" Rogers. Sisson made his escape by running out of the house. It is thought he is wounded as he was shot at a dozen times at close range. Two of the gang are still at large and went west, though the officers are close on their trail, and it is expected at any hour to hear of their capture.

But the *Elevator,* a few days later, declared:

A report reaching here that Deputy Thomas has captured the robbers appears to be a mistake. But he is still after them . . . He sent in during the week for some cartridges to be forwarded to Catoosa, which is the last heard from him.

Catoosa was a short half-day's ride northeast of Red Fork. Either Heck lost the trail, or he and his posse held a council of war and decided it was useless to pursue the robbers farther. By June 27, they had crossed the Arkansas and reached Snake Creek with the "avowed intention of capturing the Purdy gang and destroying their still."

The still was situated in a deep ravine protected on the lower side by a wall of logs and stone, and had the posse come in above this fort, they would have been spared the saddest part of the expedition. But it seems that Brewer's widow, who had given Heck the information, did not exactly understand the location of the still, or else intended that the whole raiding party be killed, or possibly Heck was too daring.

He rode boldly up the ravine in advance of his men, halted within thirty yards of the log and stone wall and called for the moonshiners to come out and surrender. Purdy and his men immediately opened fire with their Winchesters. One bullet struck Heck in the right arm, breaking his wrist. Another tore a hole eight inches long in his left side and knocked him from the saddle.

Obviously thinking that Heck was alone, the moonshiners leaped from behind the wall to finish him. A fusillade tore at them from the brush, fired by Cox, Wallace, and Childers. Purdy, in the lead, caught the full volley in his arms, chest, and legs. As he went down, Howell and Campbell dropped their rifles and surrendered.

Purdy was still alive. He was a blond giant of a man. His hard blue eyes glared, and a thin yellow beard on his face failed to hide its coarseness and brutality. Despite his wounds, he twisted over on one side, still trying to use his weapon. Cox leaped in and kicked it flying from his hands.

Heck lay on the ground, bleeding badly.

"Purdy's the son-of-a-bitch who shot you," Cox snarled. He pointed the muzzle of his own Winchester at the outlaw's head. "I'll just finish him now."

"No," Heck said.

Even under these circumstances, he would not tolerate the abuse of prisoners by his men. To cool Cox off, he sent him down to the creek for some water. When he returned, Purdy looked so longingly at the canteen that Heck consented and gave him the first drink.

Cox swore a loud oath and levered a cartridge into his rifle. "Hell's bells, let me kill him!"

"No!" Heck was adamant.

He ordered Cox to load the wounded man in the moonshiners' wagon. Meanwhile, Wallace and Childers cut up the still, destroying several hundred gallons of beer and whisky. Then the posse started to Red Fork with the prisoners. Heck rode alongside the wagon with his arm clamped to his left side to keep the blood from spurting, and his right hand hanging useless from his broken wrist.

They reached the end of the spur on the Frisco railroad within an hour. It consisted of a station and cattle loading pens. There was no doctor.

Tulsa, the Creek trading center and white settlement, lay three miles north in the big bend of the Arkansas at the historical junction where the Creek, Cherokee, and Osage nations came together. The train from Red Fork didn't leave until 6 P.M., and arrived in Tulsa any time before daylight, depending on the number of cattle to be loaded from the area.

Heck couldn't wait for the train. He had lost a lot of blood and was growing weaker by the moment.

He rode with his cargo to Tulsa. Dr. H. P. Newlin, the town's first physician, attended the wounds of his prisoner. Then Heck had the hole in his side dressed, and his right wrist set and bandaged.

The condition of both men prohibited their further travel. Heck sent Cox, Childers, and Wallace to Fort Smith with Howell and Campbell. He remained in Tulsa with Purdy.

It took some time for his wounds to heal. On one of his visits

96

to the Newlin home, Dr. Newlin introduced him to his daughter's young friend, Matie Mowbray.

"Matie's one of our schoolteachers here," the doctor said. "We've talked so much about the famous Heck Thomas that she had to meet him."

Her large, dark eyes met his, and they gazed up from what Heck recalled "the prettiest face I had ever seen."

Heck's glance matched her's, with a depth and gravity for which neither was responsible.

Then Heck withdrew his glance. "I'm honored!" he said. He swept his big Stetson from his long brown locks and bowed gallantly.

Still, in his mind's eye, he could see her. She was of medium height, neither robust nor heavy, yet showing unusual strength and suppleness in her prim, simple dress. She was still in her teens, but a full-grown woman.

And, Matie confessed, in an interview years later, "I was entranced by this tall, strikingly handsome marshal, with his well-trimmed mustache, his taste for clothes and wearing ivory-handled six-shooters. He was my ideal for a frontier hero."

Heck found himself no less impressed with Matie's parents, Reverend George W. and Hannah Mowbray: "Hannah was a small, quiet, and refined woman," who often compared the flower-covered prairies and wooded streams of the Nations with the little fields and hedges of her native England. A husky, long-bearded Methodist from Elmira, New York, Reverend Mowbray had come west in 1887 to travel and preach among the Osages. While attending the South Kansas Conference in March, 1888, the Reverend James Murray, a member of the conference and Superintendent of Indian Missions, urged him to work in the mission field, and he had moved his family from McCune, Kansas, to Tulsa where he became pastor of the First Methodist Church and took charge of the missions established among the Creeks. "He often traveled many miles into the country to deliver his sermons to the Indians and others, many times in a brush arbor; he used an interpreter with the Indians, and stayed in camp with them—a real pioneer preacher."

Heck was delighted with one story that Dr. Newlin told him:

Life in the little settlement had been very strenuous, and, when some hilarious cowboys shot the windows out of the nice new church, the former pastor had resigned. "That first Sunday, Reverend Mowbray announced that he would preach on the evils of drinking, gambling and dancing. The boys were in town celebrating pay day and had shot out all the lighted windows the night before. They sent word to him that if he preached that sermon he would dance to bullets.

"Sunday morning the boys filed in and sat down. Hannah lifted her apron and walked calmly down the aisle. 'Boys,' she requested, 'put your guns in here.' You never saw such a sheepish bunch in your life. Every last one handed over his weapon. She piled them near the front door, and after the last Amen, she said, 'Boys, come and get them.'"

But Heck was more interested in Matie. There had been only a Creek tribal school in Tulsa before the Frisco built a bridge across the Arkansas and extended its spur to Red Fork. Families of construction workers, storekeepers, and supply workers had settled there the summer of 1884 with twenty white children of school age, and the Presbyterian Mission had built a combined church and schoolroom for them in the fall. Within three years, it had become overcrowded, and many children were unable to attend because of the tuition. To take care of the latter group, Reverend Mowbray had opened a day school in the First Methodist Church, with Matie as teacher.

Heck's right hand was in splints, so he asked Matie to help him write his official report on the capture of Aaron Purdy. This second meeting ripened into a deep friendship. They saw much of each other in the days which followed. Heck told her many stories about Texas and the Territory, and Matie related her own experiences coming down from Kansas with her parents, driving a team of mules hitched to a jump-seat buggy.

"We shipped our household goods by freight, stayed the first night at Coffeyville, and made an early start into the Cherokee country next morning. Oh, it was a glorious start! The sun was bright and warm and the prairie a flower garden.

"I tried to keep track of the different flowers, but it was more than I could do. The birds were singing, so many different kinds

—saucy robins, blue jays, cardinals, brown thrush, and mocking-birds. At noon we reached the Caney River and stopped at Coody's Bluff to eat our lunch and feed the mules. The soft south wind was blowing, and the peaceful place called for a longer halt than we should have made. I shall never forget Coody's Bluff!"

She tossed back her head and sighed. She caught Heck staring at the soft whiteness of her throat, and he flushed in embarrass-ment. She looked away, toward the groves along the Arkansas where the campfires of the Creeks gleamed in the gathering twilight. Then she continued:

"We went on, came to several places on the river where we couldn't cross. We were to spend the night on the Caney at the home of John Allen, a Presbyterian missionary. But we missed the trail, drove about twenty miles out of our way. At nightfall, we reached a shack occupied by a Negro with an army of chil-dren. He told us of a short cut through the woods, but it was a new trail and very difficult to follow. Father hired one of the old Negro's sons to show us the way. After being nearly shaken to pieces and almost overturning several times, we arrived at Allen's house at midnight, hungry and so weary we hardly could move.

"Mr. Allen wasn't at home, but his wife made us welcome. She gave up her own bed and slept in the other room of the tiny two-roomed cabin with her children. She had no milk or butter, but the bacon and eggs, cold soda biscuits, and creamless coffee were ambrosia!"

Heck nodded knowingly. He had recovered from his embar-rassment. Matie's complaisance to the rough frontier life absorbed him completely as she talked on.

"We were too tired to sleep much and anxious to be on our way. The Caney was still running high the next morning, and Mrs. Allen walked a mile and a half to get an Indian to help us across. You should have seen the Indian driving us through that boiling flood! The water rolled up to the seats in the buggy, which lurched this way and that. We had to put our feet on the seats and lean first to one side, then the other, to keep from over-turning. Finally we were across, Father jumping out as soon as we landed, and blocking the hind wheels as the Indian drove up a hill that seemed almost perpendicular. The Indian gave us good directions the rest of the way and we soon arrived at our destination.

"As we came in sight of town, Father turned and said, 'Well, there is Tulsa!' I was dismayed, and asked, 'Where are the houses? Those are just old barns.' The cottonwood shacks with stovepipes sticking from the roofs looked more like they had been built for livestock than people.

"The only house we could find is the one we are living in now. It was unpainted then, with one main room, a tiny windowless bedroom, and a long shed kitchen. It was papered with newspapers, and looked anything but a dwelling place. The first day, Mother and I got two tubs of hot water, tore those old papers down, and scrubbed until we were exhausted. Our furniture had arrived, so we arranged things the best we could and went to bed early. But we had made the mistake of putting our beds close to the wall and had to get up in the night and light the lamps. We were not the only occupants of the beds—they were literally swarming with bedbugs!"

Matie laughed. But Heck, struck by her frankness rather than the humor of the situation, stared like a child left at the climax of a thrilling tale.

"Well—what happened next!" he burst out.

"Oh," Matie replied, "we had to carry everything outdoors and go over every crack and cranny with a corrosive sublimate and turpentine. We must have used five gallons of the mixture before we finally conquered them.

"But the bedbugs were not the only pests," she added, quickly. "We had no screens, and flies, mosquitoes, June bugs, and every other kind of insect came in as soon as the lamps were lighted. Hogs roamed the streets and kept coming under the house and scratching their backs on the underpinning, and fleas started coming up through the floor.

"One night Mother gave an unearthly scream. She thought a man had crept up the steps and said he had a long white beard. Father jumped out of bed, lighted a lamp, and discovered that a billy goat from the livery stable had come to visit us."

Heck began laughing then. Matie's dark eyes sparkled. She seemed pleased that she had broken the crust of seriousness that had enveloped him in his years of marshaling.

"Mother was very nervous about coming to the Territory," she explained. "She had been told she would be scalped by Indians or murdered by some criminal. So Father bought the little house, moved it close to the church, and enlarged it. One night we were awakened by such sweet music, and found a band of all Indian boys with a cornet, violin, guitars, and French harps outside. Their music was very welcome. Mother hasn't been afraid of Indians since.

"If ever this country becomes civilized and rid of its criminal element, it will be due largely to the efforts of men like you and my father," Matie concluded, and she said it with an admiration and affection that stirred Heck with a deep loneliness.

Finally, when his prisoner was in condition to travel, and Heck was ready to depart for Fort Smith, he told her:

"When you are a little older, I'm coming back after you."

Their eyes met again, as they had when he first looked upon her and he had bowed gallantly. Only this time, her eyes held his. In them he read the same hope he had just spoken aloud. Then she bade him good-by, and turned away.

12

New Courts—A New Empire

Heck reached Fort Smith with his prisoner in time for the fall term of court. The Purdy gang had been arraigned before the U. S. Commissioner on charges of larceny from a freight shipment and introducing whisky in the Indian country. All pleaded guilty and received short jail sentences, except Purdy, who faced an additional charge of assault with intent to kill a Federal officer.

While waiting for the case to go before the grand jury, Heck learned that the three train robbery suspects he had arrested near Mingo had been released. Messenger Codding, Mail Agent Colton, and members of the train crew had seen them in jail and declared "they are the wrong men."

Their trip to Fort Smith was not fruitless, however. While looking over numerous wanted posters and descriptions of fugitives in the marshal's office, Codding and Colton tentatively identified two of the bandits who had led the attack on the express car as Kep Queen and John Barber, notorious desperadoes for whom rewards totaling $7,000, dead or alive, had been offered in Texas. Queen, Barber, and a man named Whitley had committed several murders in Bell and Tom Green counties and robbed a bank at Cisco, Texas, in 1887. Whitley had been slain a short time afterward by the Rangers, and Queen and Barber had fled to the Cherokee Nation. They had been there several months, claiming to be Cherokees, and had applied for citizenship. Only two weeks before, Queen's wife, with a woman believed to be Barber's sister, had been seen in Claremore, trying to sell a small herd of horses allegedly owned by her husband.

It was certain that two men were hiding in the vicinity. Heck was preparing to go on the hunt for them when Marshal Carroll decided otherwise.

"Thomas," the marshal said, "your wound hasn't quite healed, and your wrist is still giving you trouble." But he wouldn't let Heck go because he was the chief witness against Purdy and in several other cases that were being tried at that time in the Federal Court.

Heck was disheartened. But orders were orders—and lack of his testimony "might set free these vermin for the marshals to run down again." So he requested Marshal Carroll to send two of his old comrades, Captain Gideon White and Barney Connelly, aften Queen and Barber.

White and Connelly went—and came back. Queen and Barber didn't. On the night of November 15, the deputies, with Cherokee Sheriff Bud Sanders of Coo-wee-scoo-we District, and his posse, surrounded the fugitives in an old cabin four miles from Claremore and killed Queen in a brief battle before daybreak. Barber's horse was shot from under him, but he escaped on foot, leaving a trail of blood. In a pasture nearby, the sheriff recovered seven horses which had been stolen at Cincinnati, Arkansas.

Meanwhile, White and Connelly traced Barber into Saline District. They encountered him early one morning on Spring Creek and killed him as he fled through a cornfield.

Nearly two years later, a youth who had been reared in the home of Alexander Lewis, fifty miles from Verdigris tank, confessed to J. J. Kinney, a railroad detective, that Lewis was the third member of the band, that plans for the robbery had been made in Lewis' home, and that Lewis had ridden away with the gang and returned with them following the holdup and slaying. Detective Kinney worked up some corroborative evidence, and Lewis was indicted, convicted, and sentenced to hang. But his attorney appealed to the Supreme Court on error, the case was reversed, and in his second trial, Lewis was acquitted.

Heck always believed he was the bandit who had blackened his face with mud and called himself "Captain Jack." A fourth member of the gang finally was arrested in Texas on another charge and sentenced to twenty-five years in the state penitentiary. The fifth robber was never captured.

The deaths of Queen and Barber "set White and Connelly in position to collect a large share of the reward." Heck "always felt badly" because he had not been in on the kill. He had "some consolation" when Purdy was found guilty and sent to prison.

He asked Marshal Carroll to relieve him of his Chickasaw assignment and transfer him to the Cherokee Nation. The judicial countenance of the Territory was undergoing rapid changes. With the growth of the white population and the Border States demanding a share of the "gravy" going to Arkansas as the result of the ever-increasing activity of the Fort Smith court, Congress had assigned all the region north of the South Canadian and west of the lands of the Five Civilized Tribes to the United States Court for Kansas, with court terms at Fort Scott and Wichita. The like region south of the Canadian had gone to the United States District Court for the Northern District of Texas at Graham. The area of the Five Tribes remained with Judge Parker, but the great bulk of the population was in the eastern portion of the region, with most of the business for the court coming from the Cherokee Nation.

Heck failed to mention his added interest in a certain dark-eyed girl he had met in Tulsa.

But the marshal already had made plans for him on the Canadian border of the Unassigned Lands. Boomer agitation had become so great in Washington that Congress passed a bill opening the Oklahoma country to white settlement, and issuance of a Presidential proclamation setting the date for the great "land rush" was imminent.

So Heck wrote a letter to Matie and set out for Pauls Valley and Whitebead Hill. He found the country already swarming with land-hungry people.

The month of March, 1889, marked two other events which were to determine Heck's future service as a deputy marshal. The Dawes Act of 1887, authorizing the President to allot lands in severalty to any tribe of Indians that he regarded sufficiently advanced to benefit by the change, and the Springer Amendment to the Indian Appropriation Bill, giving him specific authority to negotiate for the purchase of all surplus Indian land west of the Five Civilized Tribes, had cleared the way for the whole area to be settled by the white man. Anticipating the creation of an "Oklahoma Territory," Congress approved an act establishing the first white man's court in the Indian country at Muskogee.

Principally a court of civil jurisdiction, putting into force the laws of the State of Arkansas, it interfered with the criminal jurisdiction of the Fort Smith, Fort Scott, Wichita, and Graham courts to the extent that it was given exclusive, original jurisdiction of all offenses against the laws of the United States not punishable by death or imprisonment at hard labor. By the same act—still haggling at Judge Parker's authority by degrees "like the slow bleeding to death of an unfortunate patient under the knife of a bungling surgeon"—the Chickasaw Nation and a greater portion of the Choctaw Nation as far north as the Canadian were annexed to the Eastern Judicial District of Texas, with the court seat at Paris, and the Paris court was given exclusive, original jurisdiction of all Federal law violations within that portion of the Territory not given to Muskogee. By a special provision, appeals were authorized from the Muskogee court direct to the Supreme Court of the United States.

Thus the Oklahoma area became the direct responsibility of the Federal courts of Kansas and Muskogee. James M. Shackleford, a seasoned lawyer from Indiana, was appointed judge of the new court; Zachary T. Walrond of Kansas, prosecuting attorney; and Thomas B. Needles, a banker from Illinois, United States Marshal. A room over the newspaper office was hurriedly set up for its sessions, and the court convened at 10:30 A.M., April 1.

Heck described Marshal Needles as "a fat, good-natured man, with an air about him that was at once attractive and pleasing." From the start, Needles intended going "not a little" to make the court popular. One of his first acts was to appoint 300 temporary deputies to assist the infantry and cavalry troops stalking the Oklahoma frontiers to hold back the settlers and patroling the interior for "sooners" concealed in the woods.

Heck received one of these appointments. He also was appointed regular deputy for the Eastern Judicial District of Texas at Paris, which included fifty-five counties extending from Red River to Galveston. He wrote, "I was the only officer in federal service with authority over so vast an area and carrying commissions under three United States Marshals at the same time."

President Cleveland had signed the Oklahoma bill into law. He had been renominated by his party in the campaign of 1888, but the Republican candidate, Benjamin Harrison, was victorious. Harrison was inaugurated March 4, 1889. Three weeks later, he proclaimed April 22 as the opening day and twelve o'clock noon the earliest hour at which one could legally enter the land. Any settler entering before that time would forfeit all right to homestead. The people would gather on the borders. The first man on the land was the one to homestead it.

Hopeful thousands came from the four corners of the nation. Throughout the Border States, flags were hung from buildings, cannons fired, and bonfires lit. By mid-April, some of the border cities were nearly depopulated.

While most of the settlers moved southward through the Cherokee Outlet from Kansas, others assembled on the line of the Iowa, Kickapoo, and Pottawatomie-Shawnee reservations to the east, and on the line of the Cheyenne and Arapaho country to the west. On the south, the jumping-off place was Purcell and along the Canadian.

Here the wildest enthusiasm existed, if not a greater number of people. Men sold their rights to claims for $400 and $500, bootleggers and gamblers flourished, fights occurred daily, and Heck arrested two men for murder as he assisted the military on the Chickasaw boundary.

More than a dozen fords had been selected by which to reach the Oklahoma side of the Canadian. On the morning of the 22nd, huge crowds began gathering at the fords. Hundreds mounted on fleet horses formed long lines, jockeying for an advantage in the start. Most of them knew the treacherous quicksands of the Canadian, yet all were eager to be first to leap into its waters. The signal officer, watch in hand, waited on the Oklahoma side. Just as the second hand reached the hour of twelve, he gave the

106

signal, and before the stirring notes of his bugle reached the ears of those at the farthest end of the column, the foremost horsemen, with yells equal to a band of Comanches, plunged into the river. They came up drenched and covered with sand, and the other excited riders followed. Wagons and carriages, as thick as they could be crowded together, followed pell-mell through the fords. Reaching the opposite bank, the immense throng spread out, covering the country for miles, the advance dropping off as they reached claims that suited them.

At the same moment, the great masses from the north, east, and west surged forward to meet them in the greatest horse race in history. It was like a great den of ants swarming over a bowl of sugar. Vehicles careened crazily, overturned. Teams galloped madly with flying harness. The screams of victims trampled to death. Others leaped from the platforms and windows of trains as they rolled over the prairies along the Santa Fe. Victorious shouts, a wave of the hat, the setting of a flag or stake.

Heck, in another letter to Matie, described it in one word: "Pandemonium . . ." By nightfall, every desirable town lot and quarter section had been taken. Guthrie was a city of 15,000; Oklahoma City, 5,000; Kingfisher, 3,000. "Their campfires gleam in the darkness, their tents loom athwart the sky like an army in bivouac. Already around the campfires there is talk of mass meetings on the morrow to form local governments. . . .

"All this was gained in an afternoon," added a dispatch to the *Indian Chieftain* on April 23. "In no country save America, and in no part of that country but the great West, could such a thing be possible. It is a triumph for the Western people . . . such as they may never again have the opportunity of achieving. That they were fully equal to the occasion needs no more proof than the presence of 60,000 persons in this country last night. The conservative and leisurely East may well look at this and wonder."

Despite this enthusiasm for the embryo empire, Heck hoped the provisional governments would "take over immediately" so he could be relieved of his assignment. He was sorely disappointed. The work of the deputy marshals had just begun.

107

13

Oklahoma Organized

The land offices at Guthrie and Kingfisher—the only
two provided by the Government—were beseiged by
eager and determined men waiting to file claims.
The Guthrie office stood at the top of a long slope
east of the railroad. As the crowd grew, a "regular
jam" developed far down the line to the station. The register and
receiver did the best they could. The applicants were forced into
lines two abreast. They carried blankets and baskets of provisions
with them. Friends brought them water to drink from the engine
tank on the railway tracks. Nearby, Marshal Needles established
headquarters in a tent, flying the American flag above on a young
tree flagstaff. Heck and the other deputies were on duty day and
night to keep order.

Confusion reigned for two days. Then suddenly it grew in
dimensions.

The townsite contained 1,923 acres by actual survey, and there
were six claimants for every lot. It was the same with settlers
taking quarter sections. Many went away with empty purses and
broken hearts because they had spent much time and all their
money trying to get a piece of land and failed. Some were dissatisfied with the claims they obtained and left them or sold
them for little or nothing. Others tried to stake all the lots and
quarter sections they could, using the names of their sisters, aunts,
cousins, and even fictitious relatives, hoping to sell their "posses-

sory rights" later at exorbitant prices. Professional crooks, aided by crooked lawyers, filed contests with or without reason, forcing the poor landholder to defend his claim at the land office, where generally they would relinquish the suit for a consideration. Dealers in real estate began "operations" before two o'clock the first afternoon, saloons and gambling tents "did something more than a land-office business," and more than one man lost his claim to a land shark or on the turn of a card at the gambling table.

But most of the trouble was with sooners.

Despite the vigilance of the troops and deputy marshals, thousands "not disposed to play the game fair" had slipped into the country the night before. An hour before the opening, the prairie grass was alive with them. They came crawling out of ravines and timber, even dropping from trees. At 12:15, a dozen men from the Seminole Land and Town Company were staking out the townsite of Oklahoma City and defying the soldier-guards to run them off. Before the first train arrived at Guthrie, the townsite was swarming with sooners who had staked off most of the choice lots early that morning, and at one minute after 12, offered two townsite plots for record at the land office.

A few of the settlers who made the run from the border tried to settle their rows with sooners with fists and six-shooters.

Three miles west of Guthrie a man who had been hiding in the brush for weeks to jump a claim ordered his rival off with a Winchester. When his rival reached for a pistol, he pumped three bullets into his body.

While Heck was searching for the killer, he received a report of another slaying at Alfred, a small station fourteen miles north of Guthrie. A man named Stevens, from Kansas, and two other claimants had squatted on the same quarter section. Stevens informed them he was willing for all three to work the claim and leave the matter to the proper authorities to say who was the rightful owner. But they decided Stevens and his wife and four small children should leave and they would divide the property themselves. In the row, Stevens was shot through the lungs. He managed to reach his family and died within a few hours.

His wife was almost crazed when Heck reached her. The news

had spread over the neighborhood, and a small party of settlers soon assembled at the dead man's tent. But the murderers had lost no time in "quitting the country."

Heck helped bury Stevens in a plain box on the claim for which he had sacrificed his life. Then he took up a collection for the widow, which amounted to $11. "The woman didn't know what to do." Her neighbors advised her to hold the claim and promised that if the two men returned they would be lynched.

Before Heck returned to headquarters, news was received at Marshal Needle's tent that Martin Colbert, a wealthy half-breed from the Chickasaw Nation, had been killed at Oklahoma City in a quarrel over a claim with a man named Nolan. Deputy J. G. Varnum arrived on the scene immediately. But Nolan had made his escape.

That night, Deputy Marshal Mann returned from the new town of Noble on the Canadian, fourteen miles north of Purcell, to report one of the most exciting scenes witnessed. A band of cowboys, employed by a wealthy Texas rancher and mounted on the fleetest ponies they could procure, had started from the river on a dead run with Winchesters in their hands. A few minutes later, their mounts reeking wet from the hot and furious ride, they occupied the townsite. By mid-afternoon, they had their town government organized, a manager and city officers elected, and the new town now had 5,000 inhabitants. A settler named Goodwin had gone to Fort Reno and made a sworn statement to the post commander that his party of four, who claimed the location, had been fired upon by the Texans. His companions were slain. He had managed to escape by hiding in the thick brush along the river, making his way to the fort after dark. A detachment of Company C, 13th Infantry, under Lieutenant Buck, had been sent to recover the bodies and make a full investigation.

On April 25, J. C. Chyland, of Franklin County, Missouri, was murdered north of Guthrie by three desperate characters desiring his claim. A posse formed to capture them. They found one of the killers hiding in the brush near the Cimarron. When he refused to surrender, they "filled him with lead." Said the Oklahoma City *Times* of April 29: "The posse made no effort to conceal the killing of the assassin and rely upon the community to sustain them in their efforts to overawe the turbulent and lawless element. . . ."

But many settlers failed to sustain the scattered deputy marshals and squads of blue-shirted troops in their efforts to keep order. A very bitter feeling was being engendered against Marshal Needles' 300 deputies in particular.

"They were in Guthrie and had claims staked out before ten o'clock and then threw up their offices," read complaints to the Attorney General's office in Washington. "Under official guise they got into Oklahoma and staked off the best claims in the forenoon. The sooners in the brush saw this and they came from their hiding places and did the same thing. The marshals could do nothing because they had violated the proclamation, and so the brush men and marshals stand in together, while the multitude of settlers go homeless." One man, finding that he could not get a lot, filed on the entire townsite of Guthrie.

Marshal Needles denied these claims in a report to the Attorney General on May 17: "As far as I am concerned, I have not entered any land or lands, town lots or lots in the Oklahoma district and have no interest whatever, directly or indirectly, near or remote of any kind or nature in any land or lots in the territory. . . . I have had an intimation that one of my deputies secured a town lot in Guthrie and one or two have entered a quarter section apiece. I am not positive as to this, but will ascertain the facts at once. . . ."

He explained that he had not fully investigated the actions of these deputies because two special agents of the land office had been doing that. Their reports had been sent to Washington, and he presumed the Attorney General had been fully advised in regard to them.

In a postscript, he wrote: "If the statements made by me and the officers of the Interior Department are not satisfactory, I should like a copy of the specifications filed in order that I may furnish testimony in detail to refute them. I should like to meet my accusers face to face before you."

No accusers were forthcoming, and the case against the Guthrie townsite never went to contest.

"They were a pack of liars," Heck said—mostly men who looked

111

with contempt upon what little protection the deputies could give them and considered them hated tools of an arbitrary government that had so long denied their right to occupy public domain.

The "rider" measure of the act opening Oklahoma contained no provision for territorial government. Congress, unable to visualize the sudden building of cities and 60,000 people occupying every available foot of this million and a half acres within a few hours, had enacted no provisions to meet the situation.

The statutes in existence, framed for normal development, provided that a townsite plot be filed with the land office by corporate authorities, or with the judge of the county court in which it was situated if no incorporated town existed. With no corporate authorities, no counties and no county judges, the provisional governments were forced to take drastic steps to lay out streets and alleys, blocks and lots, where tents were so thick their ropes crossed, and passages were mere wagon tracks or foot paths winding between them. In every town, citizens held mass meetings in streets or tents and elected officials to guide them through the first wild days and nights.

Violence was to be repressed or entirely wiped out as peace-loving, God-fearing people welded themselves together. But outside the towns, where the only law was that generally applicable to Federal territory, vicious outlaws, many from the adjoining Nations, preyed upon the land. Struggling settlers lost horses and cattle. While selling, transporting, or possession of liquor in the Nations and on Indian reservations was a criminal offense, legal saloons flourished in Oklahoma. All along its borders red whisky flowed freely to those willing to cross over and get it. Robberies and murders also helped to keep the deputy marshals busy.

Heck policed the area from Guthrie to Pauls Valley and Ardmore to Muskogee, taking much small fry—whisky peddlers and thieves—to the Paris court over the Santa Fe and Texas Pacific. He continued to deliver prisoners to Fort Smith who had committed offenses in Judge Parker's jurisdiction and fled into Oklahoma or the Choctaw and Chickasaw nations.

Most of his prisoners went to Muskogee. Judge Shackleford, handing down decisions concerning the Five Nations and the

112

whole Indian country, became the busiest judge in the Southwest. One hundred eighty-six civil and criminal cases were docketed for the first term of court in June, 1889. Marshal Needles appointed twenty regular deputies and listed sixty persons wanted for crimes in his jurisdiction. By autumn, fifty-eight persons had been committed to the Muskogee jail. A new addition was being constructed to accommodate the increasing number. The commissioner for the court had issued 162 warrants besides those sent from the commissioners in Oklahoma and the half-dozen commissioners in other parts of the Nations. The court docket had quadrupled, with 528 civil cases and more than 200 criminals to be tried.

The *Indian Chieftain* of Thursday, August 29, compared the preparations for the autumn term to a threshing operation:

"There is much buzz and hum in court circles, readying the legal machine which drives its stobbs (sic) next Monday. Judge Shackleford, the feeder, will be on the ground Friday, two days in advance, to see which way to set the separator. Clerk Nelson, the band cutter, has already returned from his vacation and is now sharpening his knives that there may be no delay. The jury, the pitchers, have been subpoenaed. The marshal, the measurer, is calling in his deputies to hold the bags, and the strawstackers, witnesses, are expected to report at 8:30 Monday morning. Jailer Hisey holds a tarpaulin over the stack yard."

The same issue of the *Chieftain* lauded Heck's capture of Oscar Coulter, "the boyish murderer of a citizen of Golden City, Arkansas, who was instrumental in sending him to prison in Georgia a few years ago." Coulter had escaped and was hiding in the Nations with an $1,800 price on his head. The young desperado's hand flashed to his six-shooter as Heck stepped into his camp on the Canadian thirty miles south of Muskogee, but "upon looking squarely into the muzzle of the Winchester in the hands of the determined deputy, he changed his mind and gave up without further resistance."

The newspapers and records of the Federal courts for this period are replete with Heck's activities. Commenting on his sensational capture of Dan Pixley for the murder of Dave Givens at Tabler Springs in October, the *Chieftain* stated: "Heck Thomas has captured more outlaws than any other deputy in the Territory."

In December—the only time in his career—Heck had to stand trial in one of his own courts. Acting under orders of U. S. Indian Agent Leo Bennett, he and Captain LeFlore raided a gambling house in Ardmore and carried away all paraphernalia to be destroyed. The owner swore out larceny writs for their arrest before the United States Commissioner at Paris, Texas, but "Agent Bennett immediately took measures to see that they were properly defended and acquitted."

The same month, when Congress met, Oklahoma demanded immediate organization of a separate territory. A memorial drafted at Guthrie by a territorial convention of one hundred delegates proclaimed:

"The laws at present in force (in Oklahoma) relate only to crimes against the United States and the primitive forms of violence, such as murder and stock stealing. . . . There is no provision of law as to child stealing, attempted rape, poisoning, abortion, libel or blackmail, reckless burning of woods or prairies, burglarious entry of houses, trespass, embezzlement, rioting, carrying deadly weapons, disturbing public meetings, seduction, public indecency, profanity, gambling, lotteries, drunkenness, bribery, destroying legal process, official negligence or malfeasance, creating or maintaining a public nuisance, selling unwholesome, diseased or adulterated provisions or drink, introducing diseased or infected stock into the territory, swindling, false weights or measures, obtaining money or property under false pretense, making or using counterfeit labels; nor for many other offenses. . . .

"By the force of an exceptionally cool and intelligent and honest public opinion, there has been a degree of public order so far preserved . . . but it cannot be hoped that such conditions shall permanently continue."

On May 2, 1890, President Harrison affixed his signature to the Organic Act, creating six counties (Logan, Oklahoma, Cleveland, Canadian, Kingfisher, and Payne) and six county seats (Guthrie, Oklahoma City, Norman, El Reno, Kingfisher, and Stillwater, respectively), and extending Oklahoma Territory to include all that part of the former Indian Territory except the Nations proper of the Five Civilized Tribes, the seven small reservations of the Quapaw Agency northeast of them, and the unoccupied part of the Cherokee Outlet (but including the portion of the Outlet occupied by the Ponca, Tonkawa, Otoe-Missouri, and Pawnee tribes). Also included were the Public Land Strip or panhandle (No Man's Land) and Greer County southwest of the north fork of Red River (then in dispute between the United States and Texas) "in case the title thereto should be adjudged vested in the United States."

The government prescribed was republican in form, with a governor to be appointed by the President. The legislative assembly consisted of two houses, a council of thirteen members and twenty-six representatives. The judicial power lay in a supreme court, district courts, probate courts, and justices of the peace. The supreme court consisted of a chief justice and two associate justices, each to serve as a district judge as well as a member of the appellate court. A greater portion of the statutes of Nebraska was adopted for temporary use, and Guthrie was designated the seat of territorial operations until such time the legislative assembly and governor saw fit to establish it elsewhere.

A full complement of officers was provided by the President. George W. Steele, of Indiana, became governor; Horace Speed, a Guthrie lawyer, United States District Attorney; and Warren S. Lurty, of Virginia, United States Marshal. Lurty found the primitive new country not to his liking and returned, within a few weeks, to Virginia, without having fully qualified for the office, and was succeeded by William Grimes, a deputy, of Kingfisher. Before coming to Oklahoma, Grimes had been a sheriff in Nebraska, which even then was emerging from a pioneer atmosphere, and was well equipped for the position. Edward B. Green, of Illinois, became chief justice and judge of the first district court, to be held at Guthrie and Stillwater; Abraham J. Seay, of Missouri, judge of the second district, with court seats at Beaver (in No Man's Land), El Reno, and Kingfisher; and John G. Clark, of Indiana, judge of the third district, at Norman and Oklahoma City.

Governor Steele took office May 23. County boundaries were

defined, their population enumerated, and representatives to the first legislature elected July 8. The first Legislative Assembly met August 27. It declared Guthrie the territorial capital, passed a code of laws taken from the statutes of various states, and arranged for farming out the Territory's convicts to the Kansas state penitentiary at Lansing and the insane to Illinois.

This ended the jurisdiction of the Muskogee court and Heck's authority, for the time being, in Oklahoma.

Although the court was restricted to less than one-half its original area, by the same act it was given increased jurisdiction and power over all civil cases in the domain remaining as Indian Territory, except cases under jurisdiction of the tribal courts. Another feature was the division of the Indian Territory into three districts, with terms of court to be held twice annually at Muskogee, McAlester, and Ardmore. Fifty-six chapters from the criminal code of Arkansas were put in force to govern certain crimes and misdemeanors, the judge was given power to extradite persons taking refuge in the Territory and to issue requisitions for fugitives upon governors of other states and territories; the Federal statutes were to govern all cases in conflict with said laws of Arkansas, and the Fort Smith and Paris courts were given continued exclusive jurisdiction over all crimes and misdemeanors punishable by death or imprisonment at hard labor.

In a circular addressed to his deputies, Marshal Needles enumerated the following felonies and indictable offenses:

Larceny, forgery other than against the United States, seduction, criminal abortion, kidnapping, embezzlement, false pretenses and frauds, malicious mischief, trespass and injury to property, removing property mortgaged or subject to lien, crimes against justice, e.g., bribing jurors, etc., escape and rescue, obstructing highways and injuring bridges.

The act also conferred concurrent jurisdiction with the courts of Fort Smith and Paris in whisky cases.

Misdemeanors punishable by fine, etc., were:

Carrying on lotteries or selling lottery tickets, assault and battery, abduction, enticing females into houses of ill fame, false imprisonment, taking or injuring stock by drovers, bribing and embracery, dueling and challenges, riot, affrays, and disturbing the public peace, libel and slander, divulging contents of telegram, gaming and keno, offenses by tavern and grocery keepers, driving stock from usual range, horse racing, vagrants, profanity, Sabbath breaking, obscenity, violating the grave, carrying weapons, enticing minors from parents or guardians, cruelty to animals, acts injurious to public health, etc.

The *Chieftain* commented: "In its operations the new law ought to work a revolution in the morals of this country, as under its provisions almost any offense which can be conceived is punishable. . . ."

Other changes affecting Heck's work took place at Fort Smith. President Harrison notified Marshal Carroll by letter that he was being removed from office as soon as his successor could be named and qualified. Thomas Boles, who had served as marshal under President Arthur from 1882 and was dismissed by Cleveland in 1886, became a candidate for reappointment. An able lawyer, with three terms in Congress and former judge of the Fifth Judicial District of Arkansas, he had been an exceedingly popular officer. A petition circulated in his behalf bore 16,000 signatures. But for the sake of party harmony, Harrison gave the place to Jacob Yoes, a Republican.

Heck was an active Democrat. Nevertheless, Yoes renewed his commission. But some of the rules Yoes laid down for the deputies to follow during his term of office "rubbed Heck raw under the collar."

No transfer of papers between deputies will be permitted without the knowledge and consent of the office. Heck recalled numerous instances when such a delay in obtaining consent would have defeated his making an important arrest or prevented the service of process. *No deputy shall ever use the horses or other property of any prisoner in his charge.* Deputies had abused this privilege too often, much to the unpopularity of the force in general. But suppose an officer had his mount shot from under him and his prisoner's horse was available for pursuit of his would be assassin, what was he to do? *A deputy will be discharged promptly for conduct unbecoming an officer and gentleman while on duty.* Several had got into trouble with the court. None were angels. A few were bullies or coarse-talking, unsenti-

117

mental individuals with little regard for the rights of others. The morals of some of the best officers Heck had ridden with could be questioned. Marshal Carroll had winked at this sort of thing so long as the cause of justice was served. And Judge Parker himself had said many times, "A coward could be highly moral, but he could not serve as a marshal in the Indian country." Those who had stayed so long realized the country depended on them for the preservation of lives and property.

Maybe, Heck thought, *we've civilized it too well.*

There were other regulations—a whole eight-page pamphlet of them. What rankled Heck most, however, was Yoes's order that deputies would no longer be permitted to carry firearms when not on duty or in the city of Fort Smith!

Heck delivered his last prisoners to the U. S. jail on July 24. He decided to accept a regular commission under Marshal Needles. He still held his commission under Yoes, but he began riding exclusively for the Muskogee court.

Before the end of the summer, he got the assignment he had wanted for two years. Needles sent him to the northern division of the Territory, with headquarters in the Cherokee Nation at Vinita.

14

The Daltons Flash—

Heck made his debut at Vinita handling his first insanity case. "A dangerous maniac" had jumped off the train. The city marshal took him in custody, but he escaped by unlocking his shackles with a nail and had been "annoying the citizens for a week."

Heck cornered him in a freight car full of raw lumber parked on the sidetrack and put him in chains. He fastened the youth to a tree "from which he ate the bark," then chained him to a heavy iron safe being installed in the post office across the street, where he "stripped himself to the horror of the spectators." Finally, Heck placed him in an old warehouse and remained with him all night. Next morning the boy's father arrived on the Katy and returned him to Missouri.

Heck spent the next few weeks with his old comrades, L. P. Isbell and Barney Connelly, and "rode several expeditions with them." By september, he was off in pursuit of an Indian desperado named Rentie Smith, who had killed Fee Jefferson on Cave Creek in the Muskogee District of the Creek Nation. "The judge of the Indian court had offered a $400 reward for his capture. . . . I traced him over the Chickasaw and Comanche nations and caught him in Texas on the 27th. I then returned him to the U. S. jail at Muskogee, subject to order of Creek Nation officers" and "made application for the reward." After the added difficulty of obtaining numerous affidavits, receipts, and vouchers, he learned that

119

the Indian judge was related to the prisoner "within the third degree," which, according to tribal law, not only invalidated the reward but disqualified him to preside in the case. Heck had been out an "actual cash expense of $175" on the trip.

Disgusted, he promised himself that he would let the Indians run down their own outlaws. But he had no sooner gotten out of the Rentie Smith affair than he was offered $50 to "recover Bob Knight's mules and 'Mun' Blythe's horse" which had been stolen in the Cherokee Nation.

The offer involved no expense. The thief was a man known as "Red Buck," who stayed at the Grayson Willis home near Vinita. Heck rode out to the Willis house, found his man and arrested him, and brought back the animals.

Red Buck turned out to be a white man, which placed the matter in the jurisdiction of the Federal Court. So Heck took him to Muskogee and claimed his fees. There he learned that Red Buck's real name was George Waightman, a professional horse thief from Texas with the reputation of a killer.

He was a surly, vicious little fellow, stockily built, with a heavy mustache. He cursed a lot and swore vengeance against everyone connected with his arrest. But Heck didn't take him too seriously. He was convicted and sentenced to nine years at Detroit. When he and forty-two other prisoners, accompanied by sixteen guards, were loaded in a special prison car to be taken to the House of Correction, Heck figured it was the last he would see of him.

Waightman and two other prisoners were shackled together, but by means of a saw made from a corset steel, they managed to cut themselves apart. As the train left Lebanon, Missouri, and the car windows were opened again so the prisoners could look out, Waightman's two companions jumped from a window, feet first.

As Waightman leaped to the sill, a guard threw down on him and threatened to shoot.

"Shoot and be damned!" the outlaw snarled, and disappeared.

The guard fired twice. Waightman saw his companions fall. But he didn't stay around to see whether they were dead or where the train stopped.

He made his way to the Springfield and Memphis road, caught

a freight into Kansas, and got off the Katy at Vinita early on a Sunday morning. From there he walked to Willis' home, where he related the story of his escape. After eating breakfast and resting an hour, he disappeared, again on foot.

As soon as Heck got the news, he took a posse and scoured the countryside. They finally traced him to Big Cabin, but it was too late. Waightman, they were told, had boarded the train at the little depot two days before. By this time, he probably was in Texas.

Waightman, however, was hiding in the Nations. But Heck did not hear of him again until nearly three years later.

During autumn, Heck saw much of Matie Mowbray. He came to Tulsa often as their deep friendship developed into serious romance.

On one of his trips in October, he saw Grat Dalton, one of Frank's brothers, who was making Tulsa his headquarters. Grat had been living in California at the time Frank was murdered, but returned to the Indian Territory shortly afterward to "fill Frank's boots." He was commissioned a deputy marshal for the Fort Smith court, partly on Heck's recommendation to Marshal Carroll. On his expeditions with Frank in the Cherokee Nation, Heck had stopped often at the Dalton home south of Vinita, near Locust Hill. Later, his efforts in avenging Frank's death brought him the gratitude of the entire Dalton family, and he had come to know them well.

Sire of the Daltons was Louis Dalton, a Kentuckian who had served under General Zachary Taylor during the Mexican War. At the close of hostilities, he returned to his native state. In 1850, he moved west, settling near Independence, Missouri, where he wooed and won Miss Adeline Lee Younger, aunt of the notorious Younger brothers. They were married in 1851.

Dalton engaged in farming and stock raising. On the side he did a little horse trading and horse racing. At one time he operated a saloon at Westport Landing, but, being a temperate man, he soon sold it. He built a large house near Kansas City, which he made good use of, for he became the father of thirteen children, nine sons and four daughters. One son and one daughter died in infancy. In 1860, the Daltons settled near Lawrence,

121

Kansas, and later moved to Montgomery County, four miles west of Coffeyville, where they were respected by all who knew them.

Most of the children grew up there. The older brothers—Charles, Henry, Littleton, Grat, and William (Bill)—scattered as far as Texas, Montana, and California. On the Pacific coast, Bill married and entered politics. In 1882, Dalton moved the rest of his family to the Indian Territory and leased some land from a Cherokee Indian. Through his influence, Frank was given his commission riding for Judge Parker.

Louis Dalton's new venture proved steadily unsuccessful. He was no world-beater as a farmer, and his laziness and love of ease had begun to exert itself. His passion for fast horses kept him away from home most of the time, following carnivals and county fairs, while Frank's earnings as deputy marshal supported the family. After Frank's death, his temper soured. He returned to Coffeyville, working at odd jobs about the country. Early in 1889, he died at the home of a friend near Dearing.

When Oklahoma opened to settlement, his widow secured a claim near Kingfisher. Charles, Henry, and Littleton, home for their father's funeral, also took good claims in the western part of the territory. Two of the daughters married respectable farmers and settled down to peaceful, happy lives. Bill remained in California.

Another son, Bob, had developed a wanderlust before the family left Kansas. For more than a year he had been a deputy marshal for the Wichita court, transporting prisoners from the Osage Nation for crimes committed in that country. He rode often in Grat's posses. In 1888, he became chief of the Osage Indian police, making his headquarters in Pawhuska, while still serving as deputy marshal.

He was a smooth-faced, handsome youth, not more than twenty years old when Frank was killed. Heck remembered him as "a bit of a dandy, much given to fancy boots and guns and known to be utterly fearless. He was one of the most accurate shots I ever saw . . . shot his rifle mostly from his side or hip, very seldom bringing the gun to his shoulder." Willful, reckless, and impetuous, always wanting to be the leader, he had boasted to

122

Heck that it would have been different had he instead of Frank gone after the Smith-Dixon gang.

Emmett, youngest of the Dalton clan, was fretting for the thrilling experiences Grat and Bob wrote about. For a time he worked as a cowboy on the Bar X Bar ranch near the Pawnee Agency. The Bar X Bar lay east of the agency in the "Triangle" formed by the confluence of the Arkansas and the Cimarron. It was one of the largest pastures in the Outlet and handled most of the trail herds from Texas and Mexico. Lying as it did on the northeastern fringe of the wilderness known then as the Unassigned Lands, it also became the breeding place for outlaws. There Emmett became the saddle companion of tall, drooping mustached, sandy-haired and gander-eyed Bill Doolin, Dick Broadwell, and Bill Powers. All were seasoned cowboys, crack shots, expert riders—roughshod men who later became members of the Dalton gang.

Adjoining the Bar X Bar and stretching south along the border of the Creek Nation, in the Sac and Fox reservation, was the Turkey Track ranch, where Emmett became acquainted with Charlie Bryant, George Newcomb, and Charley Pierce. Pierce was a local product who had tried his hand at whisky peddling. Heck had arrested him once and taken him to Fort Smith, where he served a stiff sentence in the U. S. jail. Bryant was a slender, sinister-looking, trigger-happy little fellow, best known as "Black-Faced Charley." He had drifted in from nowhere and had very little to say about his past. Somewhere, sometime, his face had got dangerously near an exploding gun and he had received powder burns that left splotches of burned black powder beneath his skin. Newcomb was best known as "Bitter Creek," or "Slaughter's Kid," a nickname given him as a boy when he worked for Texas cowman John Slaughter, before Slaughter became the famous sheriff of Cochise County, Arizona. All of them rode the line together—this sextet of rowdy punchers and Emmett Dalton.

Emmett was back home when his father died. But he soon was off again, riding with his brothers as a posseman. Still a boy, he seemed not to have held a commission of his own. Nevertheless, he learned the trade riding with Bob and Grat, and was with Bob and Deputy Floyd Wilson's posse when they captured Carroll Collier and Bud Maxfield, two dangerous convicts who had escaped from the Arkansas state penitentiary.

Emmett loved excitement. But he lacked the bravado of his brothers. Perhaps he had inherited too much of the substantial quality and character of his mother. Perhaps it was because his career was cut short.

Some controversy arose over Bob's wages and he left the Osage police force. Shortly after that he got into trouble by taking whisky into the Osage country, and Marshal R. L. Walker of Kansas fired him in the fall of 1889. Bob claimed he resigned as police chief when they refused to pay his wages after the job proved too lucrative, and that he was beaten out of something over $900 due him in mileage and other fees from the court at Wichita.

"Grat got into trouble about the same time," Heck recalled. He was thirty years old—"a pugnacious fellow, but cautious. More like Frank than the others." He "wasn't much" on detecting criminals, but he made up for his lack of brilliance by careful and consistent performance. He had delivered many criminal small fry to Fort Smith. In 1888, he received a bullet wound in the left forearm while attempting to arrest a noted Indian desperado. During the first part of his services, he conducted himself as a model officer, Marshal Yoes had renewed his commission, and his bravery would have distinguished him if it had not been for that peculiar streak of deviltry that, at times, seemed to dominate his better nature.

Some men were standing in front of a store in Tulsa when Grat walked up. He had been drinking. He was talking to the men when he spied a Negro boy walking down the other side of the street, eating an apple.

"Watch me scare hell outa him," Dalton said.

He called to the Negro to halt, which the boy did, quickly.

"Put that apple on your head," commanded Dalton, "an' I'll show you some fancy shootin'."

The Negro hesitated, trembling until his teeth chattered.

124

"Mistah Grat," he stammered, "I'se afraid yuh'll miss de apple an' hit me."

"Then, by God, nigger, I'll kill you anyhow!" Grat called thickly.

By now the boy was shaking so badly he hardly could hold the apple in place. There was a prayer on his lips as he awaited execution.

Dalton raised his pistol and fired. The bullet split the apple, knocking the halves in opposite directions. A William Tell trick, although Grat had never heard of the incident. When the report reached Fort Smith, Marshal Yoes dismissed him.

As Grat himself put it, "Old Jake gave me the ax."

Bob, Grat, and Emmett could have become farmers like their brothers. There was land in the family, and more to be had on the Oklahoma frontier. In the spring, negotiations had been completed with the Cherokee Nation for the relinquishment of their unoccupied lands in the Outlet, and with the Iowa, Sac, and Fox, and the Pottawatomie-Shawnee, whose reservations lay just east of Old Oklahoma. In June, the Cheyenne and Arapaho had agreed to accept allotments in severalty and permit the opening to white settlement of their surplus lands south of the Canadian and west of the region settled in 1889 to the Texas panhandle.

Or, had they wished, the Daltons could have kept on earning fees as *posse comitatus*. It had always been the custom to allow deputy marshals to choose their posse and guards, and Deputy Floyd Wilson had plenty of use for all three of them. But a career in crime seemed easy and more rewarding. It was as simple as that.

Bob and Emmett made their last trip with Wilson and were paid off at Fort Smith on June 20. They left there and went to Claremore, where they remained until after July 4. By midsummer, gossips in Fort Smith were saying that the Daltons had gone wrong.

Those who knew Grat, Bob, and Emmett were inclined to discredit the rumors. But Heck, upon his arrival in the Cherokee Nation, had heard from Isbell's and Connelly's own mouths the story of how Emmett and Bob had visited the Osage country and stolen seventeen head of ponies and a pair of fine mules. They had tried to sell the stock to a buyer at Wagoner, but failed to make a deal and started for Kansas, trading the mules to a Cherokee Indian and disposing of the ponies at Baxter Springs.

On September 6, 1890, warrants were sworn out against Bob, Emmett, and Grat, charging them with horse stealing. While Heck was off chasing Rentie Smith, some citizens arrested Grat at Claremore and turned him over to Isbell and Connelly. At his preliminary examination before the U. S. Commissioner, no evidence could be found connecting him with the theft, though the evidence against Bob and Emmett was conclusive. Grat was released.

He had just returned to Tulsa when Heck saw him in October. Heck told him that he carried warrants for Bob's and Emmett's arrest.

"Well, you won't find them around here," Grat snorted. But he refused to say where his brothers were hiding.

"When you see them," Heck said, "tell them that if they surrender to me I'll do everything possible to help them."

Grat ruffled. "They ain't guilty of a damned thing!" he retorted. "And you or any other deputy had better not hound them!" He whirled and stomped off into the darkness.

Heck watched him go with a deep feeling of regret. They were the only outlaws for whom he ever held any sentiment.

The next day, he heard that Grat had left for California, and Heck wondered if that was where Bob and Emmett had gone.

He hoped that they were still in the Nations and would soon come in and surrender. He told their friends as much, as he rode through the Cherokee country and on his way to Tulsa to see Matie during the winter.

In Oklahoma Territory, Marshal Grimes and his deputies watched the homes of Dalton relatives near Kingfisher. Finally, warrants were sent to San Luis Obispo County on the Pacific coast, where Bill Dalton resided. But Heck had no word of Bob and Emmett until spring.

He was in Muskogee attending court when Marshal Needles handed him a flyer just received from California. Dated at San

Francisco, March 26, 1891, it "showed what the boys had been doing out there":

$3000 REWARD

Supplementing circular letter of W. E. Hickey, special officer Southern Pacific Company, dated San Francisco, February 26th, 1891, wherein is offered a reward of $5000 for the arrest and conviction of all parties concerned in the attempted robbery of Train No. 17, on the night of February 6th, 1891.

The grand jury of Tulare county have indicted Bob and Emmett Dalton as principals in said crime, and William Marion Dalton and Grattan Dalton, as accessories; the two latter named being now in jail at Tulare county awaiting trial.

The Southern Pacific Company hereby withdraws said general reward in regard to Bob and Emmett Dalton, and in lieu thereof offer to pay $1,500 each for the arrest of Bob and Emmett Dalton, *upon their delivery to any duly authorized agent or representative of the State of California, or at any jail in any of the States or Territories of the United States.*

In addition to the foregoing, the State and Wells Fargo & Co. have each a standing reward of $300 for the arrest and conviction of each such offender.

About 8 o'clock in the evening of February 6th, 1891, two armed men attempted, unsuccessfully, to rob the southbound train, No. 17, near Alila, Tulare county, California. The express messenger offered a gallant resistance, and during the interchange of shots the fireman, G. W. Radcliff, received a wound, from the effects of which he died the following day.

It is now known that the attack was made by two brothers, viz.: Bob and Emmett Dalton. On the 2nd of March they left San Luis Obispo county on horseback, and on the 8th disposed of their horses at Ludlow, a station on the A. & P. Railway, about 100 miles east of Mojave, and there took passage on the East-bound train, since which time no trace of them has been obtained.

According to an Associated Press dispatch, Bill Dalton had admitted "piloting the boys to a place of safety." He denied, however, that either he or his brothers had any part in the Alila robbery. He claimed that he had "hidden" Bob and Emmett because they were wanted for stealing horses in the Indian Territory, but agreed to "induce them to surrender" if the officers could assure him they would not be extradited to stand trial on the horse-thievery charge.

The officers refused to let him communicate with his brothers unless a deputy accompanied him. Bill insisted on going alone: "The boys are desperate; they have over 800 rounds of ammunition and will kill any man who goes with me."

In this impasse, Marshal Grimes at Guthrie announced that Bob and Emmett were not in California at all. After their escape, they had made their way directly to their old haunts in the Indian country.

"I have learned now," he advised the California officers, "that they spent one night at their mother's home at Kingfisher."

Afterward, they raided a colony of Missourians on Beaver Creek, near Orlando, and stole eight or ten head of the best saddle stock in Oklahoma Territory.

The farmers quickly organized and followed the thieves to a point near Twin Mounds in eastern Payne County. As they divided to search the dense timber along the bank of a creek, the outlaws opened fire from ambush. The leader of the posse, W. T. Starmer, died instantly, and another farmer named Thompson fell badly wounded. The rest ducked behind stumps and trees, firing in the direction from which the shots had come, but the outlaws, well sheltered behind a pile of driftwood, suffered no damage. The farmers were soon routed, and the thieves escaped on the best horses from the stolen herd, into the Creek Nation.

According to Grimes, Starmer had been killed by a Winchester rifle. He had been hit by three bullets so close together the space could be covered with one hand.

As Heck finished reading the reports, Marshal Needles gazed at him steadily. "Nobody in the Territory can shoot like that," the marshal said, "except Bob Dalton."

Heck left Muskogee immediately for the Tulsa and Red Fork area. He found the country "full of detectives and officers who were endeavoring to secure the big reward." All manner of rumors reached the newspapers as to the movements of the fugitives and those in pursuit of them. "Heck Thomas is out there," said the

128

Elevator, "and it is thought that news of an encounter will be heard of soon."

Heck had little hope of an early encounter. Bob and Emmett were thoroughly acquainted with the country, and their friends were keeping them posted.

They could not have chosen a better time to launch a criminal career. The country was in a state of chaos. Confusion was caused by many openings of new reservations and the influx of adventurers with as little respect for law and order as the outlaws. It was an easy matter to pick recruits, as needed, from this frontier rabble. With the breaking up of the cattle range by the division of the land into farms, there were many disgruntled cowboys who, loathe to go with the migrating herds or bring their daredevil natures to the subjection of change from the wild, free life, were easily fired with the prospects of making one big haul and retiring in comfort for the rest of their lives.

The first week out, Heck learned that at least two of Emmett's old comrades from the Turkey Track ranch had already joined them. Bitter Creek Newcomb and Black-Faced Charley Bryant had disappeared from a cow camp on the Cimarron the night the Daltons entered the Creek Nation.

Bryant suffered from a ravaging fever for which he had found no cure. It came on him often, leaving him deathly sick and pale. This had led to excessive drinking and a mocking contempt for life, especially his own. He had often told his companions: "I want to die in one hell-firin' minute of smoking action!" Joining an outlaw band held forth this promise.

The *Indian Chieftain* viewed the organization of this new gang with grave seriousness: "Few criminals ever turned out in the Indian Territory have been more successful in eluding arrest than Bob and Emmett Dalton. . . . That they will never surrender without a fight is a foregone conclusion."

Take your man alive, if possible; shoot it out with him, if necessary; and take your fifty-fifty chances of coming out alive. Heck had set this as a policy. With the Daltons, the chances of coming out of a gun fight alive would be less than fifty-fifty.

Heck doubted that they really felt the law would ever catch them. Few were the outlaw gangs he'd known that had not weighed the chances for and against them before starting on a course in open defiance of the law. The Daltons not only could depend on their friends and knowledge of the country to avoid arrest, but they knew every hindrance to the efficiency of the marshals who trailed them.

The Government now allowed $2 instead of $1 per day for expenses in "endeavoring" to arrest. This was supposed to cover both transportation and subsistence. Possemen still received the munificent sum of $3 per day, but they had to furnish their own mounts and pay all other expenses. If a deputy failed to make an arrest, he could not collect a cent for his work regardless of how much time and money he spent in the endeavor. It was small encouragement for hunting a desperate band like the Daltons, without finding them. The inducement was the large reward, if the officer lived to collect it.

Another hindrance was the fact that a deputy could not pursue a criminal outside his own district without first obtaining special authority from the marshal of the district into which the culprit had fled. This was true if the man were only a foot over the line. Some marshals were so jealous of deputies from other districts that, when their district was invaded, they resorted to such spiteful tactics as having the enthusiastic officer discharged on grounds that he had overstepped his authority.

By agreement among several of the marshals, an interchange of commissions had been provided for a select few. Only by this flexible system had it been possible for the deputies to make some progress in their war against organized banditry.

Heck's commission under Yoes gave him authority in the unoccupied portion of the Outlet, still under jurisdiction of the Fort Smith court as part of the Cherokee Nation. But it was the only place he could hunt the Daltons outside the Indian Territory.

In the latter part of April, he and his old posseman Burrell Cox, with Tiger Jack, a noted Euchee scout and trailer of the Creek Indian police, picked up the tracks of four riders above Polecat Creek south of the Arkansas. Their leader rode "the same large hoofed animal whose hind footprints always cut into the front hoof marks."

130

They followed the riders north all day as they split, drifted, reunited, and crossed the Arkansas into the Pawnee country.

Tiger Jack dismounted, studying the signs patiently with the canny craft of his race.

"Trail three—maybe four—hours old," he decided.

Heck squinted anxiously at the rolling timbered hills across the river. Finally he said, "We'll have to turn back."

Tiger Jack shrugged blandly. Cox began arguing. Who'd give a damn about regulations if they collected the reward? "Hell's bells, this may be as close to them Daltons as we'll ever get!"

Heck nodded solemnly. But he was reluctant to go out of his district without permission.

Cox blustered and threatened to go alone. But he followed with alacrity when Heck and Tiger Jack set off in a lope for the nearest telegraph station.

Heck wired Marshal Needles: "Request permission to pursue Daltons in Pawnee reservation."

Needles wired Marshal Grimes. Grimes welcomed the request. On May 2, 1891, he commissioned Heck deputy marshal for Oklahoma Territory.

And, on May 9, the Dalton gang held up the Texas Express at Wharton, a small way station on the Santa Fe forty miles north of Guthrie, in the Outlet.

15

—And Die!

Through the years, the technique of train robbery developed less originality than any other type of crime Heck investigated. Since the days of the Reno gang and Sam Bass, the robbers almost invariably had appeared, masked and armed, on the tender of the locomotive, put their guns at the head of the engineer, forced him to stop the train, and then attacked the express car. In some cases the express car had been cut from the train and moved down the track where entry could be gained with more safety. The single departure from this routine, introduced by the James-Younger combination, had been to signal from the track or to barricade or tear up the rails to force the emergency stop.

The regular procedure was followed in the attack on the Texas Express at Wharton. On that train, the Daltons had somehow learned, was a large shipment of cash for a Guthrie bank. When the train arrived at 10:50 P.M. and slowed to a stop for water, Bob and Bitter Creek Newcomb, masked as usual, leaped into the cab, covered the fireman and engineer and commanded them to run the train a half mile south to the stockyards where they had left their horses.

The station agent, seeing the train stop at the stockyards, remarked to himself, "That's unusual, they must have a hotbox." Hearing some shots down the track, he rushed inside the depot and put out the lights.

Emmett and Bryant, appearing from the darkness, had fired several shots down the side of the train as curious heads popped out the car windows to see what was going on. The heads were withdrawn quickly.

Then Bob and Newcomb marched the engineer and fireman to the express car and ordered the messenger to open the door. When the messenger refused, Bob stuck his six-shooter against the engineer's head.

"Tell him to open up, or I'll blow out your brains!"

"Please open up," pleaded the engineer. "They have a gun at my head. Please, please open the door."

Newcomb pumped a couple of shots into the door with his rifle for added effect, and the messenger opened it. Then the two bandits leaped into the car, covering the messenger and guard.

Emmett and Bryant covered the crew on the ground and fired a few more shots down the side of the train.

Meanwhile, Bob and Newcomb were having trouble getting the messenger to open the safe. He claimed he didn't know the combination. The big vaults were always closed and set to open at Kansas City or Gainesville, and the combination wired ahead so messengers could not open them en route, he explained. Express companies even advertised this fact on all trains running from Missouri to Texas.

But Bob knew, from experience as a deputy marshal, that such reports were designed to reach the ears of all outlaws and reassure the passengers. It was a ruse, and Bob told him so.

When the messenger pleaded the second time that he didn't know the combination, Bob's temper flared.

"You low-down, lyin' son-of-a-bitch," he snarled.

His six-shooter roared like a cannon in the confines of the car, and the bullet ripped splinters from the floor between the man's feet.

"Open that safe, or the next one goes in your belly!"

With his knees shaking and hands trembling, the messenger managed to unlock the vault. He poured its contents into Bob's sack, then opened the way safe and threw a small sack of silver into Newcomb's bag.

133

This done, Bob and Newcomb rejoined Emmett and Bryant. The engineer and fireman were ordered back into the cab and the train waved on. The quartet hurried to their horses, strapped the loot to their saddles, and galloped away in the darkness.

Before they disappeared, the station agent was chattering a wild message along the wires. When the train reached Guthrie, a large posse had been organized. Men and horses were loaded into a boxcar and started north, but by the time they reached Wharton, the robbers were miles away. In which direction they had fled nobody knew.

Heck received the details of the robbery at Osage Agency. "I immediately took my posse and headed southwest to intercept them should they recross the Arkansas. . . ."

Incomplete bits of his saga and his disconnected personal memoirs do not reveal to what extent he was successful. Contemporary reports indicate that on the morning following the robbery, he and Cox, accompanied by a Wells Fargo detective named Smith, came "close" to capturing the gang while they were at breakfast. "So close in fact," stated the *Elevator* of May 15, "that the outlaws abandoned their camp, leaving their pack horse and camp outfit, which fell into the hands of the officers."

The Daltons had faded.

For weeks, posses searched everywhere. The papers were full of the hue and cry to capture them dead or alive. They exaggerated the amount of money stolen from $25,000 to $100,000, while the Santa Fe Railroad claimed only $1,500. Reward notices were posted in all public places, and more Wells Fargo men poured in from Kansas City and California. But hope of immediate apprehension soon died.

The trail had been too hot for the gang to remain in the Nations or go near relatives at Kingfisher. Nearly three months later, Heck learned that they had holed up in an old sod ranch house in the Cheyenne and Arapaho country. There were only a few scattered ranches in western Oklahoma at that time. After three days of hard riding almost due west, they had reached the ranch of a squaw man named Jim Riley, near Taloga, on the Canadian.

Riley had been a stage driver between Fort Reno and Caldwell,

Kansas, before he married a Cheyenne woman and settled down to raising horses and cattle. He was well-to-do, and had taken no part in the robbery. Living as he did in a part of the country where his own safety depended on attending to his own business, he reluctantly had given the outlaws food and shelter.

He readily provided the officers with supplies and fresh horses when they came looking for the outlaws. By that time, the Daltons were riding again.

But Bryant wasn't with them.

En route to Riley's place, he had been seized by one of his frequent attacks of fever. The Daltons had left him with some friends in a cow camp near Buffalo Springs, in the Outlet, seven miles north of Hennessey.

In the latter part of July, he grew so dangerously ill that the cowboys persuaded him to let them take him to Hennessey for medical treatment. The doctor examined him and ordered him to bed in the hotel.

Ed Short was city marshal and carried a deputy's commission under Grimes. A blond, robust man of commanding appearance, he represented the best in frontier peace officers. He had come west from Indiana as a young man and had filled many positions as a lawman, including city marshal of Woodsdale, Kansas, during the memorable Stevens County War of 1886, and was at Caldwell in its violent heyday as railhead of the Chisholm Trail. There was not a badman on the border he would not have gone up against.

He saw Bryant when the cowboys brought him in. Glancing over reward notices and warrants for men he was hunting, he read a description of Black-Faced Charley on a Dalton poster.

Short watched the hotel. He visited with the nurse who carried Bryant his meals and medicine, and knew when he had recovered sufficiently to be released.

On August 22, Short went to the room, quietly opened the door, and pointed his six-shooter at Bryant's head. Bryant reached for a revolver under his pillow, realized the folly of it, and surrendered.

A jail for Federal prisoners was being constructed at Guthrie. Meanwhile, they had to be taken to Wichita or other points out-

135

side the territory. The next evening, Short boarded the Rock Island train for Wichita, his prisoner in tow.

He had shackled Bryant's hands behind him, but the outlaw complained so much about this position hurting him due to his recent illness that the marshal changed them, placing his hands in front. This merciful gesture cost Ed Short his life. . . .

Before the train left Hennessey, the station agent warned Short that an attempt might be made to rescue the prisoner.

"The Daltons might even hold up the train in the operation," he added.

"You ought to take along a guard," his friends suggested.

Short scoffed at their advice. He was sure of his ability to handle one man. He armed himself with a rifle, as well as the six-shooter he carried. As an added precaution, he placed his prisoner in the baggage car instead of one of the coaches.

The first stop was Waukomis, a way station and section house just over the southern border of the Outlet, thirteen miles north of Hennessey. If an attempt was made to rescue Bryant, it would be at Waukomis, Short reasoned.

The baggage car, used also as a mail car, was equipped with pigeonholes for sorting letters. In one of these, the baggage agent kept a .45 Colt. As the train approached Waukomis, Short instructed the agent to keep an eye on the prisoner while he went out on the platform "to look around."

He scarcely had gone from the car when Bryant, unnoticed by the agent, spotted the revolver in the pigeonhole and seized it in his shackled hands. Ordering the agent to silence, he stepped to the doorway.

Short had just finished his inspection when he glimpsed the prisoner standing with a gun pointed at him. Jerking his rifle to his hip, he began firing as fast as he could lever and trigger. Bryant fired at the same instant, and kept shooting until the revolver was empty and he died on the platform.

Short lived long enough to help carry the outlaw back inside the car and lie down on a cot. When the train stopped at the station a few minutes later, he was dead.

Short was the first deputy in Oklahoma Territory to lose his life in the discharge of his duty. It riled Marshal Grimes, and he became more determined than ever to bring in the other members of the gang at all costs.

Heck heard of the Short-Bryant killings in the Cherokee Nation. By the end of the summer, he learned that four more of Emmett's old cowboy companions had joined him, Bob, and Newcomb: Bill Doolin, Dick Broadwell, Bill Powers, and jaunty, almond-eyed, thin-mustached Charlie Pierce.

On the night of September 15, they held up the southbound passenger train on the Katy at Lillietta, a small flag stop four miles north of Wagoner, robbed the express car of $3,000, and fled back to their hide-outs in Oklahoma. They detained the train only a few minutes and did the job so quietly that the passengers did not know it had been robbed until they reached Wagoner.

Other events occurred now to contribute to the growth and success of the Dalton gang. On September 22, the Iowa, Sac, and Fox reservations, with the lands of the Pottawatomie and Shawnee, totaling 868,414 acres, were opened to settlement. This rush for homesteads was a repetition of the run of '89. Nearly every acre was occupied the first day and over 20,000 persons participated. From these lands, Logan, Oklahoma, and Cleveland counties were enlarged to the east, Payne County gained that portion lying south of the Cimarron, and two more counties, Lincoln and Pottawatomie, were added to the original seven. On April 19, 1892, the Cheyenne and Arapaho country was opened by a third run, adding 3,500,562 acres to Oklahoma Territory; Kingfisher and Canadian counties were enlarged to the west, and six more were designated and subsequently named Blaine, Dewey, Ellis, Roger Mills, Custer, and Washita. In both of these openings, as in 1889, thousands failed to obtain homes, and large groups of dissatisfied settlers gathered on the borders of the Outlet, pressing for entry into this only other land strip negotiated for in 1890.

Hundreds moved in, under one pretense or another, but all seeking section stones and deciphering their hieroglyphics. One party crossed over from Kansas to lay out a city. The cavalry burned their buildings and drove them out. Washington delayed the opening to keep down public expenditures until after the fall election. Cleveland was making a bid for his second term

137

in the White House. But the settlers charged it was because the cattlemen were making their influence felt and "feathering the nests" of Congressmen. Finally, the ranchers were ordered to remove their herds. The settlers set fire to vast sections of the Outlet to spur them along. One prominent cattle owner wired the Santa Fe for a hundred cars to ship his stock. "Tonight," he said, "the whole strip south of Arkansas City for a distance of sixty miles is a sea of flames."

In California, Bill Dalton had been acquitted; Grat had been convicted, but three days before he was to be sentenced, he escaped jail at Visalia and rejoined his brothers in Oklahoma. With this new turbulence in the Outlet, the new openings and constant shifting of population and lack of legal machinery, the Dalton gang moved for several months in safety.

Heck's romance had culminated in a promise of marriage. Matie's parents welcomed his visits to Tulsa. Reverend Mowbray felt great admiration and respect for him. But he thought Heck always came to see him and Hannah.

When Matie announced their intentions, her parents voiced vigorous objections.

"Why, Matie," argued Hannah, "he's old enough to be your father!"

"No matter," Matie replied. "I love him, and I'd have no other."

"How would you live—out on the prairies, under the stars?"

"That would be wonderful!" exclaimed Matie.

George and Hannah stared, exasperated. There would be no wedding, they declared.

But Matie was determined. When Heck came to Tulsa again, they eloped to Arkansas City, and Matie Thomas began a series of sleepless nights while her husband and Fred Dodge, chief of detectives for Wells Fargo and Company, rode the Santa Fe from Arkansas City to Guthrie because "suspicious characters" had been sighted near Red Rock in the Otoe-Missouri reservation.

Shortly after midnight on June 2, 1892, a train stopped at the little station. No passengers got on or off. The coaches, with their lights dimmed and sleepy heads on the reclining chairs showing through the windows, looked innocent enough. While the engine hissed idly, the station agent delivered some parcels to the ex-

138

press car and returned, whistling softly. Everything appeared regular, except the smoker behind the express car. It was in total darkness. Inside, Heck and Chief Dodge crouched with rifles ready to spit flame at the first sign of trouble. Nothing happened, and the train moved on.

At 1 A.M., a second section—the regular express—came roaring in from the north and stopped at the station. This time the Dalton gang went into action. Pierce and Newcomb jumped suddenly into the cab from the tender, covering Engineer Mack and Fireman Frank Rogers with revolvers, and commanded them to run the train down to the stockyards. When the train stopped, they were joined by Bob, Emmett, Grat, Broadwell, Powers, and Bill Doolin. They marched the engineer and fireman back to the express car and ordered them to open the door.

E. C. Whittlesy, the messenger, and J. A. Riehl, the guard, anticipating what was going on, had blown out the lights and refused to allow anyone to enter. The gang opened fire from all sides, sending lead whipping through the wooden walls and windows, even shooting from under the car through the floor. But Whittlesy and Riehl stood their ground and courageously drove back the robbers.

Bob seized a coal pick from the engine, handed it to the fireman, and told him to break open the door. This placed Rogers between two fires. Realizing that it meant death to his companion, Engineer Mack begged the men inside to stop shooting.

Whittlesy and Riehl allowed Rogers to approach the car. He chopped a hole in the door large enough to admit a man's body.

"Now, crawl in there and unlatch that damned door!" snarled Bob Dalton.

The moment Rogers was inside, Riehl ordered him to go to the opposite end of the car and lie down. Then he shouted to the bandits that the first one to enter the opening would be killed.

Another fusillade poured through the car while Whittlesy and Riehl hugged the floor. After this siege, Bob Dalton yelled: "Lay down your guns and come out with your hands up, and you won't be hurt!"

Rogers pleaded with the two men to give up, and finally they surrendered. Grat and Doolin entered the car. Using a sledge hammer and chisel, they broke open the way and through safes and dumped their contents into a grain sack. After taking Riehl's gold watch and both men's rifles and revolvers, the gang walked to their horses and rode off into the night.

The first report of the robbery that flashed over the wire claimed they had escaped with $70,000 annuity money being expressed to the Sac and Fox agency for payment to the Indians. This shipment, however, had gone through on the first train under the guns of Heck and Chief Dodge.

Again the gang's take was less than $3,000. But, for the third time, the Daltons had gotten away without a scratch.

Heck and Dodge combed the Creek Nation border from the Sac and Fox agency to the Cimarron. Two posses totaling twenty-five men under Chief Deputy Marshal Chris Madsen and Sheriff John Hixon, of Logan county, set out to the north and searched the Outlet for sixty miles west of Red Rock. A third posse raced south from Caldwell. Another headed east from Fort Supply, and a fifth under the personal leadership of Marshal Grimes hurried west to the South Canadian.

They beat the country from the Canadian River to the Kansas border to the Texas panhandle and No Man's Land. They picked up a trail in the Cimarron hills and followed it south to the ranch of Jim Riley, where the robbers had obtained fresh horses, then vanished completely. Their hide-out in this western isolation could not be found. Four horses which the gang had abandoned was all that the marshals brought back with them.

"The James boys, with all their deeds of outlawry, surpassed in no way crimes that the devilish Daltons have been known to commit!" cried the territorial press. "The time will come when they must give up their liberty or life, but *when* and *how?*"

With Oklahoma Territory getting too hot for them, they left their western lair and, by some circuitous route, returned to the Cherokee Nation, where they bivouacked two days on Grand River, a few miles beyond Pryor Creek station on the Katy Railroad.

Already the gang had planned its next raid. On the evening of July 14, they held up the northbound passenger train at Adair. It was the most daring feat yet accomplished by the Daltons.

Thirteen Indian police and special guards were riding the train with a valuable express shipment from Muskogee. The bandits poured in a withering fire as they tried to leave the cars. Several officers and passengers were wounded during the onslaught, and a prominent citizen, Dr. W. L. Goff, was slain as he fled for shelter from the porch of a store nearby. This time the gang took $17,000.

Their bold attack on such an armed force, which they must have known to be on the train, spread great alarm throughout the territories and Border States. It shook political circles all the way to Washington, and territorial officials were ordered to resort to every means at their disposal to wipe out the bandits. The Katy, the Santa Fe, and Pacific railroads and Wells Fargo and Company pooled their resources to raise to $5,000 the reward for the apprehension and conviction of each member of the gang, making a grand total of $40,000—the most money ever offered for an outlaw band in America.

At Arkansas City, Wells Fargo manager, Amador Andrews, outfitted Heck and Chief Dodge for "a long journey and a hard siege." Said the Arkansas City *Traveler:* "They were furnished with pack horses and saddles, cartridges, flour and other necessities. They were joined here by Burrell Cox, who has served under Thomas on many expeditions . . . and Sunday evening the trio left for the Cherokee Nation to find the Daltons. They were last heard from in the Osage, and were making good time toward their destination. . . ."

Heck was "not surprised" to find that there had been "no pursuit by men of experience in that country." Even a call for volunteers to go after the gang immediately following the robbery had met such little response that the project was abandoned. The reward called for their apprehension and conviction, and these people recalled the Dalton vow never to be taken alive.

"I figure," Heck told some of his old comrades in his easy drawl, "that I can talk the boys into surrendering if we get them cornered. Knowin' Bob and Grat like I do, I don't believe they'll crack down on me."

"Then you'd better go alone," his friends replied.

So Heck, Dodge, and Cox continued their quiet hunt without

141

assistance. Manager Andrews was the only person they kept advised of their movements as they "picked up reports of the gang in all directions. . . ."

First, they had camped near Blue Springs, east of Grand River, for two days following the robbery. "Some of Gaskell's sawmill hands ran into the bandits with Winchesters stacked and a blanket spread on the ground covered with six-shooters and a big pile of money. They told the sawmill men they had business back the way they had come and to go attend to it. The advice was taken. . . ."

Obviously, the gang had divided the loot and split up here. On September 21, three of them took dinner at the Wiley Mayes's home in the Grand River hills. Mayes recognized Grat Dalton, and his description of the other two fit Broadwell and Powers. They had "bought some chickens, eggs and butter . . . and weren't particular about the price they paid." That night the same men rode past the house of Willis Woods, three miles east of Big Cabin, in the direction of Vinita. They had not been seen afterward.

The citizens of Catoosa "felt confident" that three more of the gang had visited there the same day. "They purchased some gun oil and a few things to eat." After leaving town, they met an old Negro named Charley Robbins, on Hominy Creek, and "questioned him as to whether he had seen any posses or marshals."

"The descriptions fit Doolin, Pierce, and Newcomb," Heck reported. Apparently they were making their way southwest to their hide-outs and friends in the old Sac and Fox reservation. By the end of July, he had "the other two members of the band accounted for. . . ."

Bob and Emmett had beat a course almost due west into the Osage. To avoid any posse that might be expecting them at the main ford on the Arkansas, they had plunged down the treacherous, precipitous banks of the river at its confluence with the Cimarron during a storm. They had managed to fight their way across the muddy, roaring flood, but their pack animal had floundered, lost its footing, and been swept away in the deep swirling waters. Its body was discovered when the waters receded several days later. Heck recognized the bald-faced brown horse which the Daltons were known to have acquired since losing another pack animal and their camping outfit to his posse in the Osage. It bore the same brand and was a mate to the rangy sorrel Bob Dalton rode.

Heck made an important decision. Bob Dalton was the leader. He and Emmett had always stuck together. "We'll stay on their trail," he told Cox and Dodge.

Eventually, he theorized, the gang would reassemble around Bob and Emmett.

Emmett Dalton, in an account of his outlaw life written years later, admitted that Heck Thomas became their "nemesis." He tried to "bait" them into various traps. He knew most of the friendly ranches and isolated cow camps where they visited and planted his confederates in the guise of cowboys to "take them unprepared." But their friends proved their "reliability." They gave them "forewarning" and Heck's traps "yawned unsprung."

But his theory soon proved correct. Toward the end of September, 1892, the gang gathered in their last bivouac north of Tulsa. Only Doolin, Pierce, and Newcomb weren't there. Doolin had proved "too undisciplined," "wild and unruly," and "mentally awkward," and the "rampant foolhardiness" of Pierce and Newcomb, according to Emmett, had proved "too dangerous" to include them in their plans for a last big raid from which they could gain a fortune and "retire to South America."

With indignant territorial officials, an outraged society, rewards so great to cause even their trusted friends to turn against them, and Heck Thomas "pressing close," they feared capture, Emmett declared.

Encouraged by their successful escapades, Bob's mad ambition was to commit a robbery so daring and sensational that the entire country would be shocked. The Daltons knew the little town of Coffeyville, its inhabitants, and their habits intimately. They decided to eclipse anything the James and Youngers had ever done and rob two banks in the town in broad daylight on the same day.

Heck noted: "We located their hide-out on October 3, got full information that five men still composed the gang, and were ready to take them, when they suddenly pulled out for the north. We followed them to a camp on California Creek (about twenty miles south of the Kansas border), which they had left about eight o'clock the evening before (October 4) . . . and were starting to Onion Creek when word came that they had been killed on the streets of Coffeyville."

An account of this battle is of no consequence here. It has been recorded many times in fact and fiction. It can be found in minute historical detail in David Stewart Elliott's *Last Raid of the Daltons.*

For Heck, it was the end of the Dalton trail. The gang rode into Coffeyville that crisp fall morning at 9:30. Bob and Emmett entered the First National Bank, and Grat, Powers, and Broadwell entered the C. M. Condon. Despite their false beards and mustaches, they were recognized the moment they entered the city. The townspeople darted into their homes and stores for weapons. When the outlaws emerged from the banks, they were met with a barrage of gunfire.

Five minutes later, Bob and Grat Dalton and Bill Powers lay dead in the streets and alley, four citizens had been slain and two wounded. Broadwell managed to cling to his horse and ride a mile out of town before dropping beside the roadway. Emmett Dalton had a bullet in his hip, another in his arm, and a charge of buckshot in his back. He survived his wounds and was sentenced to life in the Kansas state penitentiary.

Heck and Chief Dodge proceeded to Coffeyville to "make proof" of the Daltons' death for Wells Fargo. Afterward, Manager Andrews wrote Heck this letter: "While it has not been marked by capture, we feel that your work, more than anything, brought about the extermination of this gang . . . and are happy to hand you, from our railway and express pool, a check herewith in the amount of $1,500."

Manager Andrews was scarcely correct, however, in stating that the band had been exterminated. Down on the Cimarron, Bill Doolin, Pierce, and Newcomb alternately cursed and thanked their lucky stars that they had been dropped from the outfit before the disastrous invasion. The fearful slaughter of that day should have made them reconsider their program for the future. They realized, though, that they were outlaws, still being hunted throughout Oklahoma Territory and the Nations. In no time they became the nucleus of a new Bill Doolin gang more vicious than the Daltons.

16

A Nail for Bill Doolin's Coffin

First to join Doolin, Pierce, and Newcomb was Bill
Dalton. He had never looked with favor upon the
crime-smashing work of his brothers. After his arrest
and acquittal in California, his sympathies turned
with their criminal activities. He had left his wife
and children with relatives in Merced County and was visiting
in Oklahoma when news came of the killing of Bob and Grat
and the wounding of Emmett. Arriving at Coffeyville with his
mother from Kingfisher, he swore vengeance for the slaying of
his brothers:

"The boys were wrong in trying to rob the banks, but they
were right when they shot the men who were trying to kill them!"

His mother, frightened half to death, begged him to keep still.
"They can't bluff me," he cried. "I say what I please!"

Next he threatened to sue the city for damages, alleging as
his cause of action that, while the bodies of his brothers were
in charge of its officials, unauthorized persons were allowed to
rifle their pockets of money and valuables, which had not been
turned over to him or the family:

"I know that one of the citizens robbed the bodies of $900
which Emmett claimed they had before coming to Coffeyville."

"This is the sheerest nonsense," stated the Coffeyville *Journal*.
"The chances are that it is only a bluff game, played in order to
force those who took the articles and are keeping them as relics
to return them. He claimed that one of the ablest attorneys in

145

the state is backing and instigating the suit on a contingency fee, but refused to name him. . . . Will's actions and words and his bank account are all interesting straws to watch when considering the question of his being a silent partner in the late firm of 'Dalton Brothers, bandits and outlaws,' whose business cards should have borne the inscription: 'Train and bank robbery a specialty.' "

After reading the paper, Bill Dalton entered his hotel, "fuming mad." When he sighted Heck sitting in the lobby, he stepped up to him and said: "I came near going over just now and shooting me a newspaperman. By God, the next one that braces me *will* be shot!"

Heck didn't blame him much. It had been a rather unfair thrust. But Bill was not very popular in Coffeyville, and the statements he had been making on the streets "made him less so."

His other complaint was about a horse that Bob Dalton rode in the raid. Identified by a man from the Indian Territory as one stolen from him a few weeks before, it had been released to him by the authorities. Heck had "some personal knowledge" that Bob had purchased the animal, and he helped Bill obtain papers of replevin, which "Bill made the mistake of flashing about, and led everyone to believe he had been appointed a deputy marshal."

The rumor reached Washington. Congressmen demanded an explanation from Attorney General W. H. H. Miller, and Miller in turn demanded to know on what basis a man like Dalton had been commissioned.

This brought separate denials from the United States Marshals of Kansas, Arkansas, and the Oklahoma and Indian territories. Wrote Marshal Walker of the District of Kansas at Topeka:

Wm. Dalton does not now, nor has he ever held a commission under me. Bob was a deputy under Col. Jones when I came into this office, and I retained him for a few months, but removed him in the fall of 1889. . . .

Marshal Needles of Muskogee replied:

I am in receipt of yours of the 22nd Ins't, in which you enclose an abstract from a letter rec'd by Senator Vest, as follows—"This very day Bill Dalton, one of the notorious family of that name, is walking

146

through the streets armed with a repeating gun and a commission as deputy United States marshal, with authority to scour the territory on our border"; and asking me as to the truth of the statement.

In reply I have to say that Bill Dalton, nor no other Dalton, has now, or ever has had, a commission from me as deputy marshal.

Marshal Yoes of Fort Smith was even more emphatic:

If William Dalton holds a commission as deputy U. S. marshal, it is not from this court, as he has not been appointed and never will be!

Marshal Grimes of Guthrie sent a lengthy report. Since it contains a full explanation of the matter and the role Heck played, it is worth quoting here:

Hon. W. H. H. Miller
U. S. Atty. Genl.,
Washington, D. C.
    Sir,—
My attention has been called to certain statements in regard to one William Dalton, who it is claimed has received a Commission as Deputy U. S. Marshal either under this office or under the Marshals of Kansas or Indian Territory.

While I am not in the position to know what the other Marshals may have done, I desire to state that the following reports have reached this office:

Shortly after the killing of the Daltons at Coffeyville, a man appeared at that place and claimed that one of the horses ridden by the Daltons, and which was held by the authorities, had been stolen from him a short time before; that upon his statements to this effect the horse was turned over to him, and he left with it for the Indian Territory. One of the deputies under this office, Heck Thomas, had sometime before that tried to buy the horse from the same man but had failed to do so, but had learned from reliable parties that the horse had been sold by this man to Bob Dalton and that he had paid $100 for the same. The man who claimed the horse and who got it has been considered as being closely connected with the Dalton gang for some time past and I understand that he is now in hiding some place in the Indian Territory. Upon learning the facts in the case, Mr. Thomas informed William Dalton that the horse did really belong to his brother Bob, and it is understood that William Dalton then tried to get lawful possession of the horse, but has so far failed to find the man; it is also understood that the papers which were supposed to

147

be a Commission as a deputy marshal, or which some people have spoken about as being such, were simply summons issued by a Justice of the Peace for the witnesses in the case if the horse should be found by William Dalton.

These are the reports which have reached this office . . . and I think the facts are substantially as set forth.

I am personally acquainted with William Dalton, in fact every deputy on the force here knows him, and he came to this office the day after the Coffeyville affair, to inquire about the truth of the alleged killing of his brothers, and requested me to furnish him a certificate that he was not one of the Daltons who had been hunted by the officers for a long time, this in order that he might go to Coffeyville and see his brothers without being arrested. I notified the Mayor of the town about his going there and informed him that while we had a suspicion that William had had more or less to do with his brothers on the outside, we had no proof against him whatever, and that there were no warrants out for him in this District. While the Daltons have all been a bad set of men, William has been somewhat more quiet or careful in his doings and has never been convicted of any of the crimes for which the rest of them have been tried; he is . . . a bright young man, but is considerably given to bragging and no doubt would be willing to take a hand in anything that would give him a reputation like his brothers had, but I think he lacks the nerve to do so. He has never had a Commission under this office nor would he ever get it under any circumstances. . . .

Very respectfully,
William Grimes
U. S. Marshal

Marshal Grimes underestimated both Bill Dalton's nerve and ambitions. Failing, finally, in his Coffeyville efforts, he threw aside all pretense of respectability and sought out Doolin in his camp on the Cimarron.

At first Doolin resented his presence. He still regarded being cut out of the Dalton gang as an insult. Maybe Bob Dalton hadn't liked the way he strutted up and down the depot platform at Adair when the shooting started, or the erratic bravado of Pierce and Newcomb when they proposed to rush into the coaches after the express car had been robbed and finish the fight with the Indian police and deputies. Perhaps he had thought them too sure of themselves. Certainly, Bob had been

148

displeased with the way they hobnobbed with their friends and other persons who concealed them.

He had been especially disturbed by the politeness of Bill Dunn and his five brothers and cousins, all Oklahoma farmers, who hid them in their cabins and dugouts along Council Creek near Ingalls, an isolated little settlement eleven miles east of Stillwater. "Someday you fellows," Bob had warned Pierce and Newcomb, "will get shot in the back. . . ."

"You're too damned suspicious, Bob," Doolin had replied, with irritation. "They ain't no suckin' calves!"

Doolin figured now that including another member of the Dalton family, with the peculiar prestige that went with him, would jeopardize his complete control of the gang. Dalton, however, entertained a certain respect for Doolin's ability and experience, and told him so. He soon convinced him that they should join hands. Doolin could lead the organization; he would aid him and be as helpful as possible.

Next, Doolin contacted "Little Dick" West, a bantam-sized, spindle-legged youth, trigger-quick and wiry, with eyes that darted about like those of a wild animal, and as ignorant of his antecedents as anybody. Little Dick's earliest known history began on the Three Circle ranch of Oscar Halsell in west Texas. Halsell, a big-hearted cattleman, had picked up the wandering, undernourished waif on the streets of Decatur and put him to wrangling horses when he was thirteen.

Asked about his origin, he replied: "I was just dropped on the prairie somewhere. Ma died soon after, and pa broke his life-long rule about sleepin' under a roof. He got caught, and I ain't seen him since."

Rain or shine, he always ate his meals in the open and slept on the prairie. As he put meat on his bones and grew older, his animal qualities gradually disappeared. But he continued to eat and sleep in the open, and the wild look never left his eyes.

He developed into an excellent cowhand, and when Halsell expanded into the Indian Territory and established his HX Bar ranch on the Cimarron, thirteen miles northeast of the future site of Guthrie, Little Dick went along. He worked for Halsell until the opening in 1889.

On the HX Bar he met Bill Doolin. Doolin was the son of Mack Doolin, an Arkansas cotton farmer. With no education and scarcely able to read or write, he had drifted into Oklahoma and got a job with Halsell cutting logs for cabins and corrals. He could use an ax, and Halsell's cowboys couldn't. Soon he became a top hand, bronc rider, and an expert shot with either Winchester or six-shooter. When Halsell quit ranching and entered the wholesale business in Guthrie after the opening, Doolin had gone to work on the Bar X Bar.

Little Dick had drifted into the Osage, where he lived for a time on money he had saved as a cowboy and discovered a cave which Doolin considered an excellent stopping place while riding with the Daltons. Little Dick's habit of sleeping in the open when others were seeking cozy beds and warm houses would make him a valuable member of the band. Should officers attack their rendezvous, he would always be on hand to flash a warning. Little Dick held great admiration for Doolin, and lost no time transferring his gear to the Cimarron hide-out.

Doolin added Bill Raidler, a well-educated youth of Pennsylvania Dutch ancestry, who had become fascinated by the cattle ranges and worked a number of years for Halsell. Forced to seek other occupations, he was easily persuaded that Doolin's method was a faster and more exciting way to get rich.

It is not known how Doolin became acquainted with Red Buck Waightman, whom Heck had arrested for horse thievery and who had escaped from the prison train at Lebanon, Missouri, in 1890. Early one morning he rode into camp with seven fine saddle ponies he had stolen and which Doolin decided they needed.

By this time the roster included Dan Clifton, another Texas horse thief who traveled under the alias "Dynamite Dick"; Jack Blake, a Creek Nation hijacker, known as "Tulsa Jack"; Ol Yantis, a local farmer with a checkered past whose sister had settled a claim near Orlando, north of Guthrie; and Roy Daugherty, alias Tom Jones, alias "Arkansas Tom."

Arkansas Tom hailed from Doolin's native state. His parents were religious people, and two elder brothers had been educated for the ministry. When he was ten years old, his mother died. A nagging stepmother, it is said, made life more miserable than

150

a sensitive boy could tolerate, and he ran away to the Indian Territory when he was fourteen. He had worked as a cowboy on a ranch in the Cheyenne and Arapaho country that Doolin often visited, and the tales of Bill's exploits with the Daltons had set the boy concentrating upon a quick draw rather than a quick rope.

The excitement of the Dalton raid had scarcely died down when an alarming announcement swept southeastern Kansas. The survivors of the gang had reorganized and were coming back to wreak vengeance on valiant Coffeyville!

An anonymous letter, mailed to Coffeyville from Arkansas City on October 12, has been credited to Doolin. From its tone and contents, Heck always believed it to be "the work of revenge-crazed Bill Dalton":

I take the time to tell . . . the citizens of Coffeyville that all of the gang ain't dead yet by a damn sight . . . and we shall come and see you. I would have given all I ever made to have been there the 5th. You people had no cause to take arms against the gang. The bankers will not help the widows of the men that got killed there and you thought you were playing hell fire when you killed three of us but your time will soon come when you will go into the grave and pass in your checks. . . .

Immediately the irate citizens again prepared to defend themselves against this threatened invasion. Emmett had been removed to Independence for trial. Bill Dalton had accompanied his mother there and disappeared. He had not been seen since, and Heck was down in Oklahoma trying to get a line on him, hoping that he would lead him to Doolin, Pierce, and Newcomb.

The morning after the letter was received, the agent at Wharton wired Chief Dodge that a large band of desperadoes had passed his station "presumably en route to Coffeyville to wipe out the place." Dodge wired the mayor of Coffeyville.

The excitement intensified. Telegrams were sent to Parsons and Kansas City asking that all available rifles and other weapons be shipped at once. By nightfall, the whole town was ready to fight. A Katy Railroad car stood at the depot, barricaded and full of armed agents and guards. A huge bonfire was built on

151

the plaza to furnish illumination. But the expected attack did not come.

Apparently it had been part of Doolin's strategy to draw the full attention of the country to Coffeyville. While Bill Dalton and the others were having their fun, Doolin took Newcomb and Yantis and rode west to Ford County. At 3 o'clock the cloudy, raw afternoon of November 1, the trio descended on the bank of Spearville, relieved Cashier Baird of $10,000, fired several shots to frighten the citizens, and left town, going south.

Sheriff Chalk Beeson of Dodge City was notified at once and headed southeast with a posse to intercept the robbers. A party of hunters returning to Spearville, sighted the bandits, and opened fire on them. The gang escaped unscathed, separated and disappeared. Sheriff Beeson split up his posse. He took Yantis' trail and followed it into the Outlet.

In his haste to put as much distance as possible between himself and Spearville, Yantis pushed his pony too hard. By the time he reached the Oklahoma border, his pony was staggering so badly he was forced to dismount. Orlando lay fifteen miles away. Leading the animal, he started east to his sister's home on foot.

As he stumbled along, footsore and frantically combing his back trail, he met a farmer riding a fine bay. Yantis demanded that he exchange mounts with him. The farmer refused and, without further argument, the outlaw whipped out his six-shooter and blew him from the saddle. Turning his worn-out pony loose on the prairie, he mounted the fresh horse and galloped away.

The murder aroused the whole community. Neighbors formed posses to hunt the killer. When Marshal Grimes received the news at Guthrie, he dispatched Heck and Chief Deputy Madsen to the scene and wired Deputy Tom Houston at Stillwater to proceed west to Orlando and assist in the search. Meanwhile, Sheriff Beeson had come upon Yantis' pony. The line-backed buckskin, with its black mane and tail, had enabled him to trace the fugitive from Kansas. Madsen recognized the pony at once, and knew Yantis' sister lived nearby.

The officers reached the farm before daybreak. Beeson and Deputy Houston covered the front of the house. Madsen stationed himself at one corner of the barn where he had discovered

152

the murdered farmer's horse. Heck took a position between the barn and the house, behind a stone fence.

At daylight, a man came to the door and peered out. Finally he emerged, carrying a six-shooter in one hand and a sack of grain in the other, and started toward the barn. His furtive movements convinced Heck he was the man they were seeking.

When he was alongside the stone fence, Heck rose quickly.

"Throw up your hands, Ol—we're officers!"

The outlaw swung his revolver, blazing away before the last words left Heck's mouth. Heck ducked to safety as chips flew from the rock wall above his head. Other shots followed almost with the rapidity of machine-gun fire.

The outlaw's sister dashed from the house, screaming: "Run, Ol, run!"

Heck scuttled to the end of the wall and rose again to fire at the outlaw just as the woman ran between them. Heck hesitated, and Yantis again swung his six-shooter to kill him.

Madsen's rifle cracked from the barn fifty feet away.

His well-placed shot knocked Yantis off his feet. As he lay writhing on the ground, struggling to lift his weapon, Heck sprang forward and kicked it from his grasp.

The terrified woman flung herself across her brother, moaning and begging the officers not to shoot again. Yantis looked up at Heck and snarled:

"Too damn bad I didn't get you!"

He might have done just that, Heck thought. He examined the outlaw's revolver and found one cartridge left. Madsen's shot had come in the nick of time.

Yantis had been hit in the left groin and was bleeding badly. The officers loaded him in a wagon and took him to Orlando to a doctor. Despite all medical attention that could be given, he died that night. In a belt about his waist, they found $4,500 of the loot taken in the Spearville robbery. It was returned to the bank by order of the court.

Heck checked the first member of the Doolin gang off his list, and thanked Madsen for saving his life.

The stocky, barrel-chested little Dane glanced down at the saddle gun in his hamlike fists, then looked up at Heck, and his

153

blue eyes twinkled. In an accent as thick as cheesecake, he replied: "Dot is goot." Which meant that he was pleased to have been of service. They were the best of friends from that day to Heck's death, but before that Heck and this tough little former army scout and Indian fighter would ride many another trail together.

As a starter, they had driven the first nail in the coffin of Bill Doolin.

154

17

Tom King Opens the Jail—

On November 8, 1892, Grover Cleveland was elected to his second term as President. That night, shortly before the southbound passenger train was due at Wharton, a lanky, pock-faced stranger, armed with two six-shooters and a rifle, entered the station and bought a ticket at Orlando. He inquired if the train was on time, and when assured that it was, took a position outside at the end of the platform.

The agent, his suspicions aroused, wired Madsen at Guthrie that he expected a holdup. Madsen boarded a special with a posse and started for the place at once. In the rush to reach the station by the time the train arrived from the north, the engine jumped the tracks above Orlando. The posse unloaded their horses and continued toward Wharton as fast as their mounts could carry them. The delay saved the robbers.

When the train stopped at the station, the conductor thrust his head from the baggage car. The stranger on the platform ordered him to put it back, and fired a shot from his rifle to emphasize the command.

Immediately two more bandits appeared, wearing masks. They fired a fusillade to intimidate the train crew, then entered the passenger car. One man carried a sack for the passengers to drop their valuables into; the other bandit walked behind, pointing

155

two ugly-looking Colts to see that his companion's orders were obeyed.

When E. Bee Guthrey, a newspaperman on his way home from Kansas City to Stillwater, saw the pair approaching, he searched his pockets, found $3.75 in silver and held the money in his hand until it was his turn to donate. He told the man holding the guns that he would like to keep out enough to pay hack fare to Stillwater.

"Drop 'er in!" the gunman commanded.

As the man carrying the sack moved down the aisle and the gunman came alongside Guthrey, he turned and asked, "Do I know you from somewhere?"

Guthrey, convinced by now that the man was Bill Doolin, said: "We met once in a cow camp, Bill."

"So we did!" the bandit readily replied. "What's the fare of that damn hack?"

Guthrey told him it was $1.25, whereupon the bandit ordered the man with the sack to hand him back that amount.

This done, they left the coach, compelled the engineer to detach the express car from the rest of the train and run it south to Cow Creek. Here they blew open the safe with dynamite, wrecking the entire rear of the coach. Finding no money, they stole the guard's shotgun and a Winchester rifle, mounted their horses, and rode off in an easterly direction.

Madsen and the posse reached Wharton nearly half an hour later. They obtained descriptions of the robbers, proceeded to Cow Creek, and picked up their trail. It was easy to follow because of recent rains. They rode all night and most of the next day. After crossing the Arkansas, the gang had separated and vanished in the Osage.

Since the killing of Yantis, Heck had been in Arkansas City with Matie. When he was assigned to the case the latter part of December, this robbery had been credited to the Doolin gang. He doubted Guthrey's identification—the bandit had seemed too anxious to acknowledge that he was Bill Doolin—and the pock-faced rifleman who had stood guard at the platform rang a bell in Heck's past.

"He's a dead ringer for Jesse Jackson, who used to sell whisky around Nowata," Heck told Madsen. His running mates, Heck informed Chris, were a half-breed Delaware youth named Ed Newcome and the notorious young Cherokee outlaw Henry Starr, now being hunted in Indian Territory for murder. On December 14, Starr had killed Deputy Floyd Wilson, who was attempting to arrest him on a whisky warrant in the California Creek country. "I'd like to do some checking up there."

Chris nodded. "You have dot authority."

Marshal Yoes at Fort Smith had resigned with the advent of Cleveland's election, and George J. Crump, the acting marshal, had renewed Heck's commission.

"Work both sides till this gang iss captured," Chris said. "Do you vish someone to go mit you?"

"Deputies Rufe Cannon and Ike Rogers handle that section," Heck replied. "I'll contact them when I get there."

Heck departed for Nowata. By January, he had unraveled this story:

Jesse Jackson was the bandit who had purchased the ticket to Orlando. The Santa Fe agent recognized him from a photograph. Newcome had carried the sack through the passenger coach. His companion who brandished the pistols and passed for Doolin was Ernest Lewis, a white man "about thirty years old and a dangerous character" wanted for murder in the Chickasaw Nation and for killing another man in the state of Washington before fleeing to Indian Territory. The trio had returned to the Cherokee Nation after the robbery. Following a quarrel over their failure to find any money in the express car, the gang broke up. Jackson and Newcome rode off with Henry Starr. Lewis had disappeared.

On January 20, Deputies Cannon and Rogers came upon Starr, Newcome, and Jackson near Bartlesville. In a running fight, "during which nearly a hundred shots were fired," Cannon "shot off Jackson's right arm and sent another bullet through his side before he surrendered." Starr and Newcome escaped.

Heck hurried to Bartlesville, claimed the prisoner, and took him to Guthrie. He confessed the details of the Wharton robbery, but didn't know where Lewis could be found.

Meanwhile, deputy marshals remained on the trail of Starr

and Newcome, who became the most hunted desperadoes in the Border States and the Territory.

Quickly, the fast-shooting, hard-riding pair robbed stores and railroad depots at Chelsea, Pryor Creek, Choteau, Nowata, and Aldrich, Missouri, climaxing their foray at Caney, Kansas, in March, with one of the most unique bank robberies in border history. Except for the ten employees and citizens who were quietly placed in a row, no one in town knew about it until it was over and the bandits had departed with $2,000.

With his share of the loot, Newcome decided to visit his mother on California Creek north of Nowata. Deputies Gideon White and J. C. Wilkerson, who had been watching the house, "took their man-boy without firing a shot" when he appeared, April 20.

Since most of his crimes had been committed within the jurisdiction of the Western District of Arkansas, it was agreed that he should be tried before Judge Parker. Heck talked to the prisoner before White and Wilkerson left with him from Nowata.

He told him: "Lewis put the marshals on you and Jackson to get the $1,500 reward offered by the railroad."

He was lying, of course; but it produced the results he expected.

"The double-crossin' bastard!" Newcome exploded. "Why, he engineered the whole thing himself. He even took the guns we got from the express car."

"Do you know where those guns are now?" Heck asked, casually.

The outlaw hesitated, as if sensing the ruse. But he replied: "Why, they're in his hotel room at Pawhuska."

Inadvertently, he had revealed where Lewis was hiding.

Heck left for Pawhuska. He found the killer sitting on the hotel porch, "heavily armed with two revolvers and a dirk knife." As he started to make a play, Heck warned:

"Better not, Lewis. I have a warrant for you, and it is a fugitive warrant."

Lewis knew Heck's reputation from down in the Chickasaw Nation, and a fugitive warrant meant that the marshal could bring him in upright or horizontally.

Lewis' moment of hesitation was all Heck needed. He sprang to the porch beside the outlaw, covering him with his rifle. He

158

relieved him of his weapons, then snapped on the handcuffs. In Lewis' room, he found the guns stolen from the express car.

Heck delivered the weapons and his prisoner to Madsen at Guthrie. With his inauguration in March, President Cleveland had announced that there would be a new group of territorial officials. Twenty-two applicants already were seeking the job of marshal. Disgusted, Grimes had gone to his farm at Kingfisher, leaving Chris in charge.

A number of prisoners were housed in the new territorial jail, which had been built by a stock company of Guthrie men and leased to the Government. But there were some sections yet to be completed, and some of Lewis' friends had arrived in town and were talking about "springing him."

"We take no chances mit such a desperate character," Chris decided, and transferred him to Oklahoma County.

His work on the Wharton case finished, Heck returned to Arkansas City and Matie. He had been home only a short time when Chris wired him that Lewis had broken jail at Oklahoma City with the help of a female horse thief named Flora Quick Mundis, alias Tom King:

. . . They stole two horses near Edmond and are headed for Kansas or the Creek Nation. Tom is about medium height, rather prepossessing, of dark complexion and badly tanned. In man's attire, she has the appearance of a well-proportioned boy of seventeen. . . .

Heck knew Tom King. He had seen her in Guthrie in 1892, when she was a resident of the city and a familiar figure on the streets, representing herself as a Cherokee half-breed, dressed in a stunning costume and always riding a good horse of doubtful ownership.

The youngest daughter of Daniel Quick, a wealthy farmer and stockman near Holden, Missouri, Flora had "grown up" in a saddle. When she was fourteen, her father had sent her to Holden College, where she remained only a few weeks. Restless, too full of nerve and energy for confinement, she was soon back at the ranch, herding cattle. About a year later, her father died, leaving an estate of 2,400 acres of land and $13,000 to be divided among nine surviving children. Flora sold her share of the property,

159

married a "disreputable, drunken whelp" named Ora Mundis, despite the protestations of her sisters and brothers, and galloped away to Oklahoma.

Their life together at Guthrie was fast-paced, brief. They spent their nights in the saloons and gambling halls—until Flora's money ran out; then Mundis galloped away alone.

But Flora never intended to be lonely. She became acquainted with Jessie Whitewings, the fleshy, flaxen-haired, 23-year-old former mistress of an Indian gambler. Flora was an apt student, and in no time had her own place at the corner of Grant and 4th streets. She "traded" for horses or money. No scandal was attached to her name until she had a warrant sworn out for one Doc Jordan, charging him with assault with intent to rape. Doc didn't stop long enough even to deny the charge, but deeming discretion the better part of valor, hied himself away, and the case was dropped.

Flora's business was ruined, however. She quit "trading" for horses and began stealing them. Dressed as a man, riding under the curious appellation of Tom King, she operated in Logan, Canadian, and Oklahoma counties, finally landing in the Oklahoma City jail. But iron bars do not a prison make. She displayed her charms to a none-too-bright turnkey, left him locked in her cell, and galloped away this time with Killer Lewis.

Lewis had painted her a rosy picture of the profits in train robbery. While the officers searched for them, they went into camp at the Santa Fe bridge on Black Bear Creek, between Red Rock and Wharton. For this job, they engaged the services of a half-wit, and former acquaintance of Tom's, named Manvel.

Manvel boarded Train No. 408 at Wharton the afternoon of June 29, with a Winchester wrapped in his coat and a Knights of Pythias sword buckled to his waist, and secreted himself in a closet of the smoking car. As the train approached Black Bear crossing, he leaped from the closet, covered Conductor Al Glazier with his rifle, and forced him to pull the bell cord.

When the train stopped, the desperado ordered him out of the car to the ground, following him closely. In stepping from the car, Manvel tripped on his sword. Before he could recover,

Glazier leaped upon him, seized the rifle, and knocked him down. Some passengers jumped out and helped tie him up with the bell cord. In his pockets they found two small pistols and four sticks of dynamite with the fuse already attached.

"What shall I do with him?" asked Conductor Glazier in his wire to Madsen. There were no officers along the road in the Outlet. "I think I better take him to Wichita."

At Wichita, the prisoner stated that two companions with the horses had waited for him near the crossing. Madsen and Marshal Grimes, who had returned to Guthrie that morning to wrap up the details of his last day in office, went up to the Black Bear on a special engine to look around.

They found a water hole near the tracks where a man and a woman had camped. From the size of the footprints, they guessed that it had been Lewis and Tom King, and learned afterward they had guessed correctly.

Chris wired Heck to proceed to Wichita and bring back "a member of the Lewis gang and a *bad* man." Then he sat back, chuckling to Grimes: "I'd like to see the expression on Heck's face when he arrives in full regalia to take charge mit the prisoner."

It was just as well that Chris wasn't there. Heck was "mad enough to have killed him and Grimes both. . . . He was the sorriest looking bad man I'd ever seen, with that sword, and his hair sticking out through holes in his hat and his feet in an old pair of plow shoes." Heck bought him a new hat before taking him out of jail.

He cursed Chris all the way to Guthrie. To make matters worse, nearly a thousand spectators had gathered at the depot, pushing and scrambling for a glimpse of the territory's "most dangerous train robber." Heck shoved through the crowd with his prisoner, flushed, and without speaking.

Afterward, Chris tried to apologize. He told Heck that it wasn't because he was ashamed to be seen with the prisoner that made him mad, but because the jailer at Wichita had let Manvel have his sword and he was scared!

"That didn't make things better," Chris wrote Matie, in describing the event to her years later, "but after we had been to Frank and Low's restaurant and had a good dinner, Heck quieted down and everything was all right until one day Heck and I, Joe McNeal (a local banker) and Glazier happened to be on the same train going to Oklahoma City. We got to talking about Manvel, and I asked Glazier what had become of him. I had not heard anything about him since he went to the lunatic asylum at Bloomington, Ill. Al got mad at once and told me that I knew very well where he was, but that I just wanted to make fun of him because Manvel had once been elected chairman of a Democratic county committee somewhere. Al, who was a strong Democrat, felt that it reflected on him to have had dealings with that kind of a man, and then Heck chipped in and wanted to join Al so the two of them would whip me and McNeal, me because I had turned the prisoner over to him, and McNeal because he owned the jail where they had to take the prisoner.

"We did not, like old Wilson, go to Versailles to draw up a peace treaty, but settled it in 'Two Johns' bar at Oklahoma City."

What happened to Tom King and Ernest Lewis?

Heck "next heard from Lewis in Colorado, where he killed another man and was sent to prison. After serving eight years, he returned to Bartlesville, got into a gun fight with the local constable, Pussyfoot Johnson, and both of them died together."

Tom remained in the Territory another two years and "kept stealing horses." Heck arrested her twice, and each time she escaped jail by "tricking or confusing some hapless turnkey."

Once, when Heck and Chris arrested her and were bringing her to El Reno in a spring wagon they had hired, she asked Chris:

"What's the name of the jailer where you're taking me?"

"Vy do you want to know?" Chris asked.

"Every jailer in Oklahoma has his price. If I know which one this is, I'll know his."

Tom finally seduced one man too many. Who and where is not known. She escaped again. When apprehended in Kansas and brought back to the territory, she was pregnant. With a baby on her hands and a trial staring her in the face, "no judge could be found who would re-sentence her for a minute's service anywhere."

162

She left Oklahoma and drifted to Tombstone, Arizona. But she never reformed. Nobody ever knew her real end. Heck told a reporter several years later what was supposed to be her end—a matter of a young man being killed in a holdup in a remote border town, who, upon burial, proved to be a woman whose body scars and measurements tallied with Tom King's.

18

—And Doolin Strikes Again

Heck and Matie moved to Guthrie in the spring of
1893. Heck had become a strong, twenty-third candidate for United States Marshal of Oklahoma. Early
in January, many leading members of the Democratic
central committee of the territory had "cheerfully
endorsed" him as "one of the oldest officers working out of Judge
Parker's court at Fort Smith . . . a man of irreproachable character whose allegiance to the party is beyond dispute." Judge
Parker, in a letter to President Cleveland on February 21, stated:
"He is entirely familiar with the country and the people living
in it and has done very much service for the Government in
breaking up lawless bands of murderers, train and express robbers. . . . I regard him as peculiarly qualified to meet the emergencies which are likely to arise in that office."

Heck prided himself on being a "working" marshal. Since
Cleveland's election, he had been in the field trailing the Wharton
bandits, so had no time to spend lobbying in Washington. He
was not yet a familiar figure in Guthrie—the center of all political
activity of the territory—and attention turned to a local businessman, Evett Dumas Nix.

Nix was thirty-two years old. He had come from Kentucky to
Oklahoma a few months after the opening in 1889. He had no
law enforcement experience, although his father, a lieutenant in
the Confederate Army, had served as deputy sheriff of Callaway

County, at Murray, for several years following the war. He had been in the hardware and furniture business since he was seventeen.

At Guthrie, he entered the retail grocery business with a man named Ed Baldwin. Within a year he sold out and formed a partnership with Oscar Halsell. By 1891, Nix, Halsell and Company had become the largest wholesale firm in Oklahoma. Later, when the Commercial Bank of Guthrie closed its doors in the first banking failure of the territory, Nix had been appointed receiver, under bond of $450,000, and disposed of the affairs of the ill-fated organization so satisfactorily that the people looked upon him with great confidence in his executive ability to conduct the affairs of the office of United States Marshal.

Despite the fact that the political "wah hosses" of the territory ridiculed the idea of his being a candidate, pointing to him as a mere boy who had done nothing for democracy, Nix "held onto the pole and finally knocked the persimmon."

"This is a young man's country," declared the editor of the *Daily Oklahoma State Capital.* "The new pace set down here has dazed age, while the young men have gone on producing wonders on which the world looks with admiration." Heck admitted it was Nix's "incorrigible energy, persistency and good cheer that got him this big plum."

Throughout his campaign, Nix had labeled the bandit problem in Oklahoma as "acute, hampering the development of legitimate business and making it almost impossible for money and merchandise to be successfully transported through the territory." He pointed to the fact that big Eastern dailies had "proclaimed it a horrible society in which it is possible for outlaw gangs to roam at will," and "at a time when Oklahoma needs new people and new capital." And he made much of such bitter comments in the territorial press as: "A tidal wave of criminality is sweeping the country. There is scarcely a county that is not the scene of bloodshed, suicide, rape, robbery or gigantic thefts. About one murderer in fifty is brought to justice."

Heck felt it was "hardly a true picture." Marshal Grimes, with a half-hundred deputies to police thousands of square miles of raw frontier, had done his best to cope with the situation. "He

165

has proven himself an able and conscientious officer," said the Guthrie *Daily News,* "and he lays down the insignia of office and leaves the same, bearing with him the respect and hearty good will of all his fellow citizens. . . . Deputy Madsen, who retires to private life, for the present at least, with Marshal Grimes, has likewise proven himself a tried and trusty man who, when duty called, was never found wanting."

The wiping out of the Dalton gang at Coffeyville and the slaying of Black-Faced Charley and Ol Yantis should have relieved the impatience of the citizens. But the formation of the Doolin gang had aroused new threats against the peace and welfare.

Nix declared it would be his sole purpose to apply himself to the solution of the outlaw difficulties and return to civil life and the pursuit of his own business as quickly as possible. As Heck predicted, "he little realized how strenuous a life he would lead those next few years, nor how gruesome a trail of blood his organization would be forced to leave behind in their efforts to establish law and order."

Nix took office July 1, 1893. He appointed John M. Hale as chief deputy. Hale was even younger than the marshal, but a man of "equilibrium," "depth of character," and "unquestionable bravery." He had considerable experience as an Indian trader in the Osage Nation and was well acquainted throughout the territory. Nix appointed his father, S. S. Nix, chief clerk because of his experience as an officer in Kentucky, and named W. S. Felts, a young cashier from a Guthrie bank, head of the accounting department. These three men, together with two assistant clerks and two stenographers, comprised his office force.

This done, he turned to the problem of picking his field deputies. He asked Grimes's men to stay on until he could make a satisfactory selection for the various places to be filled, and told a *Daily News* reporter: "No man who drinks can have a place on my staff. They will, above all, be courteous, of unimpeachable character and good standing in their communities. . . . The time has gone by for swashbucklers; for men who fence themselves in with revolvers and cartridges. A revolver, with the men I appoint, will be for business, and not for show. Men shall be treated as innocent, when arrested, until the law and evidence

166

shall prove them guilty, and will not be dragged from their homes nor carried five hundred miles around the country for the sole purpose of putting dollars in the pockets of the officials who arrest them. . . .

"He uttered these sentiments in no Utopian sense," the *News* continued. "They were the spontaneous outburst of a man who knew that the record of his life was clean . . . that in his career he had done unto others as he would that others should do unto him."

But the *State Capital,* suddenly doubtful of its earlier opinion of this "exemplar of young democracy," replied: "This means that none but Y. M. C. A.'s need apply! It will seem queer to see a lot of dyspeptic cadavers going out to trail the class of criminals who produce the 'holdups' in this territory. Think of a gentlemanly moralist, running onto a tough out in the jungles and, in a plaintive voice, declaring: 'My deah suh, we have been sent for you, suh, and we would like you to hold up youh hands and be ouh prisoner; if youh don't, suh, as much as we dislike to, we will be compelled, suh, to pull ouh guns on you!' And how beautifully 'moral suasion' worked, the deputy would have to discover in heaven, for the daisies would grow on a premature grave. And think of Mr. Nix searching the ranks of democracy with a microscope to find this brand of Sunday school moralists from which to make sleuth-hound saviours of banks and express trains."

Interviewed by both papers, Heck voiced no opinion pro or con. Personally, he agreed with most of Nix's policy, though he read into it some earmarks of the old Yoes regime at Fort Smith.

He looked upon the new marshal as a man of discrimination and keen judgment—a rare combination of courage and youth, of high moral tone—and told him so in the rear of Patton's store, where Grimes had moved his quarters while closing the business of his term and settling the accounts of his deputies.

"But," Heck added, frankly, "the strength of your backbone will be shown more by the striking force than the character of the men you choose or the way they wear their weapons."

"There are fifty deputies in office at this time," Nix said. "I'm a businessman, Thomas, and I've been asked by the Department of Justice to reduce that number to thirty to cut expenses. Do you think it will work?"

"Yes, if they are an effective body of men," Heck replied. The words of Judge Parker seemed suddenly to burn through his brain. "Cowards may be highly moral, but they can't serve as marshals in this territory," he said.

Later that evening, Nix sought him out at Frank and Low's restaurant. He spoke of his campaign in Washington, and said: "It was clean on the part of every man who sought the office. I hope I have made no enemies."

On the contrary, Heck admired him for being outspoken: "The more I knew of him the better I liked him." Their deep mutual understanding made Nix realize that Heck had a sincere interest in assisting him, and Heck was glad to be appointed one of the first field deputies in his organization.

Here is the list as given out by Marshal Nix himself on July 15th:

John Hixon, Morris Robacker, Frank Hindman, J. O. (Joe) Severns, Joe Pentecost, of Guthrie; J. M. Jones, John Quinby, Charles Colcord, Sam Bartell, John Hubatka, of Oklahoma City; William Banks, Cheyenne; J. H. Gill, Tecumseh; Charles L. Roff, El Reno; Frank Farwell, Anadarko; C. H. Marx, Osage Agency; J. A. Cooper, Kingfisher; James Vandeventer, Orlando; Thomas Tipton, Chandler; C. W. Reynolds, Perkins; Wm. Ivey, Choctaw, I. T.; Alonzo Poling, Chandler; S. T. Butner, Crescent City; George Smith, Norman; HECK THOMAS, Guthrie.

Robacker, Banks, and Severns had served under Grimes. Hixon was selected because of his experience as a pioneer peace officer in Kansas and as sheriff of Logan County, in Oklahoma. Although Hixon had waged an energetic campaign for the position of marshal, Nix held him in highest respect. Commented the *State Capital:* "Most of the appointees are known and tried men, and all are undoubtedly good and brave."

Next, Nix turned his attention to the sheriffs and deputy sheriffs in the counties adjoining the Nations. Too often crimes were committed in these counties and they did not have the authority to cross the border in pursuit of offenders. The Organic

Act gave the marshal concurrent jurisdiction with sheriffs in all criminal cases. Nix carefully compiled a list of eligible local officers and deputized them all as Federal men.

"This made it possible for all officers, regardless of politics, to work toward one end," Heck recalled.

These appointments, at no additional salary expense to the government (regular deputies now received $250 per month, in addition to fees), gave him a force of nearly 100 men.

Having selected his deputies, Nix called them together at Guthrie for a three-day conference on policy and procedure, urged them never to forget that they would be going up against some of the worst characters on earth, and always to make sure they safeguarded their own lives and the lives of citizens, then ordered them to their respective stations to begin work.

Meanwhile, the Doolin gang staged two of the boldest robberies of its career. They stopped the California Express on the Santa Fe west of Cimarron, Kansas, shot the express messenger, and escaped with $1,000 in silver and the contents of the way safe. Returning across the Outlet, they held up the southbound train at Wharton, guarded its crew until the arrival of the train going north, then looted both trains of several hundred dollars, a quantity of registered mail, and the valuables of gaping passengers.

Doolin could not have picked a better time to demonstrate the striking power of his band and his own generalship. It was as if he were attempting to "ridicule the new marshal and his little army." Nix was too busy completing his appointments and assignments to give immediate pursuit, and, in addition, on August 16, his force was shouldered with the responsibility of policing the Outlet, together with the surplus lands of the Tonkawa and Pawnee, which President Cleveland proclaimed would be opened to settlement at high noon September 16.

For nearly a month the crowds were greater and the scenes reproduced on almost a larger scale than in the openings of 1889, 1891, and 1892 combined. On the northern border, from Arkansas City to Caldwell, and on the southern border, from the Cimarron to Orlando and Hennessey and to the Texas panhandle, scrambling, fighting hordes gathered to await the zero hour. Nix's deputies, assisting the military, patroled the southern border. Immediately after the opening, they were to move in on the townsites to keep order. Four land offices were established on the sites of Wharton, on the Santa Fe; Enid, on the Rock Island; and Alva and Woodward, on the Southern Kansas Railroad. These would become the boom towns, and the deputies' primary targets.

Nix would need more men to handle the situation. When he suggested a force of 150 deputies to the Department of Justice, there was no objection, although this was twice the number ever allowed a territorial marshal.

Naturally, Nix added Democrats where possible. But he smartly set aside partisanship to accomplish his objectives. He found Chris Madsen willing to accept a deputy's commission, and instructed him to take charge at Enid, Alva, and Woodward and other points north and west. Heck was glad that Chris was back in the saddle again.

He was happy also when Nix recommissioned Bill Tilghman, with orders to take charge at Wharton. Tilghman had served under Grimes since May, 1892. Before that he had been a buffalo hunter and army scout on the Kansas frontier. In 1875, he had settled at Dodge City and stayed fourteen years, serving one term as undersheriff of Ford County and three years as a city marshal in Dodge when it was the toughest town west of Kansas City. He had come to Oklahoma in 1889 to play an important role in the early building of Guthrie, and settled a claim near Chandler in the Sac and Fox opening of 1891. Although Heck had worked very little with Tilghman up to this time, he listed the handsome, blue-eyed, soft-spoken officer first among his admired friends.

Then, during the last week of August, Nix's office learned that the Doolin gang, flashing the proceeds of their robberies, were rendezvoused at Ingalls, in eastern Payne County.

Here they came openly, spending their stolen money for provisions, whisky, and ammunition and enjoying the hospitality of most of the hundred or more citizens of this isolated settlement, who informed them when officers appeared in the neighborhood and even joined in their festivities. Only a few miles to the north

170

lay the wild, unsettled Pawnee country, and to the south, the hills and timber along the Cimarron, where escape was easy. To the east, along Council Creek, were the dugouts and farmhouses of the Dunns, who had sheltered Doolin, Pierce, and Newcomb since the days of the Dalton gang, and beyond there were the Creek Nation and the hundreds of places to hide. Marshal Nix was on the border of the Outlet. Chief Deputy John Hale was attending court at Stillwater. Heck and John Hixon had been left in charge at Guthrie to handle any emergencies which might arise during the absence of Nix and Hale.

Hixon conceived the idea of organizing a posse and going into Ingalls in covered wagons. "Everywhere homeseekers in covered wagons are crossing the country for the Outlet," he told Heck. "We'd just look like another party of homeseekers headed for the promised land."

Heck had seen too many such expeditions fail. In the past, he always had gone after his quarry alone, or accompanied by one or two possemen, and been successful. Even while trailing the Daltons, he had used, at the most, only three men.

He warned Hixon that it was a fool's errand and wanted no part of it. Hixon appeared irritated. "I reckon *one* of us ought to stay in Guthrie," he said.

Quietly he organized his posse. Three were former Grimes deputies: Dick Speed, city marshal at Perkins; Tom Houston, now serving as a constable at Stillwater; and Lafe Shadley, who had been a deputy sheriff in the Coffeyville vicinity at the time of the Dalton raid and stationed under Grimes at Pawhuska among the Osage Indians. Other lights included several local citizens, all fine shots and anxious to exterminate the outlaws, like Jim Masterson, brother of the famous Bat Masterson. Jim had been a policeman at Dodge City during its cowboy days. A first-day settler of Guthrie, he was a well-known figure about town, and had been acting as a deputy marshal since.

On the night of August 31, two white-topped wagons left Guthrie en route to Ingalls. Each wagon boasted a single driver, but carefully concealed beneath their flapping canvas were a cargo of arms and ammunition and thirteen men.

On the morning of September 1, they made camp in a ravine

171

southwest of Ingalls, and two scouts went ahead to study the town.

At 9 o'clock, they were back with a report. Seven of the outlaws had ridden in, left their horses in the livery barn next to the Ransom and Murray saloon, and separated, Arkansas Tom going to the hotel, the other six entering the saloon.

Hixon, perhaps a little shaken now by Heck's warning, decided the odds of thirteen against seven desperate criminals were not enough. He dispatched a messenger to Chief Deputy Hale at Stillwater. Hale gathered a posse and started for Ingalls at once.

Meanwhile, Hixon decided to scatter his men to block all avenues of escape. Masterson, with one of the wagons and half the posse, circled the town, stopping in a grove of trees to the east.

Speed drove the second wagon in from the west. Hixon, Houston, Shadley, and the others dropped from under the canvas, taking positions behind buildings, fences, and trees.

Then Speed turned the empty vehicle down main street past Light's Blacksmith Shop and stopped in front of the Hostetter livery stable, a block north of the Ransom and Murray saloon.

Inside the saloon, the outlaws were playing poker. They had seen the first wagon disappear in the grove on the east edge of town, but thought nothing of it since this was a favorite camping spot for travelers. When the second wagon lumbered in from the west, Bitter Creek grew nervous and left the game to investigate.

Speed had climbed down from the wagon with his Winchester and was standing in the doorway of the livery stable. He saw Bitter Creek step into the street and start toward the wagon.

At that moment, 14-year-old Del Simmons came out of the blacksmith shop. Speed called to him: "Who is that fellow coming up here?"

The youth stared incredulously. "Why," he exclaimed, "that's Bitter Creek Newcomb!"

Bitter Creek heard and lifted his rifle. Speed whipped his Winchester to his shoulder and fired.

His bullet shattered the magazine on Bitter Creek's weapon and drove a piece of it into his right leg. The outlaw flinched

172

with pain as he fired, and his shot went wild. His rifle would not work for a second shot. As he mounted a horse standing nearby to escape, Speed stepped from the doorway to kill him.

Arkansas Tom heard the shots in his room on the second floor of the hotel, and ran to the window. As Speed stepped from the stable, he fired at the officer, killing him instantly.

The other possemen began shooting at Bitter Creek as he rode south out of town. Doolin, Dalton, Tulsa Jack, Dynamite Dick, and Red Buck opened fire from the saloon, covering his escape. In the melee, young Simmons was shot dead as he fled down the street.

Hixon and his men concentrated their fire on the north side and rear of the saloon. Masterson and his party moved from the grove and advanced through a row of residences to cover the front of the saloon and the stable where the gang had left their horses.

Lead ripped into the building from front and rear. Ransom was hit in the leg, and his partner Murray received a wound in the left side and a broken arm. The outlaws decided to make a run for their horses.

Doolin went first, then Red Buck and Dalton, then Dynamite Dick and Tulsa Jack, each segment, with guns blazing, covering the other as they gained the stable entrance.

Hixon and his men shifted positions to cover the stable. Houston moved to the corner of an old granary to fire into the rear door of the barn. In the hotel, Arkansas Tom, unable to assist his comrades now from the window of his room, had crawled into the attic. He poked a hole in the roof with the muzzle of his Winchester and shot Houston through the left side and bowels.

At that moment, the five outlaws rode from the stable, Dalton, Red Buck, and Tulsa Jack from the front door, Doolin and Dynamite Dick from the rear. Hixon shot Dalton's horse in the jaw. The horse stopped. Dalton put spurs to his mount. Then Shadley fired, breaking the horse's leg.

As the screaming animal went down, Dalton leaped clear and ran toward the other outlaws, who had reached a barbed wire fence at the head of a draw. Dalton realized the only pair of wire cutters among them were on his saddle, and he started back to his injured horse.

He saw Shadley run for the shelter of a storm cave near the fence. Whipping up his six-shooter, he fired three bullets into the deputy's belly, and kept firing at the other officers until he obtained the wire cutters. He cut the fence. The five outlaws, on four horses, vanished down the draw into the timbered hills toward the Cimarron.

Only Arkansas Tom remained, hidden in the hotel attic. The officers virtually riddled the roof and upstairs with bullets, but, miraculously, after another hour of fighting, Tom was still alive and seemed to have an inexhaustible supply of ammunition.

Hale arrived from Stillwater. He sent his posse in pursuit of the escaped outlaws, and joined the officers around the hotel, demanding the killer to surrender.

"Go to hell!" yelled Arkansas Tom.

Masterson went to his wagon and returned with two sticks of dynamite which he had brought along for just such an emergency. "Come out with your hands up," he shouted, "or we'll blow you to kingdom come!"

Inside, Mary Pierce, who owned the hotel, pleaded with the outlaw to spare her place. After obtaining a promise from Hale that he wouldn't be lynched, Arkansas Tom finally strode from the building and surrendered.

Hale, with possemen Ike Steel and W. C. Roberts, returned to Guthrie with the prisoner, a half-dozen witnesses, and three citizens whom they had arrested for harboring. Steel led Tom's horse, which the gang had left in the stable, and Roberts carried Bill Dalton's saddle.

Hixon accompanied the body of Dick Speed and the wounded Houston and Shadley to Stillwater, where they suffered through the night and died. The Stillwater *Gazette* lamented: "Three brave and fearless officers . . . cut down in the prime of life by assassins while in defense of our homes and firesides." And the Guthrie *Daily Leader* demanded that "the scoundrels be caught and made to pay the penalty, or killed as one kills wild beasts."

Heck guessed they would be some time accomplishing that.

On September 16, the bugles blew, the signal shots were fired, and the struggling, pushing, cursing hordes swarmed over the Outlet. Dust and sand rose in dense, mighty clouds. Men ran each other down as they raced onward. Women shrieked and fell fainting, only to be trampled and left dead on the prairie. Vehicles of all kinds were smashed and lay useless. Knives and guns were drawn over claims. Cities sprang up within hours. Seven new counties (Kay, Grant, Woods, Woodward, Garfield, Noble, and Pawnee) were added to Oklahoma Territory, with county seats at Newkirk, Medford, Alva, Woodward, Enid, Perry (a mile north of Wharton), and Pawnee, respectively.

By nightfall the opening day, Enid had 12,000 people camped on eighty acres. Other cities boasted from two to eight thousand. Twenty-five thousand occupied the government townsite of 320 acres, on Perry proper. This was not big enough, and, as the afternoon waned, there sprang up on the government land around it a North Perry, a West Perry and Wharton, or South Perry, each the same size.

Thrown, pitched, tumbled into place, the city appeared "stretched all over the face of the earth and piled three or four deep." Tents and rude structures were being erected by the light of flaming torches. "About the temporary saloons was pandemonium . . . elsewhere a thousand campfires twinkled in an inextricable mix-up of horses, mules, equipage and men . . . a half dozen people seemed holding down each lot."

While every city in the Outlet had its townsite difficulties and violence, Perry suffered most. Within a week, it became so tough, and vice so rampant, that Marshal Nix ordered Heck to Perry to assist Bill Tilghman.

19

Hell's Half Acre

Heck found conditions in Perry even worse than Nix had described them.

The mass of tents and shacks, wagon covers and dugouts sprawled upon the prairie, wholly without form. When one moved about, it was over guy ropes and wagon tongues and loose lumber to be met by continuous and profane orders to "Get off this lot!" Streets and alleys, park sites and government reserves had been ignored and pre-empted helter-skelter.

As Heck noted: "It was everybody for himself and the devil would have had a very busy time taking the hindmost."

Hundreds of businessmen had squatted on the four sides of the courthouse square facing the streets. Few were legitimate merchants. The speculators and lot boomers had been first, and the buildings erected were merely for the purpose of holding the lots and suitable only for restaurants, saloons, and real-estate offices.

They had been informed by some unknown person that this was open for settlement instead of the block lying immediately south of it, and were accusing the authorities of changing the government plot of the townsite for mercenary reasons. Supporting their accusation was the fact that a company of soldiers, there as purveyors of peace, either posted as to the trick or mistaken, had refused to allow them to occupy the block to the south and kept it clear of claimants until certain favored ones allegedly had been located before turning over the balance to public settlement.

The matter finally went to the courts, but the settlers lost.

Orders came from Washington: "Clear the square of squatters!"

This kept Sheriff J. C. Scruggs and a score of deputies busy. The county officials established quarters in tents and hastily constructed shacks on the square. Heck and Tilghman shared the sheriff's quarters and assisted him. They mingled with the crowd constantly, admonishing one here and there and attempting to establish a friendly atmosphere.

Honest men and thieves, bankers and paupers, adventurers and those who just wanted homes moved in frantic disorder. The tramp of thousands of human feet and the hoofs of animals rendered the air unbearable almost to the degree of suffocation from the dust created.

"It was days," Heck wrote, "before one could see the distance of two feet ahead in the government acre."

The wind drove the strongly akaline dust into his ears, mouth, and nostrils "until it bit and burned." Black sand covered everything. Men went to Cow Creek to wash their clothes and hang them out to dry, leaving friends to guard their lots.

Each lot had from one to a dozen claimants. Several fist fights broke out. The feeling was intense.

Two young men pulled their guns in a dispute over a lot. In a twinkling Heck and Tilghman were upon them, the guns were wrested away, and the men hustled apart without a shot being fired.

"That's Tilghman and Heck Thomas," flew the talk. And there was no other trouble around the land office.

The office occupied the government acre in the heart of Perry. Restaurant men in tents clustered about, serving lunches and coffee with little regard for sanitation. Bunco artists and cardsharps were scattered through the crowds, and, although Heck and Tilghman prevented them from carrying on a very profitable business, they attracted the masses. The shell game seemed the most popular. Sometimes a minister could be found, mounted on a box, preaching to an interested congregation.

All over the acre, lawyers had pitched their tents. "Only now is the ground being cleared and the cormorants thrown off," the Kansas City *Times* reported. It estimated that 500 lawyers were in Perry before the process began. "Probably 200 or 250 are still there. Many are reputable men, representing firms of the highest standing in Oklahoma and Kansas . . . but the majority are jacklegs, pettifoggers and low-down police court advocates who disgrace the profession. It seems a shame that honest homesteaders should be exposed to the wiles of these unprincipled shysters . . . and a pity they weren't thrown off long ago. It is claimed that these sharks are the ones who have caused all the talk about bad administration of land office affairs."

At first, nearly 12,000 eager homesteaders gathered about the office. Had they been compelled to hold their places in line, hundreds would have died from fatigue and exposure. Then someone hit upon a numbering plan. The line, from the man whose turn it was next to file, was divided into companies of ten, each under a captain. As new filers were added to the line, they were organized and numbered.

A man in company 801, for instance, could figure that company number 800, or 8,000 men, were ahead of him. Figuring an average of the filings each day, he knew pretty well the day he could file, and could go home for a week, or even a month or so.

The homesteaders agreed among themselves upon this plan and the Government agreed to recognize it. "Even with this system," Heck recalled, "nearly two hundred were always in line at the office."

With the immediate problem of orderliness in the lines at least temporarily solved, Heck and Tilghman turned their attention to the cancerous section which had bloomed out in the east part of town along the Santa Fe tracks known as Hell's Half Acre.

"During the short weeks it existed," quoted the *Times*, "in all its pristine and unchecked exuberance, it discounted anything in history, either sacred or profane. Killings averaged a man and a half a day. That is, two men were killed every three days."

Yet killings were regarded as only a minor part of the devil-

178

ment going on among the most dissolute women of the West, the worst riffraff of the entire Indian Territory, and the cream of toughs and thieves and desperadoes of half a dozen states, which swarmed in Hell's Half Acre.

The first establishment erected had been a combination saloon, dance hall, and gambling den, owned by a woman called Black Nell. Other resorts were soon running in competition, but Black Nell's held more than its share of patronage. Whisky was the one beverage in demand.

"It was first sold over the tail-boards of prairie schooners," said the Perkins *Journal.* "A few enterprising settlers erected bars in the open by the very simple process of laying a board across two barrels, on which was displayed all or most of their stock in trade. . . ."

But Black Nell, with her following of women, Mexicans, and half-breeds, had a house of pine boards. Along one side ran the bar, behind which canteens and bottles were arranged on shelves and barrel tops. On the other side of the room were tables for poker, faro, keno, and craps. Crowds of unkempt, sullen-faced, and desperate men thronged the place, hoping against hope that they might win enough to take them out of the territory and back whence they came. In another canvas-walled addition was the dance hall, where, nightly, wild and uncouth revelries occurred as could be seen only in a frontier town.

The Buckhorn, a similar establishment, did business from the first hour of the opening in a large tent which resembled Barnum's. With water so scarce, beer sold for one dollar a bottle. Its proprietor brought in 33,000 bottles, which he disposed of at this figure in the first few days, and amassed a fortune.

The point of entry nearest the Perry townsite was on the Outlet border east of Orlando. The record for distance run was claimed by Jack Tearney, conspicuous in Guthrie sporting circles before coming to Perry. He reached the townsite from this point in thirty-one minutes and had his Blue Bell saloon operating at 4 o'clock.

One establishment, with foot-tall letters, proclaimed: "The best whisky in town for $1.00." The Carolina, the Ark, the White Elephant, and the original Red Light saloons were all on the

179

acre. Others bore such names as Hawkeye, Oriental, Pawnee, Anchor, Midland, and Board of Trade.

Not for a moment did Hell's Half Acre belie its name. No night passed without the promiscuous discharge of firearms while every person sleeping in a tent lay a little closer to the ground or set up bullet shields. A bale of hay was the favorite protection from lead screeching through the canvas above.

Several homesteaders were wounded. One morning Heck found one poor fellow in his tent, dead. A bullet had entered his right eye and passed through his head.

Heck had no authority to close or regulate these activities, only to police the throngs and keep the peace.

As to the throngs, according to the *Times,* "the Midway Plaisance of Chicago was scarcely in it." There were the same "eternally restless crowds," and "had the architecture of Old Vienna and Cairo street and all the rest of 'em been combined, it could not have surpassed for variety the architectural nightmare in Perry. Anywhere here the Javanese or Japanese could get pointers on lightness, and especially airyness, of construction. Auctioneers are fully as strong lunged and certainly as adept liars as the Midway fakirs. . . ."

As for entertainment: "On a minute's notice any of the dancehalls will furnish an exhibition besides which the muscular gyrations of the Turkish damsels weren't a marker. To be sure, there's no Ferris wheel, but just go into any saloon and watch the roulette!"

Every place had its music. The fiddler and the piano were the limit of orchestration, and the latest popular airs were on tap at all times, sung better or worse, depending on the alcoholic condition of the singer. "After the Strip Is Opened," an appropriate and touching parody of "After the Ball," was the favorite among the vocal classics. It sold on the streets at ten cents a copy, and one singer in the Blue Bell made $23 by singing that many verses or one verse that many times to a disappointed homeseeker who had run up against a sooner and was trying to drown his sorrow.

Violence reigned supreme as more than one desperado "shot it out" with another.

A slow, easygoing Westerner named Billy Haney presided on

the midnight till morning shift in the Buckhorn. The Buckhorn was patronized regularly by a cheap outlaw and tinhorn gambler named "Three Fingered Jack." Jack had his "Lady Lou," also a patron of the Buckhorn, who became enamored of the bartender Haney.

At 2 o'clock one morning, with business quiet, Lou was sitting on Haney's lap at the head of the bar when in walked her three-fingered lover. Jack pulled his gun and fired. The bullet struck the woman in the arm. A shot from Haney's revolver, and Jack fell mortally wounded. Coolly, Haney walked around the bar, gathered up his victim, carried him across the railroad tracks and dumped his body behind a dance hall, where it was discovered shortly after by early morning revelers.

Jack Baugh, a big, tough, six-foot Negro meatcutter, met L. E. Belopue, another bartender, coming along the railroad track at night and decided to rob him. When Belopue resisted, Baugh put a bullet through his hat, and "got hell blowed out of himself" for his efforts.

Several fugitives from the states sought refuge in Perry the day of the opening. Heck arrested one notorious killer, whom he turned over to Sheriff Ike Ault, of Sedgwick, Kansas.

In September, S. H. Harris, a prominent Norman lawyer, was appointed prosecuting attorney for Noble County. He received so many complaints of robberies and homicides in and around the gaming places that he decided to put a stop to it.

On October 3, in accordance with an order from William C. Renfrow, the new territorial governor, Sheriff Scruggs, Heck, Tilghman, and half a dozen other deputies, raided all the gaming establishments. By the end of the day, wheels of fortune, faro layouts, and chuck-a-luck tables were "piled in innocuous desuetude on the outside of the principal resorts," and the most pretentious places like the Buckhorn and Blue Bell "looked like deserted tabernacles."

Meanwhile, in the greater and better section of Perry, business pluck, push, enterprise, energy, and capital combined to set the city rolling at almost startling velocity.

"You can see it day by day. At morning stands a vacant lot, at night the framework of another house or store building. Another day it is inclosed and another the stock is being moved in even with lathers and plasterers still at work. If the town keeps this up much longer," the *Times* concluded, "it will have every other Oklahoma city by both the hair and the heels."

Governor Renfrow issued a proclamation, declaring Perry a city of the first class and calling for an election. Four wards were created, conventions held, and many tickets placed in the field. "The campaign was as unique and exciting as any that ever happened. . . ."

On October 21, John M. Brogan, an Oklahoma City grocery-man, defeated his nearest opponent by 108 votes for mayor. A treasurer, city attorney, city clerk, and an assessor were chosen. Alonzo Jacobs became police judge, and eight councilmen, two from each ward, were selected. With the exception of two councilmen, both saloon men, the entire first body of lawmakers for the new city was Democratic.

They held their first meeting in a saloon and gambling house owned by one of the councilmen. "The gambling tables were brought into legitimate use while the hired help took a welcome rest for the night." The first ordinance offered and adopted defined the corporate limits. Mayor Brogan appointed Bill Tilghman city marshal and Heck as assistant. Four extra policemen, one from each ward, and other appointive officers, were named at that time.

Then followed daily meetings of this group with an almost continuous string of resolutions and ordinances being proposed, authorized, tabled, or otherwise disposed of.

"This first council," continued the Perry *Daily Times*, the town's first newspaper, "set the precedent for future management by establishing an honest and economical government. It was liberal and progressive and from the beginning resisted the assaults of individuals inspired by selfish greed, seeking to grasp the most valuable franchises and give in return only a mess of potage. . . . And there was a 'cleaning up' by the police force, which gradually pushed out the vicious element—or at least drove it under cover. . . ."

Marshal Nix granted leaves to both Heck and Tilghman but

continued their commissions so that they could attend to any government work in the locality.

Elsewhere in the Outlet he appointed new members to his force. He placed Jack Love in charge at Woodward, Gus Hadwinger and E. W. Snoddy at Alva, W. A. "Pat" Murphy at Pond Creek and Enid, and brought Deputy Madsen back to El Reno as chief deputy in charge of the western half of the territory.

By an act approved December 21, 1893, Congress added two territorial justices for the new section. President Cleveland named Andrew G. C. Bierer and John L. McAtee to these positions. Thus the membership of the supreme court and the number of judicial districts for Oklahoma Territory increased to five.

Judge Bierer had the fourth district covering the eastern half of the Outlet with headquarters at Perry, and Judge McAtee was in charge of the fifth district comprising Kingfisher, Grant, and Garfield counties, with headquarters at Enid. John H. Burford, of Indiana, had been appointed to the vacancy created by Judge Seay of the second district, who resigned to become territorial governor in 1891; Frank Dale, of Kansas, succeeded Judge Green in the first judicial district at Guthrie and Stillwater, and Henry W. Scott succeeded Judge Clark at Oklahoma City and Norman.

Of these first men on the bench in Oklahoma, only Judge Burford remained until statehood eliminated the territorial courts. His jurisdiction included the extreme western counties and No Man's Land, where settlers were few and the cattle range ideals still prevailed. He dealt with more cases of killing than all the other judges combined, and Marshal Nix found it necessary to assign some of his best field deputies to this remote section to assist in the proper service of papers, the accumulation of evidence, and maintenance of order.

Heck and Tilghman continued to work at Perry. "These are wonderful men," said the *Daily Times* of November 23, "and their appointment had a wonderful effect. The most notorious characters in town skipped out at the first intimation that they were not wanted. Others are going."

The 110 saloons were reduced to fifty-two, with the license fee fixed at $300 a year. Gambling rooms were permitted on payment of so much per table each month. But they could no longer operate on the ground floor flush with the street, and moved upstairs. Dissolute women were ordered to keep off the streets or get out of the city. During the winter of 1893-94, Police Judge Jacobs' dockets particularly were replete with cases where "such kindliness was exhibited that nothing was barred save sex—previous condition, race and color are welcomed with no questions asked and . . . has set his honor to wondering what the next variety presented will be."

As the city passed through its first transformation, the streets were cleared; tents and shanties gave way to permanent frame buildings; three brickyards were started outside the limits; the post office moved from a rough board building on the government acre to a commodious room in a new structure at the other end of the square, and plans got under way for the construction of a courthouse and jail. A Board of Trade was incorporated under the laws of the territory and chartered for twenty-one years.

The important work it accomplished consisted in disseminating throughout the United States information relative to the surrounding Outlet, its fine farm lands, outcroppings of coal, and the finest beds of cement rock in the country, "in the center of which is Perry, bigger and richer, livelier and wider awake, and with more vim and go in her to a square inch than either Guthrie or Oklahoma City to the square foot." With electric light and street car companies already figuring on franchises, and a corps of Rock Island surveyors laying out a line from Enid, through Perry and Stillwater, to McAlester, it "should continue a banner city and the most important metropolis between Kansas City and the Gulf."

At home, the board's efforts were directed toward promotion of commercial and municipal enterprises. Bids were made for the trade from the nearby Indian reservations and steps taken to incorporate the large residential districts in the townsites adjacent to Perry proper.

The one objection seemed to be that Heck and Tilghman had tamed the town too well. With their tight rein on the saloons and gambling dives, most of the proprietors quit business, the buildings were moved away, and Hell's Half Acre, almost deserted, was given over to a show lot for small tented aggregations that visited the city.

There was an axiom among border men that where saloons and gambling houses flourished, there was a good town. And despite their honesty and high standard of official rectitude, some members of the council became convinced that Perry would die if a wide-open policy was not re-established. They pointed to Guthrie and Oklahoma City as wide-open towns, and even forcibly impressed this fact upon the minds of their constituents.

"It merits Marshal Tilghman's consideration," demanded Councilman Gregg. "What is an officer for, anyway? It certainly is not to give roughshod condolence for loss sustained."

Tilghman had gone to make a brief check on a small string of racing horses that he kept at his farm near Chandler. This was his hobby. The star of his stable, named "Heck," after Thomas, was unbeatable up to 4½ furlongs, having a strain of quarter-horse blood. Tilghman and his partner, Neal Brown, another deputy, had raced the string on the tracks at St. Louis in 1892 and 1893. Their winnings had been enough to make the hobby a profitable one, and they planned to race again that year.

For the time being, Heck was in charge at Perry. He read into the town's dilemma the old situation that had confronted Longhair Jim Courtright in Fort Worth. But he did not, like Courtright, move on to clean up another tough settlement.

He did not even wait for Tilghman's return to "settle Gregg's hash." The issue came to a head at a council meeting the night of February 7. Gregg offered an amendment to the ordinance providing for the payment of occupation tax or saloon license for the quarter ending April 30, resulting in a tie vote which Mayor Brogan decided negatively. Mayor Brogan explained that the funds were needed if they expected him to maintain an effective police force.

Councilman Flock, who voted for the amendment, explained that he was more interested in justice for the "working" man. He wanted ordinances passed in consonance with the territorial statutes. "Do things right or not at all."

185

Councilman McGinnis spoke of the city of Perry which "the working man had started and would see finished." This speech was "lost among the plaudits" of three hundred representatives of the saloon league and others looking on.

Encouraged by this response, Gregg introduced his amendment the second time. Upon motion, the rules were suspended and it was introduced for the third time. Again the amendment was voted upon, receiving five yeas and one no.

Confident now of support from the other councilmen, Gregg announced that he intended to ask for the resignation of a certain gentleman filling the office of assistant marshal. He further stated that the city already had paid out an aggregate amount of $500 for his protection, and a dwindling population was all they had to show for it.

In the course of time, Heck made a reply. He commenced calmly enough, but soon his temper arose. He accused Gregg of saying things "which are not true" and being sore "because I arrested one of his pimps—I mean, one of his gentleman friends."

The councilman evidently saw no distinction between the words quoted and "You are a liar!" No sooner had they passed Heck's lips than Gregg leaped to his feet. Seizing the city clerk's massive inkstand in a firm grip, he let it fly at Heck's head. Heck dodged the missile, as did Mayor Brogan, who was near him. Such of the contents that had not decorated Heck's shirt front "frescoed the wainscoting and nearby window lambrequins."

A motion to adjourn was immediately made, seconded, put and carried, and everyone went outside to "regain his equilibrium."

At the next council meeting, however, their differences were resumed. Gregg's motion to dispense with Heck's services was promptly seconded and carried.

There are no details of what happened next. The Guthrie *Daily Leader* of February 25, 1894, carried this item: "News came from Perry last night that Officer Thomas and Councilman Gregg became involved in a quarrel during which Thomas hammered Gregg over the head with a gun, breaking his skull. Gregg is reported to be in a dangerous condition."

Gregg recovered. Heck supposedly was fired in February, but city records show he was still on the payroll in April, when W. A.

186

Stone, a Republican, became mayor, and named a new police force.

Heck returned to Guthrie. Judicial and business affairs of the Outlet having settled down to peaceable routine, Nix's staff was able to concentrate its effort on a campaign against the Doolin outlaws.

"Almost daily," Heck jotted in his memoirs, "the people of the territory appealed to Nix for relief from the terrible suspense hanging over them by reason of this vicious band's depredations. . . ."

The evening of January 5, 1894, two members of the gang had entered the post office at Clarkson, in Payne County, covered Postmaster Waltman with six-shooters, and looted the place of all money and registered matter. Shortly after 3 P.M., January 23, Doolin himself stepped into the Farmers' and Citizens' Bank at Pawnee, placed the muzzle of his revolver against the head of Cashier C. L. Berry, and snarled:

"Open the vault, or I'll blow out your brains!"

Berry told him he had just placed all surplus funds in the safe and set the time lock for 4 o'clock, when daily balances were made. Doolin put his ear to the safe. Hearing the time lock clicking, he became convinced that it could not be opened readily. He waltzed the banker back to his desk, took what cash was in sight, nearly $300, then marched Berry outside where Tulsa Jack and Dynamite Dick waited with the horses.

A curious crowd started toward the bank. The robbers opened fire on them with Winchesters. As they scurried for cover, the robbers mounted, Doolin taking Berry up behind him so the citizens would not return their fire. With wild cries and another volley of shots, they went tearing down the street across Black Bear Creek into the timber. Three miles away, Doolin ordered Berry to "pile off," which the banker did with alacrity.

Sheriff Frank Lake and his chief deputy, Frank Canton, met him walking back to town. They combed the wilderness with a posse. At Gray Horse ford, they found signs that the trio had been joined by a half-dozen other riders, but the trail vanished.

The gang rode west through the Outlet. At 1 o'clock the morning of March 13, Doolin and Dalton entered the railroad hotel at

187

Woodward, went upstairs to the room of the station agent, George W. Rourke, awakened him with six-shooters, and ordered him to dress quietly. They marched him downstairs to the depot, forced him to open the safe, and sacked up $6,540 in currency consigned to the army paymaster at nearby Fort Supply. They then proceeded to the stockyards a half mile east of town, left their victim bound and gagged, and rode southwest with the loot.

A passer-by discovered Rourke at daylight. Deputy Marshal Jack Love and a posse took the trail of the robbers. Lieutenant Kirby Walker, with twenty cavalrymen from Fort Supply, joined the hunt. From El Reno, Deputy Madsen headed northwest to the scene with another posse. A courier from Ochiltree reported that at least eight riders answering the description of the Doolin gang had been seen traveling west. Love, Madsen, and their posses hurried to Lipscomb, on South Wolf Creek, obtained fresh horses, and continued in hot pursuit, but the outlaws had vanished in the canyons and gulches of the Cheyenne country.

At Guthrie, Marshal Nix and Hale questioned Arkansas Tom about their hide-outs. Arkansas Tom laughed at them. He believed that the whirlwind methods employed by his former companions in flitting from one crime to another and disappearing successfully and completely were confusing the marshal and his "little army," as he styled Nix's force of deputies, and said:

"You boys make me weary."

In April, he was taken to Stillwater, chained and under heavy guard, and arraigned before Judge Frank Dale for the murder of Speed, Houston, and Shadley. He was tried in the May term of court, convicted of murdering Tom Houston, and sentenced to fifty years in the territorial prison at Lansing.

Heck was one of ten deputy marshals stationed about the courthouse during the trial: "A well-founded impression had been created among the officers that an attempt would be made by Doolin to liberate Arkansas Tom, and we took every precaution to prevent any such foolhardy proceeding. . . . No one was allowed to enter the court room without first being searched for concealed weapons."

When he had sentenced the prisoner, Judge Dale, overwrought

by details brought out in the trial of the killings at Ingalls, called Marshal Nix into his office.

"Quit trying to bring this gang in alive," he said. "Bring them in dead!"

It was the first order of its kind ever issued by a Federal judge in the territory.

Nix laid his problem before the Department of Justice in Washington. He wrote in a letter to the Attorney General:

By reason of a thorough knowledge of the country, this gang has been able to establish and maintain retreats in different parts of the territory, and when they are pursued and pressed by the authorities . . . they flee from one rendezvous to another, making it impracticable to effect a capture.

A very important element which contributes to their safety is the fact that the inhabitants of the parts of the territory infested by them are either on friendly terms with them, or have been so terrorized and intimidated by threats against their lives and property, that they dare not and do not volunteer the slightest information, or take any step that would lead to the discovery of their acts, whereabouts, or intentions. . . . The difficulties heretofore attending the organization of a posse of men possessing the necessary qualifications to make a successful raid on the outlaws have been and now are the want of an adequate pecuniary inducement to tempt them to incur the preliminary expenses which are unavoidable, and to expose themselves to almost sure death. . . .

I am fully aware that it is the policy of the U. S. government to induce men to conduct such raids by offering what is considered an adequate reward for the capture and conviction of each of the desperadoes, but I beg to impress upon you the fact that the men who will engage in such an enterprise and upon whom absolute dependence can be placed, are men without means, who are poorly able to properly equip themselves to insure more or less success in a raid of this character.

I am convinced that if the federal government will authorize the organization of a competent posse possessing the necessary qualifications, and will take upon itself the responsibility of defraying the actual expenses incurred in equipping and conducting a raid of this character, the territory will, in a very short time, be rid of these outlaws.

I, therefore, earnestly recommend that the U. S. Marshal for Oklahoma be authorized to organize such a competent posse . . . the actual expense of which to be defrayed by the United States government not to exceed Three ($3.00) Dollars per diem for each man, (to include) the cost of daily living of the men, the cost of preparation in the way of ammunition, etc., and the hiring of horses owned or hired by the men. In this connection, I beg to suggest also that the killing of horses owned or hired by the men be considered an extra expense they would be reimbursed for. I mention this item because of the entire probability that such losses will occur. . . .

The officers are at the mercy of these vicious characters, who have no regard for human life whatsoever, and take advantage of every opportunity to waylay them. (Yet) there are men who hold themselves ready and willing to go after this desperate band if authority is given them to organize and properly equip themselves, and it is a matter entirely worthy of the consideration of the federal government and its most vigorous aid in efforts looking towards the relief of our citizens. . . .

Washington wired Nix that it would give a reward for each member of the gang, or in lieu thereof, "pay the expenses of a posse to hunt them down." It was "impossible to pay both a reward and expenses." Nix decided it would be better to pay the expenses of a posse. He deposited two thousand dollars of his own money in a "posse fund," and invited other corporations and citizens throughout the territory to make any private contributions that would ensure success of the operation.

Heck and Bill Tilghman were to spearhead the campaign until the last member of the Doolin gang "was in prison or under the sod." Chris Madsen soon joined them. Through their efforts in the desperate months to follow, they became known as "The Three Guardsmen" of Oklahoma.

20

Clouds of Portent

Heck knew that Doolin had many friends among the settlers south of Pawnee and along Council Creek between the little settlements of Lawson and Ingalls. To most of them he had given money to buy groceries and seed for their crops during the first year of their struggle for existence in this new country. They appreciated his kindness, and, though he was a fugitive with a price on his head, they would ride to Doolin at midnight, if necessary, to warn him of the approach of officers. It was almost impossible for a posse to travel together without being seen by someone who would give the alarm in time for the outlaws to escape.

Besides the regular members of the gang, there were a score of others who acted as "fences" and furnished them with shelter. The most active of this class were the Dunn brothers. Bill Dunn seemed to be their leader. He and G. C. Bolton owned a meat market at Pawnee. Bolton attended the butcher shop, and Bill Dunn rode the range and furnished stolen beef, until Sheriff Lake and Deputy Canton finally obtained sufficient evidence against Bolton to send him to prison at Lansing. Canton also had obtained a warrant charging Bill Dunn with cattle thievery. He had been arraigned before the United States Commissioner at Pawnee, bound over for trial in district court, and released on bond.

Heck knew all this, and knew that at least Doolin, Pierce, and Newcomb spent much of their time between raids at Bill Dunn's cave on Council Creek or the cabin of Dal and John Dunn nearby. It was here, if at any place, Heck theorized, that the band "might be trapped in a bunch."

Madsen's brother-in-law, Ed Morris, who was unknown to the outlaws or residents of the area, was equipped with a cowman's cook wagon, loaded with guns, ammunition and supplies, and sent into the country. Deputies I. S. Prater and William Banks, of El Reno, rode with him, concealed under the canvas. Heck and Madsen left Guthrie singly, at different times, to meet on Tilghman's farm near Chandler. Thence they proceeded secretly to the camp established by Morris.

Here they made plans to attack Bill Dunn's dugout. The cave sat at the top of a hill in a fork on Council Creek. Crawling up the slope through the tall grass in the dark hour before dawn, Madsen and Tilghman took positions where they could "shoot the outlaws down as fast as they came out." Heck and the others circled and moved up from the rear.

At daybreak, Heck called for the occupants to surrender. When there was no response, he tossed a stick of dynamite on the roof.

The blast sent chunks of earth and rock splashing skyward. Before the debris had settled, a man ran out with his hands up. Then, one by one, seven others appeared and surrendered. To the chagrin of the officers, none were the important quarry they were after. All were wanted for crimes from robbery to whisky peddling, however, and admitted that Doolin and four members of his gang had left the hide-out during the night. They were shackled and left under the guard of Morris, Banks, and Prater, while Heck, Madsen, and Tilghman set out on the trail of Doolin and the others.

They followed the five down the creek to the Cimarron and along the river to a lonely cabin. A young Indian came to the door. He told them to tie up their horses and feed them, then come inside, that his woman would have dinner ready shortly.

"You were expecting us?" Heck asked, puzzled.

The Indian nodded. "The other part of your outfit stopped for

192

breakfast and told us you would be along about noon and would be tired and hungry."

The marshals looked at each other ruefully, but did not inquire whether he classed them with the outlaws or the outlaws had told him they were officers.

After they had enjoyed a good meal, Madsen asked how much they owed him. The Indian said "so much for the breakfasts and so much for the dinners."

"Vy do we owe for the breakfasts?" asked Madsen.

"The others had no money and say you pay for all," the Indian replied.

Madsen paid the bill. He explained to Heck and Tilghman afterward: "We might come this way again, and I wanted to leave the Indian satisfied."

Heck called off the chase. The outlaws knew they were being followed, and further pursuit would be useless. He "never knew how Doolin had been warned."

Heck next heard of the five at Southwest City, Missouri. The afternoon of May 20, they swooped down on the thriving little farming and mining center on the outer rim of the Ozarks in one of the most daring raids of their career. While Little Dick West terrorized the citizens, the others entered the bank and relieved the president and cashier of nearly $4,000.

This job, however, did not go off as smoothly as the ones at Pawnee and Spearville. The moment the townspeople realized they were being robbed, they armed themselves and cut down on the outlaws as they left the bank. The gang had to shoot its way from the city. A shoemaker was badly wounded, and the city marshal shot through the thigh. Oscar Seaborn and his brother Joe, a former state auditor and a popular man in Missouri, stepped from their store just as Bill Raidler rode past with a revolver blazing in each hand. He fired in the direction of the two men. The bullet passed through Oscar's body, without serious effect, and struck Joe, killing him instantly.

And exactly at 3 o'clock, three days later, on the afternoon of May 23, Bill Dalton with other members of the gang took $2,500 from the First National Bank at Longview, Texas, and fled back to the Chickasaw Nation. They divided the loot and scattered. But this time the marshals had their inning. Deputy Loss Hart and a posse traced Dalton to the Houston Wallace home, twenty-five miles northwest of Ardmore at Elk. They surrounded the house at 7 o'clock the morning of June 8, and killed him as he jumped from a window.

With Arkansas Tom in prison and their lieutenant dead at the hands of officers, the gang must have wondered which of them would be next. Their depredations lulled for a few months. So long, in fact, that the newspapers ventured "the territory is rapidly becoming law-abiding."

Marshal Nix read into this nonactivity "lull before a storm." Citizens and property could never be safe until the last member of this "band of border terrors" was dead or behind bars.

Heck "bent every effort to trap them." With Bill Tilghman, he revisited the Dunns: "Our raid on the dugout, and the fact that they now faced charges of harboring federal fugitives, made them restless. . . . They soon agreed to our proposition that they would not be prosecuted if they would furnish us information and cooperate with us in capturing Doolin and the others."

In addition, Heck promised them a share of any rewards collected. He and Tilghman would even use their influence to have the cattle thievery charges dismissed in Pawnee County.

All this, of course, was dependent on their willingness to sever relations with Doolin and other outlaws, obey the laws of the territory, and make good citizens.

A conference was arranged with Nix and the United States Attorney at Guthrie. These men were dismayed. From the beginning, Nix had declared that any deputy using a posseman of bad character, or one guilty of a felony, would have his commission revoked.

Heck didn't relish the idea, but he'd never been squeamish where the means justified the end.

He and Tilghman argued, and finally won their point. The Dunns need not participate in the capture. All that would be expected of them was positive information as to the time of arrival and the place the outlaws were stopping. Marshal Nix would collect any rewards, and turn all the money over to the Dunns, after deducting the actual expenses of his deputies.

The brothers agreed to these terms. After promising to report at intervals, they were allowed to return to their homes.

"You have placed your lives in their hands," Nix told Heck and Tilghman. "They could easily lead you into ambush, where you would not have even a fighting chance."

"They also know that if they have us killed, every officer in the territory will hunt them down," Heck replied. "On the other hand, if we are successful, they will go free with a good reward."

Under the circumstances, Nix decided they would play the game fair.

Nothing happened for a couple of weeks. . . .

Then, shortly before midnight, April 3, 1895, the gang stopped the Rock Island train south of Dover, robbed the express car of $50,000 consigned to pay United States troops in Texas, and fled west into the sand hills.

At daybreak, Madsen, Prater, and Banks, with a posse of nine men from El Reno, reached the scene by special train, unloaded their horses from a boxcar, and picked up the trail. They followed it west all morning, then northwest to Hoil Creek, in Major County. At 2 o'clock in the afternoon, they topped a hill forming the edge of a small basin, and came suddenly upon the robbers fifty yards away, resting themselves and their horses in a patch of stunted blackjack.

Tulsa Jack sighted the posse first and gave the alarm. Deputy Banks, leveling his rifle, fired, killing him in his tracks. Billy Moore, one of the posse, yelled: "Throw up your hands, you sons-of-bitches!"

The outlaws answered with a volley from their rifles and fled for their horses. The posse dismounted. Hugging the ground, they pumped lead at the robbers, while bullets cut the trees all around them.

Nearly 200 shots were exchanged. None of the posse was hit. They killed three horses. After a forty-minute running battle, the outlaws mounted, four of them on two horses, and escaped down a ravine which had been left unguarded.

195

Banks and Prater took the body of Tulsa Jack to Hennessey for identification and to claim the rewards. Madsen and the posse continued in pursuit of the outlaws. On April 6, they came upon the body of an aged preacher named Godfrey, shot through the head. Red Buck had murdered him when he refused to give up his team and wagon.

Red Buck drove west into the Gloss Mountains, where tracking was almost impossible. The rest of the gang scattered to their haunts in the old Cheyenne and Arapaho country. On the night of April 29, Newcomb and Pierce returned to the weather-beaten log house of the Dunns in Payne County.

Tall, rawboned Bill Dunn, wearing a false mustache and side whiskers, called on Marshal Nix at his office. Twelve hours later, Heck and Tilghman were encamped near his dugout and "in eye-shot" of the house of his brothers. Bill Dunn told them the outlaws had gone to Ingalls to get whisky, but that Pierce's sweetheart was in the house, and they would return shortly.

They did—a few minutes after midnight on May 2. In the moonlight, their figures were "easily discerned" as they put up their horses and entered the cabin. The officers, accompanied by Bill Dunn, took positions about the house so that all doors and windows were covered.

At Heck's signal, each man fired, alternately, one shot, as an alarm. There was a "wild commotion" inside, and the lights flickered out. Almost simultaneously, the front door opened and Pierce appeared with a Winchester. As he loomed in the doorway, a female voice inside cried: "Don't go, Charley!"

Pierce could not see his antagonists, but his figure in the moonlight afforded a bull's-eye target for the officers. In three seconds, "his chest was transformed into a lead mine." As he fell back into the room, the leaden hail continued, bullets being planted in his arms, legs, and even the soles of his boots.

Newcomb tried to climb out a window, shooting as he climbed. A bullet struck him in the head, tearing away a portion of his brain and skull. Another shattered the stock of his Winchester. He fell back into the room, his right forefinger still working the trigger.

Dal and John Dunn were in the house, but neither had fired

196

a shot. The officers ordered them outside with the woman. After making sure both bandits were dead, they entered and removed the bodies.

Dal and John hitched a team to a wagon, loaded the bodies and covered them with a tarpaulin, and set out for Guthrie to claim the rewards. Bill Dunn stayed at the cabin "to obliterate all trace of blood." Heck and Tilghman remained in the vicinity "in case other members of the gang showed."

The Dunns reached the capital with their cargo at 2 o'clock in the afternoon, and pulled up on the east side of the water tower. Dal jumped down and raced to Marshal Nix's office. Within a few minutes, Spengel's undertaking barouche went speeding down the hill, the two bodies were removed from the wagon and hauled to the undertaking parlor. As news of "dead bandits" spread, the crowd of curious people became so great and the pressure so strong that Nix found it necessary to throw open the doors of the establishment and allow the public mind to be satisfied.

For three hours people streamed through the rooms, viewing the forms that lay stretched on embalming boards. They pointed to the bullet holes in the soles of Pierce's boots, the wounds in Newcomb's head and neck and his right arm stiffened and raised as though warding off a blow. A wild rumor swept the city. The Dunns had "taken the bandits into their home, got them drunk, and then riddled them with bullets while they slept."

Heck and Tilghman denied it when they reached Guthrie. But their efforts to take upon themselves the glory of the killings were in vain.

Bitter feeling arose against the Dunns in Payne County. Friends of Newcomb and Pierce openly swore vengeance. The Dunns barricaded their home and turned it into a veritable arsenal for weeks before their vigilance relaxed and they felt free of molestation.

As they grew more and more unpopular, the cattle thievery warrant for Bill Dunn was renewed in Pawnee County. He blamed Frank Canton for his plight, and rode into Pawnee to kill him.

Canton had just stepped from a restaurant where he had

served some papers. As he started up the sidewalk in the direction of the courthouse, Dunn stepped in front of him. His hand was on his revolver as he spoke:

"God damn you, Frank Canton, I've got it in for you."

When Canton glanced at Dunn's face, he saw murder in his eyes. He drew his revolver instantly and fired. The bullet struck Dunn in the forehead. As he dropped, he pulled his revolver, which fell on the sidewalk near his body.

21

The Dark Clouds Fall

Heck might have washed his hands of the whole mess. But he had made a deal with the Dunns, and he stuck to it.

With Nix's permission, he appointed them possemen. Despite their unpopularity, they had proven a willingness to work on the side of the law. The law needed the information they now obtained, and they needed its protection. Most of all, they wanted a share of the $5,000 in rewards on the head of Bill Doolin.

In August, Heck learned that Bill Raidler, who was to have joined Newcomb and Pierce at the Dunn place, had gone to an old hide-out near Bartlesville. Dynamite Dick and Little Dick West had fled to Texas and New Mexico, and Red Buck was still hiding in the El Reno district.

Doolin's whereabouts was a mystery. Family responsibilities as well as crime had occupied him during 1894. In 1891, he had married Edith Ellsworth, a storekeeper's daughter, at Ingalls. In 1893, the Ellsworths had moved to Lawson (now Quay), in the northeast corner of Payne County, where Mrs. Doolin gave birth to a baby boy. Doolin had eluded officers many times to see his wife and son. An old bullet wound in his left leg, received during his flight from Spearville, was giving him trouble, and he had talked often of pulling out, taking his family far away from the territory, and settling down. With the proceeds of the Dover robbery, and his gang scattered, it was likely he had done just that. For, during the summer of 1895, Edith loaded her child in a wagon and disappeared in the Osage.

Heck conferred with Nix and Chief Deputy Hale. Flyers on Dynamite Dick and Little Dick West were sent to major points in Texas and New Mexico. Madsen would search for Red Buck. Heck and Tilghman would go after Raidler and try to pick up the trail of Doolin's wife and son.

According to Heck's information, Raidler was at Little Dick's old cave in the hills between Bartlesville and Pawhuska. He enlisted the aid of Deputy Marshals W. C. Smith and Cyrus Longbone, of the Bartlesville district, and two Osage scouts, Spotted Dog Eater and Howling Wolf. The party split. Heck started northwest from Bartlesville with the Indians. Tilghman, Smith, and Longbone worked northeast from Pawhuska.

Heck and his scouts were first to spot the hide-out. Raidler opened fire from ambush. Heck cut down on him with a .45-90 Winchester. The bullet ripped through the fingers of Raidler's left hand and tore the rifle from his grip. The Dutchman howled in pain, and sped off in the brush.

They followed him through the hills to Mission Creek, and lost the trail. All Heck gained were a couple of souvenirs. Raidler was nervy as well as tough—two mutilated digits lay on the bank of the stream. Instead of waiting until he could have them dressed, he had whipped out his knife and cut them off, then hid in a tree nearby while Heck and his scouts combed the vicinity.

He told Heck about it several days later. . . .

Tilghman, Smith, and Longbone, after a week of weary hunting, learned from a friendly Indian that the fugitive was hiding in the timber and taking his meals at Sam Moore's ranch, eighteen miles south of Elgin, Kansas. They went to the ranch, determined the direction from which he usually came, and posted themselves.

At dusk, September 6, Raidler came riding confidently up the lane on his way to supper. He put up his horse and started for the house. Tilghman stood in the shadows at the corner of the corral, and Raidler passed so close he could have touched him.

200

When he was a few steps away, Tilghman called: "Throw up your hands and surrender!"

Raidler had no notion of doing such a thing. He whirled, whipping out his revolver, and fired in the direction of the officer. Less than ten feet separated them. But the outlaw's shot missed. Tilghman's Winchester spoke as the fire flashed from Raidler's weapon. His bullet tore through the outlaw's right wrist.

Raidler dropped his revolver and began running. Smith's shotgun roared from the other end of the corral, and the outlaw was knocked off his feet.

Moore and his wife ran from the house and helped carry him inside. They did what they could to stop the flow of blood. No one believed he could survive. He had received five wounds besides the broken wrist, one in each side, one through the neck, and two in the back of the head.

But the little Dutchman had the grit to live. He told the deputies:

"I'd have made a fight if you'd been a hundred strong!"

They loaded him in Sam Moore's wagon and took him to Elgin. A doctor dressed his wounds. A few days later, he was moved by train to Guthrie, where he "talked like a sailor and entertained 200 people with stories of his exploits." He slowly recovered in the Federal jail, was tried at Kingfisher for the Dover train robbery, and sentenced to ten years in Lansing. In prison, he developed locomotor ataxia as a result of his wounds. The doctors gave him only a few months to live, so the President issued him a pardon "to die among friends."

The capture of Raidler had put Heck and Tilghman a step closer to Doolin. While attending the wounded outlaw at Elgin, they learned that a man named Tom Wilson, but answering Doolin's description and favoring a bad left leg, had stopped to buy supplies for his wife and baby. He had been dressed in ragged clothes, giving the appearance of a "played-out" Oklahoma farmer, and drove a "poor" team hitched to a dilapidated lumber wagon. The family had gone north.

Tilghman stayed in Kansas to pick up the trail. Late in December, he located Mrs. Doolin and the child at Burden. They were living in a tent near town, and affected such poverty that, at Christmas time, the ladies of Burden had solicited a purse and a basket of food for the "poor suffering" woman and her infant son.

Tilghman watched the tent for a week, but Doolin didn't show. He watched the trains, but Doolin didn't return. He checked the mails, but there was no communication between the couple. Finally, on January 6, Mrs. Doolin made a visit to Winfield.

The postmaster there informed Tilghman that she had picked up a letter from a Mr. Wilson at Eureka Springs, Arkansas. The contents? Well, Mr. Wilson's leg was better. The baths seemed to help his "rheumatism." He would stay a little longer. . . . Before Tilghman got back to Burden, Mrs. Doolin and her child boarded the train for Perry.

He wired Heck to shadow the woman. Heck soon advised him that she had gone to her father's home at Lawson. Convinced that Doolin would not return to Burden, Tilghman hurried to Guthrie.

He told Nix and Hale: "I'm going after him."

Heck offered his assistance. Tilghman insisted on going alone. "One man won't be noticed," he said.

It was all right with Heck—Tilghman had developed the lead and it was his case.

But Nix protested. "Doolin will shoot you on sight."

Tilghman stepped to the coat rack and donned the marshal's long-skirted Prince Albert. Next, he put on Deputy Hale's black derby. "I'm going disguised as a preacher," he said.

The others stared in surprise. He had always dressed in rough clothes while on duty in the territory. In a hat and coat of these styles, he hardly could be recognized. From a local tailor, he obtained the other items necessary to complete his costume. At 5 P.M., January 12, 1896, he boarded the train for Arkansas.

On January 15, he wired Nix: *"I have him. Will be there tomorrow."*

Here is the story of the capture as Tilghman related it to the territorial press:

"I arrived in Eureka Springs at 1:30 Wednesday morning. Walking up town, one of the first men I met was Bill Doolin. He didn't see me at that time. I soon learned he was stopping

202

at the Davy Hotel under the name of Tom Wilson, the same name he had used at Burden.

"I went to a carpenter and ordered a box made in which I could carry a loaded shotgun . . . and walk about (town) until I met him again, the box being arranged so that with a slight movement of the thumb it would drop, leaving the gun in my hand ready for action.

"While the carpenter was making the box, I decided to take a bath in the mineral waters and went to a bathhouse nearby. When I stepped into the gentleman's waiting room, whom should I see but Bill Doolin sitting on a lounge in the far corner, reading a paper. He looked up sharply . . . for a second he seemed to recognize me, but I walked briskly into the bath rooms, calling to the clerk that I wished to take a bath at once.

"Inside the door I turned so I could watch him. His view of me was shut off by the stove. I noticed that for several moments he watched the door through which I had passed, but finally relaxed his vigilance and returned to reading his paper.

"Now was my chance. With my gun in my hand I slipped quietly into the room up to the stove, then jumping around it to a position immediately in front of Doolin, I told him to throw up his hands and surrender.

"He got up, saying, 'What do you mean? I have done nothing,' but I grabbed his right wrist with my left hand as he raised it to get his gun, and with the revolver in my right hand leveled at his head, ordered him to throw up his left hand. He put it up part way, then made a pass toward his gun. I told him I would shoot if he made another move.

"When I first called on Doolin to surrender the room was full of men. In half a minute we were alone. I called to the proprietor to come in and help me, that I was an officer. He came tremblingly to the door, and I finally persuaded him to come over where we were. After two or three attempts he managed to get Doolin's vest open and take his revolver from under his arm, then wanted to hand the revolver to me notwithstanding the fact that I had both hands full. I told him to get out (of the room) with it, and he ran into the street, holding the gun at arm's length.

"When Doolin's vest was opened, he made a final effort to get loose, and even after his gun was gone, protested that he had done nothing. I then said:

"'Now, look at me; don't you know me?'

"He looked me in the eye and said: 'Yes. You are Tilghman.'

"I then shackled him, got his gun and started for his hotel. I said, 'Bill, you know you are in the hands of no sucker. To get good treatment all you need to do is behave yourself.'

"Doolin said, 'I give you my word that if you will take these shackles off I will give you no trouble.' I told him I would take his word, and took them off, telling him that if he made a single move to escape I would drop him in his tracks.

"We went to the hotel, got his effects, went to the bank and got $100 he had deposited, and left on the first train. . . . Doolin rode in the seat in front of me and was perfectly quiet, nobody knowing who we were until we got into Oklahoma."

News of his capture brought people swarming into Guthrie from all over the Territory. They packed the grounds at the Santa Fe depot and the hill beyond, and congregated at the jail. When the train arrived at 12:25 P.M., there was a great pushing, scrambling, and crowding for a glimpse of the "king of outlaws." As Tilghman stepped from the coach with his prisoner, they saw, instead of a booted, spurred, and bearded desperado, a tall, slender man, with sandy mustache and pleasant blue eyes, with a smile on his face, dressed in a well-worn suit of clothes and walking with a cane.

One little lady, inching in close to the bandit leader, commented on his docile appearance, and said, "Why, Mr. Doolin, I believe I could capture you myself."

Doolin's smile broadened, and he replied: "Yes, ma'am, I believe you could."

Heck, Nix, and Hale were waiting with a cab. Doolin was put inside with Tilghman, Nix, and Hale. Heck rode with the driver.

They drove the prisoner to the Federal jail, where everyone who wished could pass through and see him. "A number of ladies and leading citizens shook his hand," said the *Daily Leader*, stating that they were "very happy to meet him," and "of course, courtesy demanded that he make the same remark." Tilghman was the "hero of the hour." Hundreds of friends congratulated him and "spoke enviously" of the rewards he could collect upon Doolin's conviction. Marshal Nix rejoiced and termed the capture "the climax of a continuously successful campaign against outlawry inaugurated at his advent to office."

There was more rejoicing March 5. On that date, Deputy Madsen and a posse of farmers located Red Buck in a dugout near Arapaho. They gave him an opportunity to surrender. He came out shooting, and they killed him.

A few weeks later, deputy marshals in Texas arrested Dynamite Dick on a whisky charge and recognized him while he was serving a thirty-day sentence at Paris. By the end of April, he was in jail at Guthrie with Bill Doolin.

The Federal jail was a long, two-story building with stone walls eighteen inches thick. Inside, a steel stairway led from the main office to the upper floor, where a big barred door opened into a corridor that ran across the front of the jail. Behind the corridor was the bull pen where prisoners were allowed their freedom in the daytime. Across the back ran a tier of cells where they were locked up each night. The most dangerous prisoners were kept in a block of cells next to the corridor, with a passageway to the bull pen down the center.

Doolin took his confinement quietly enough. About the first of July, he complained so much about the pain in his left leg that he was allowed the freedom of the bull pen to exercise it. On Sunday morning, July 5, Heck came in with a whisky peddler from the Osage. Dynamite Dick's cell was in the block next to the corridor, and Heck observed Doolin in the passageway talking to him. As he passed with his prisoner, Doolin's voice dropped to a whisper, and he could not catch his words.

Before leaving, Heck warned the head jailer: "Doolin's planning something."

"I'll watch him," the jailer promised.

That evening two guards, J. W. Miller and J. T. Tull, were on duty. Shortly before 9 o'clock, Miller removed his revolver, placed it in a box near the corridor door as was customary and, with keys in hand, was let into the passageway by Tull to lock the prisoners in their cells.

George Lane, a huge, half-Cherokee and half-Negro desperado, stood near the door. A bucket of water sat outside where the prisoners could reach through the bars to get a drink. They were in the habit of filling tin cans with water to take to their cells at night. Lane's can was too large to pass through the bars, and as Miller started to the rear of the jail, he asked the guard at the door to fill it.

Instead of waiting until his partner returned, Tull unlocked the door and handed in the bucket. The brawny half-breed seized him about the shoulders and hauled him into the passageway. Three other prisoners leaped upon him, flung him to the floor, and grabbed his weapon.

As Miller came running from the bull pen, Doolin sprang through the door and snatched his revolver from the box. His docility had gone. His eyes shone, the hair on his head bristled, and his teeth set in a death's head grin. He shoved the gun against Miller's breast and ordered him to open the combination lock to Dynamite Dick's cell or die.

The rest was easy. The keys were taken from Miller, a half-dozen other prisoners in on the plan were released, and the two guards locked in cells.

Then, with Doolin and Dynamite Dick in the lead, they marched out of jail, down the stairs, and disappeared in the darkness.

It was nearly an hour before the break was discovered. By this time, the prisoners had reached a point a half mile north of town and separated. As Doolin started on, his leg gave out. He met a young man out buggy-riding with his girl friend, took the horse and buggy, and sped away into the night.

Sheriffs and deputy marshals converged on the area from every point in the Territory. Special posses combed the Pawnee country, others watched to the west, and hundreds searched north and east along the Cimarron to the Ingalls area and the Creek Nation in the greatest man hunt in history. One prisoner, William Beck, came back to the jail and surrendered. Another, Ed Lawrence, was captured at his father's home near Enid. The others had vanished.

When Heck got the news of the break, he was at home with Matie.

"Those men will want guns," he told her. "They know I have several fine guns, and know where we live. I want you to hide them."

After he rode off on the hunt, Matie took the rifles and six-shooters outside and hid them in the brush and tall grass.

"When Heck returned," she related, years afterward, "he was terribly put out. 'Why, woman,' he said to me, 'those guns will rust—I wouldn't have them rusted for anything.' And he put in a lot of time rubbing them after I helped by hiding them, too!"

Heck spent several more days and nights looking for Bill Doolin. His son, Albert, who had finished school in Georgia the year before and returned to the Territory to live with his father and Matie, accompanied him. Already the youth had proved his worth as a posseman. Deputy Marshal Rufe Cannon, who had helped capture the Lewis gang, came over from the Nations and joined them in camp in the Ingalls vicinity below the Cimarron.

Heck was confident that Doolin had found refuge with friends. His wife was still at Lawson. Sooner or later he would contact her.

Through the Dunns, Heck had become acquainted with Tom and Charlie Noble, two young blacksmiths at Lawson. Charlie was courting the Dunn boys' sister. They promised to watch Mrs. Doolin closely.

On August 23, Mrs. Doolin, with the help of her father, loaded a covered wagon with some household effects, a plow, a cultivator, and a coop of chickens. In the afternoon, she brought a team to the blacksmith shop to have them shod. This meant a long journey. A messenger sped through the night. Heck received the word and started for the Dunn place with Cannon and Albert.

In 1920, a petty thief living in the Lawson area started a story of how Bill Doolin had died of consumption; that when the officers arrived, they made a deal with his widow for the body, promising to give her a share of the reward; that Doolin's body was then propped against a tree and a charge of buckshot fired into it. It was published in the newspapers, and yellow journalists have repeated the scurrilous tale ever since.

Here, in Heck's own words, is the true version:

"We made the drive by 2 o'clock (the next day) and, after picking up the Dunns, rode to a point beyond Lawson. Met the Noble boys and some others with fresh news (Doolin's horse had been seen in a shed behind Ellsworth's store)—and crawled up close enough to watch old Ellsworth's house with field glasses.

"We waited a long time (until midnight) without seeing anyone, although there was considerable stir about the store. . . . We learned afterwards that Doolin's wife had told him that some of the neighborhood boys had been spying around there too much and that someone was around that night.

"Finally, he (Doolin) came out of the stable and, to our great surprise, started down the lane, coming west. The store was situated on high prairie. If he had wanted to have made his escape, he could have had open roads north, south, east, northeast, southeast, or northwest through the pastures to the high hills. . . .

"He came straight down the lane, leading his horse by the tip ends of the bridle reins, walking slow in the bright moonlight, Winchester in both hands, well out in front of him, nearly in position to shoot. He was walking slow, looking first to one side and then the other. He was sure on the prod for the neighborhood boys who had been spying on him, intending to shoot them up a little, when I hollered to him and had one of the boys on the other side of the road to holler to him right after I did.

"He shot at me and the bullet passed between me and the Dunns. I had let one of the boys have my Winchester and had an old No. 8 shotgun. It was too long in the breech and I couldn't handle it quick, so he got another shot with his Winchester and as he dropped his Winchester from glancing shot, he jerked his pistol and some of the boys thought he shot once with it. . . . About that time I got the shotgun to work and the fight was over."

The body had twenty-one holes in it. Heck loaded it in a wagon and hauled it to Guthrie. The escape and death of the desperado gave many of the companies that had offered rewards "a chance to crawl out of their propositions." Heck finally collected $1,435—$25 from the U. S. jailer, $500 from Wells Fargo, $500 from the Missouri State Legislature, $160 from the citizens of Southwest City, and $250 from the Government in marshal fees. He divided the reward money between his posse.

Bill Doolin was buried in the Summit View Cemetery at government expense and a rusty buggy axle driven in the ground to mark his grave. In reporting the last rites, the Stillwater *Gazette* commented: "His left leg will get a rest."

22

Dynamite Dick—
Then Little Dick West

Following Doolin's arrest at Eureka Springs, Marshal Nix announced that his purpose in office had been accomplished. He returned to the wholesale business in Guthrie, and Patrick S. Nagle, a young lawyer from Kingfisher, who already occupied a prominent place in political affairs of the territory, had been appointed for the months remaining of his term under Cleveland.

While the politicians gave Nix credit for having "captured or killed most of the members of the major outlaw gang infesting the country," there were "numerous accusations" and complaints that he had "squandered the government's money at an enormous rate," and Nagle promised a reduction of the large force of deputies "to the barest number possible for effective operation."

In the midst of the shake-up, Madsen had gone east to take a youth to the Federal reform school at Washington. While in the capital, he dropped by the Attorney General's office for a visit, and was asked if he would like to go to Kansas City as office deputy under the famous Confederate general, Joe Shelby, then Marshal of the Western District of Missouri. Shelby needed a man who understood government red tape. An inspector had just examined his books and recommended that he obtain an expert to put them in order.

Chris's wife, Maggie, had always been a delicate, frail girl, a gentlewoman. She had borne admirably the fear and anxiety of his long days and nights in the saddle, while caring for their two small children. But her health was beginning to fail. Chris welcomed the opportunity to spend more time with his family. He returned to Oklahoma, moved to Kansas City, and assumed his new duties on July 1, 1896.

Tilghman's commission had been renewed, but he talked of retiring to his farm at Chandler and throwing his hat in the race for sheriff of Lincoln County.

Heck continued his work as field deputy at Guthrie. Matie liked their big home there, and had made many friends. Often, when Heck was away, she visited her parents in Tulsa. In August, 1894, she had given Heck a son, christened Henry Hale, in honor of Nix's chief deputy. The child had died in infancy. But nothing else marred their happiness. She was proud of Albert. And Heck was proud that he had come to live with them. He wanted to make a peace officer out of the boy. And Albert thought it was a fine thing to uphold the law.

"My father loved to play tricks on me," Albert wrote in a letter on September 10, 1957. "Early in July, with possemen Bill Crane and myself, he made a trip from Guthrie to about 15 miles northeast of Stillwater, looking for Doolin. We camped overnight, and the next morning, Crane and I got to scuffling around the campfire. I stepped on a corncob, fell and, as it developed later, broke a small bone in my right ankle. Father loaded me in the bottom of his spring wagon, with my leg resting on a pile of bedding, and started back to Stillwater, stopped in front of a drug store and, as I remember it, bought a bottle of Mexican Mustang liniment and a bag of candy. He pretended he thought I might cry while he was rubbing my leg with the liniment and told me I could have the bag of candy if I didn't. (Of course, I didn't.) The druggist decided my ankle was really broken and recommended I be driven back, as quickly as posssible, to Guthrie.

"The following is what really got my goat: While lying in the wagon, a reporter from a Stillwater paper came by and, recognizing my father, stopped to shake hands. Father told him I was a young horse thief he had tried to arrest the day before and shot in the leg in order to capture me!

"Well, the reporter wrote an account of how Heck Thomas had

come through Stillwater with a wounded horse thief and went on at length to describe how tough and hard-boiled I looked and how Heck Thomas was to be commended for getting another outlaw. This account was printed on the front page of the paper. My father procured several copies and mailed them back to family and friends in Georgia. Of course, the true story was printed later, but I didn't hear the last of this little incident for some time."

Albert lauded his father's record. From 1893 to 1896, Nix's force of deputies had made nearly 60,000 arrests for violations of Federal statutes. While Heck had been concerned primarily with running down the Doolin gang, his record books for these years—containing case numbers of warrants, for whom issued, dates and places served, and fees collected—show that he was responsible for the apprehension of more than 300 criminals in every part of the Territory. Heck was re-commissioned the day Nagle took office.

Heck was now assigned the duty of running down the remaining members of the Doolin gang, Dynamite Dick and Little Dick West. This included the fugitives still at large who had participated in the jail break of July 5.

Through some Negro friends in the territory, he learned that George Lane, the half-breed desperado, whose daring had effected the wholesale jail delivery, was hiding at Greenwood, Missouri. The postmistress there, in a letter to Heck, promised to keep tabs on the fugitive.

On November 19, Heck arrived in Kansas City with a warrant for Lane's arrest. Being outside his jurisdiction, he asked Madsen to go with him. Chris obtained another warrant from the United States Commissioner in Kansas City "to make things legal in case the outlaw resisted."

They took the train to Greenwood, passing through the settlement so they wouldn't be seen getting off the train, then hired a livery rig and drove back to town. The postmistress told them Lane had just been in to call for his mail. They checked about town and learned that he had gone to the home of a lady friend a half mile away.

He had boasted never to be taken alive, and the officers took

212

no chances. At dusk, they drove near the house and left their team. There was a door in each end of the cabin. Heck went to the rear door and Chris to the front. As they rapped simultaneously, the Negro woman stepped to the front door and opened it. Lane, who had been sitting before the fire whittling, stepped to the back door, the knife still in his hand. Heck "covered him so quickly that he offered no resistance, and his hands shot into the air obediently."

The marshals handcuffed him and drove back to Greenwood. A crowd gathered to see "the bad man who had been bragging how tough he was down in the Indian country." When the Negroes taunted him for submitting to arrest without killing somebody, he pointed to Heck's Winchester and replied meekly:

"I know when to quit."

Lane had served time in Texas for horse stealing. He had been in the Federal jail for selling whisky to the Indians. In his youth he had attended Lincoln Institute, at Jefferson City. En route to Guthrie, he talked well and readily, expressing no chagrin at having been captured:

"After I broke jail, they hunted me night and day. Many times I could have reached out and touched them. Once I swam the Cimarron with shots whistling around my head. Another time I stepped over the sleeping bodies of the Osage chief of police and two assistants, secured a gun and walked away. I could have killed them all as they slept.

"I knew the country better than my pursuers. But it was a dog's life I led. Green corn was ripe, thank God, or I would have starved. Once for three days I didn't have even that. . . ."

Two months later, Heck captured Lee Killion—one of the prisoners who had leaped upon Guard Tull and seized his weapon as Lane dragged him into the passageway. The *State Capital* of February 6, 1897, gave this brief account:

"Killion was in Colorado until a short time ago, when he came back to his old home and got into trouble as usual. . . . Thomas found out he was in the neighborhood of Joplin and, after he had him fully located, quietly walked in on him and brought him back to Guthrie yesterday."

Heck hardly had Killion behind bars when the Sac and Fox agency, sixty miles east of Chandler, was looted one afternoon by three masked riders.

They swooped down first on the agent's office to rob him of $46,000 that was to be paid as annuity to the Indians. The money had not arrived, so they rode to the store of Fannie Whistler, covered the occupants with revolvers and Winchesters, and took $486 from her safe.

They held up J. W. Miffit's store, taking $59 and a gold watch, then robbed Chief Keokuk's place of $80 and $3,000 in notes.

The traders were too frightened to resist. After robbing Keokuk, the bandits dashed through the grounds of the Indian school, discharging their weapons, and galloped madly away across the Deep Fork of the Canadian into the Creek Nation.

The leader, "a big, heavy set man, and well muscled," had been identified as Dynamite Dick!

Heck and Albert picked up the trail and headed northeast into the Creek country with the Dunns as possemen. Twenty miles west of Sapulpa, they "ran into Dynamite Dick and two others" camped in a ravine. Heck wrote: "We opened fire and a pitched battle followed. The outlaws, having the worst of it, took flight, leaving behind their baggage and one riding horse. Darkness coming on, we were unable to pursue them. . . ."

In the baggage, they found a marriage license issued to Bob Reagin and a girl living near Chandler. Reagin headed for Arkansas, but decided to return for his bride. Heck followed the girl and arrested him at "a protracted meeting." Reagin implicated John Spurgeon, "a tough character and seemingly proud of his reputation, whom I had suspected for two years of different crimes." Heck arrested him the next day near Carney. Dynamite Dick, he learned, had gone into hiding on "the Sid Williams place," ten miles west of Checotah.

Deputy Marshals George Lawson and W. H. Bussey, of the Muskogee District, went to Williams' farm and "hid on the trail several days." Early on a Sunday morning, they sighted their quarry riding through the timber from Williams' house. The Muskogee *Phoenix* reported his demise as follows:

"The officers pulled down on their man and ordered him to

surrender. But Dynamite Dick, who had terrorized the country for eight years and boasted that no officer or man or set of them could take him, knew that surrender meant death on the gallows and obeyed not.

"In a twinkling, he lifted his Winchester and fired. A ball from Lawson's rifle broke his arm and knocked him from his horse. He dropped his Winchester and took to the brush.

"The officers followed him by the blood from his wound. They lost the trail during the day. About dark they came upon a little cabin hid in the woods and circumstances which led them to believe the wounded desperado was inside. . . .

"They stationed themselves on either side of the cabin. After repeated threats of burning the building and a few grazing shots to intimidate the occupants, an Indian woman and boy emerged. The officers ordered them to set fire to the cabin, threatening instant death unless they complied. The officers could hear someone moving around inside, knocking clinkers from between the logs to make an opening to fire through. Again they commanded the woman and boy to set fire to the house.

"As they started to obey, Dynamite Dick threw open the door and jumped out shooting. With one arm shattered, he was badly handicapped, and the officers brought him down. He lived only a few minutes after the fierce fight was over.

"They loaded the body into a wagon, and after driving all night landed in front of the marshal's office this morning. The remains of the daring outlaw were removed inside the jail stockade until identification was made. The identification was thorough and complete, and all that was mortal of Dynamite Dick was buried at government expense."

Heck got $700 for the capture of Spurgeon and Reagin, which he split with his posse. He never received a cent of the $3,000 in rewards for Dynamite Dick, although his information sparked the hunt that had led to the outlaw's death.

In the summer of 1897, he was hunting the Jennings gang. According to Heck, they were "the most comic band of robbers" to win notoriety in the Territory.

Little Dick West was the leader. The others were rank amateurs. Al and Frank Jennings were lawyer sons of the probate judge of Pottawatomie County. Pat and Morris O'Malley, a couple of Tecumseh "plow-pushers," had served as possemen under some of the deputy marshals, but had been discharged for padding accounts. Temperamentally averse to doing any work and imbued with the idea of becoming heroic bandits, they fell in with Little Dick the moment he returned from New Mexico.

The gang jumped into prominence the night of August 16, when they attempted to hold up the Santa Fe passenger train at Edmond, north of Oklahoma City. They climbed over the tender, covered the engineer with six-shooters, then went back to the express car and tried to batter down the door. In the excitement, they forgot to capture the conductor, and when this veteran leaped off the train, holding a lantern aloft, and demanding, "What are you doing there?" they "leaped on their horses and flew like bats out of hell."

The conductor knew the Jennings and O'Malley boys and had recognized their voices. Within twenty-four hours, Heck and Bill Tilghman had a sworn statement from him. Warrants were issued for all five bandits. Thus they bore the label, even if they hadn't earned it.

An attempt to stop the Katy passenger train near Muskogee two weeks later failed. The engineer sighted some ties piled on the track, increased the speed of the train, and raced through them.

They went to Purcell to loot the express station on the Santa Fe. A night watchman spotted them hiding in the yards and gave the alarm. The city marshal rushed to the station with a dozen armed men, and they fled in the darkness.

Their plans to rob the bank at Minco were abandoned when they discovered a group of citizens guarding the place day and night.

Down to their last penny, their clothes in tatters, and taking only such meals as they could obtain from scattered farmhouses, the gang grew desperate.

Finally, on October 1, 1897, they held up the Rock Island train, eight miles north of Chickasha, in daylight.

Pat O'Malley captured the fireman and engineer. Morris O'Malley and Frank Jennings stood the trainmen and passengers outside

216

the coaches, then went down the line, collecting $300 in cash and the conductor's silver watch. Al Jennings and Little Dick West broke into the express car. The messenger couldn't open the safes. Al had brought along some dynamite, but had no experience in the use of it. He placed the sticks on the through safe, set the way safe on top of them, lighted the fuse, and leaped outside. The blast tore the side from the express car. The safes stood in the smoking ruins, unharmed. Unable to obtain anything of value, they rode off with a two-gallon jug of whisky and a bunch of bananas.

Heck and his posse loaded their horses on a special train to Oklahoma City, transferred to the Choctaw line, and went to Shawnee. They searched the country, watching all the roads and crossings, hoping to cut off the robbers if they headed home.

But the outlaws had ridden west through the uninhabited Wichita reservation, made a meal of bananas and whisky, then circled north to the house of a friendly farmer on Cottonwood Creek, southwest of Guthrie. Here they divided the loot, giving their host the conductor's watch. They had operated nearly two months, and their total take had netted them $60 each. Disgusted, Little Dick left them. After resting a couple of days, the others headed east down the Cimarron.

Heck next heard of them in Payne County, where they entered Lee Nutter's store at Cushing in the middle of the night, exchanged their tattered garments for warm clothing, helped themselves to tobacco and groceries, took $40 from the till, then rode into the Creek Nation. Heck wired the marshal at Muskogee that the gang had entered his district.

Deputy Bud Ledbetter and a posse rode after them. He picked up their trail on the Pittsburg and Gulf Railroad at Barren Fork, near Checotah, and followed it north into the Cherokee Nation, where the gang robbed the little post office at Foyil, and headed south again. On November 29, he located them at the Spike S ranch, between Snake Creek and the Arkansas, where a furious gun battle took place. Morris O'Malley was captured. The others escaped in the thickets along Snake Creek. They held up two Euchee Indian boys in a wagon, took their outfit, and headed toward Okmulgee. Ledbetter got the report and hurried to the crossing on Rock Creek. On December 6, the bandits jolted down the frozen trail through a deep cut into the muzzle of Ledbetter's rifle, and surrendered.

The gang was lodged in jail at Muskogee. Al Jennings got life in the Columbus, Ohio, state prison for assault with intent to kill Ledbetter in the fight at the ranch. The others received five years each. On June 23, 1900, through the persistent efforts of his family and Judge Amos Ewing, who was a friend of President McKinley, Al's sentence was commuted to five years. In 1902, President Theodore Roosevelt issued him a "citizenship pardon," which he displayed afterward in theaters across the country with the movie *Beating Back*, the story of his career, that actually had covered a period of less than four months.

When the Jennings boys were captured, Little Dick West was hiding at the home of a friend in Lincoln County. On Christmas Day, he returned to the Cottonwood Creek vicinity, hiring out as a farm hand on the Ed Fitzgerald place, under an assumed name. Harmon Arnett owned the next farm west, and Little Dick made frequent visits to his place for extra work until spring.

One day Mrs. Arnett remarked to a friend that she thought Fitzgerald's hired man was trying to get her husband in trouble. The friend mentioned the fact to the wife of the district clerk, who told Sheriff Frank Rinehart. Rinehart told Heck. Heck's eyes "fairly sparkled" when he heard the description.

He talked to Chief Deputy Bill Fossett. They organized a posse, consisting of Rinehart, Bill Tilghman, Policeman Ben Miller and Albert. Here is Albert's story of this expedition:

"We left Guthrie after dark (April 6th), using a covered wagon and team and my saddle horse 'Limber Jim,' which I rode. Miller drove the wagon, and the others rode inside. We made dry camp about a mile from the house, and an hour before daybreak moved in and separated—Fossett, Rinehart and Miller taking a stand a hundred yards or so in front of the house, and my father, Tilghman and myself taking a stand about the same distance in the rear. Just before daybreak lamps were lighted in the house and, in accordance with mutual understanding, Fossett and his party advanced to the front door, knocking on it and demanding entrance, which was given them immediately.

218

"They thought that if West was in the house, he would run out the back right into our arms, but there was no evidence that he was around, except a horse in the corral that fully met the description of the one he had been using.

"Although we could not get an admission from the farmer or any of his family that they had ever heard of Little Dick, their explanation as to the horse being a stray was not very convincing. Knowing of the other farm house about a half mile away, and a dugout in the side of a small hill about the same distance in a different direction, we again split up, my father and Tilghman heading for the dugout, Fossett and Rinehart going to the other house, and Miller and myself to the horses and wagon with the understanding we would all meet at the second place.

"Miller and I had almost reached the wagon when we heard a half-dozen shots in quick succession in the direction of the house where we were to meet—then two more shots at intervals. We made a run for the horses. Miller drove the wagon, and I rode 'Limber Jim' on a dead run toward the firing. I can see in my mind's eye right now Ben standing up in the wagon, lashing the horses with the ends of the reins, trying to keep up with me, but of course 'Limber Jim' and I beat him by at least a hundred yards to the scene, which by this time had switched to a road on the far side of the house.

"Little Dick West was dead, lying on his back, his right arm stretched above his head, his cocked six-shooter in his hand. This is what happened: As Fossett and Rinehart approached the house, they saw a man step into the breezeway to look close at them. He then stepped from view, but reappeared beside a little building at the rear, walking toward the stable yard. They yelled that they wanted to speak to him, but he jerked his six-shooter, firing and running toward the wire fence enclosing the lot.

"Both men fired at him as he dived under the last strand, one shot going under his right shoulder blade and through his body. He ran, I would estimate, about 150 yards beyond the fence, reloading as he ran, and had turned in the act of firing again when he died.

"Sheriff Rinehart was using my Remington 10 gauge shotgun loaded with buckshot. I had loaded the shells myself. It was

219

claimed that Chief Deputy Fossett, who was using a Winchester, killed West, but my father and Tilghman, after examining the wound in his body, were of the opinion that it was made by a buckshot.

"My father and Tilghman loaded the outlaw into the wagon and hauled him into Guthrie. He was the last member of the Doolin gang."

23

End of an Era

For twenty years now Heck had been a peace officer in some capacity. Eleven of these he had spent in continuous service as a Federal deputy. He deserved one of the top positions as marshal. But, as he often put it, "these jobs almost invariably were given to politicians, and then seldom lasted from one administration to the next."

Nagle had resigned in June, 1897, after holding office little more than a year, following the advent of William McKinley's inauguration as President. Within a week, there were fifteen applications on file in the Attorney General's office. The "plum" had gone to Canada H. Thompson, a lifelong Republican and big ranch owner near Enid, who had come to Oklahoma at the opening of the Cherokee Outlet. A political whip in the territory, he had canvassed the western counties in Dennis T. Flynn's behalf when the latter was running for Congress, and had been instrumental in the appointment of Cassius M. Barnes as fourth territorial governor. His law enforcement experience consisted of a term as sheriff of Marion County, Kansas, and as special agent for the Rock Island Railroad.

He held great respect for Heck and admired his reputation, and Heck always felt "the fact that I was a Democrat" again had prevented him from becoming chief deputy. Thompson assumed his duties on November 8, with W. B. "Bill" Fossett, a former railroad detective, of Kingfisher, as chief assistant.

Said the Guthrie *Leader:* "He was besieged with callers and pie-eaters all day, but he seemed to enjoy the diversion. During the afternoon the following field deputies were appointed: Ned E. Sisson, Garfield county; William Tilghman, Lincoln county; and Heck Thomas, Logan county. No more appointments will be made until November 15th."

Heck's job seemed secure for a few more years.

Tilghman moved his family from Guthrie to Lincoln County after the killing of Little Dick. Finally, he did the thing he had been planning. He ran for sheriff and was elected.

In March, Madsen resigned his office in Kansas City—the climate there was worse for Maggie's health than in Oklahoma. He brought her back to El Reno. He mortgaged his farm and hired the best doctors. On May 2, 1898, she died from consumption. Then the United States declared war on Spain. A telegram came from Colonel Leonard H. Wood, requesting Chris to come to San Antonio, where the Rough Riders were being organized. Soon Chris was back in the army as quartermaster sergeant.

The Three Guardsmen were still friends, but they were no longer a fighting combination. Heck lost "the best posseman he ever had" at the same time. Albert joined the Rough Riders. Albert's bunkmate at San Antonio was Policeman Ben Miller, who had ridden with them after Little Dick West.

Two new hungry mouths graced the Thomas household, both baby girls. The first, Harley, was born in 1897; Beth in 1899. They occupied Matie's time and affection.

For Heck, things went on about as usual. Now and then, someone robbed a store or post office. Most of the time, however, he was chasing timber stealers, horse thieves, whisky peddlers. Life was still exciting, but the days of the big bandit gangs were over.

The complexion of the whole territory was changing. The Kickapoo reservation, lying east of Old Oklahoma and comprising most of western Lincoln County, had been opened by the last great run in 1895. In 1896, the United States Supreme Court upheld the 1890 act defining the Territory as extending to the south fork of Red River, and Texas lost the extreme southwest corner of Oklahoma comprising Harmon, Jackson, Greer, and part of Beckham counties.

On August 6, 1901, the surplus lands of the Kiowa-Comanche and Wichita-Caddo tribes, known as the "Fort Sill country," were settled by lottery. This method was used to avoid the confusions, disputes, and bickering which characterized the earlier openings. The proclamation divided the region into three counties—Comanche, Kiowa, and Caddo—and reserved 320 acres as a townsite at each county seat—Lawton, Hobart, and Anadarko, respectively.

At the same time the entry of lands began, the sale of lots in these towns began also. They were sold at auction to the highest bidder for cash, the funds to be used for the erection of courthouses, jails, and other public buildings and to build roads and bridges and pay the expenses of county governments until taxes could be levied and collected. The auctions attracted men of wealth, and this region developed more quickly than any other part of Oklahoma. Only 13,000, less than 10 per cent of those who sought the smiles of Lady Luck, were successful, but over 160,000 persons poured into this area of 4,639 square miles.

Lawton became the queen city—and the wildest, woolliest, and wickedest. Marshal Thompson sent Heck to tame it.

It was reminiscent of his days at Whitebead Hill. The scenes of Perry and Hell's Half Acre were repeated. The pattern, it seemed to Heck, was always the same: "Picture a place about a mile square, staked off in lots, with canvas tents pitched in long rows with broad streets and alleys in between, then multiply any good carnival company by ten, and you have it."

As town lots were sold, buildings sprang up like magic. There would be a pile of lumber on a lot at sundown. By morning, another saloon was doing flourishing business. The first two buildings in Lawton were a long, low wooden structure which housed the land office and a boxlike shack about 16 feet by 20 feet, occupied by the First National Bank. The bank had no vault, no steel cages, only a pine counter. But on the outside sat two determined men with high-powered rifles carelessly resting across their knees. Two different men sat on guard all night.

There was no difference between day and night as far as activity was concerned. Shell games, wheels of fortune, street shows, and fakirs were everywhere. Gamblers, confidence men, and prostitutes did more business than the "locaters," real-estate agents, and land lawyers. Gun-hung toughs swaggered the streets looking for their "man for breakfast."

Through this bawdy, violent picture strode Heck, as Longhair Jim Courtright had strode, many years before, through vice-ridden Fort Worth. Coming to Lawton with a reputation like few other lawmen of his time, Heck kept terrorism by gangs at a minimum. Gunslingers feared him.

Unlike Courtright, he won the co-operation of local officials and the courts. He represented the Federal Government, and carried an additional deputy's commission under C. C. Hammond, Comanche County's sheriff.

Within a few weeks he had been elected Lawton's first chief of police. He organized a three-man police force that finally grew to fourteen, and equipped them, as had Courtright, in blue uniforms with brass buttons, and black hats. Heck wore a white one.

"We were very busy keeping order," recalled Stephen A. Woody, one of Heck's first appointments. "There was one saloon with gambling devices of every kind and dancing all under one tent that covered a block. There was a big wheel on a platform, built seven feet high where everybody could see it. The operator would holler: 'All ready, all ready—go!' Then the wheel would start revolving and all games would start. You could hear money clinking as they started betting. When the wheel stopped, the games stopped. This method was repeated around the clock. Indians and their squaws liked the roulette best. Some were lucky.

"Three of us went to this tent one night to quiet some drunks. We arrested fifteen. There was some shooting, and the bartender got hit in the leg.

"We had a big bell at police headquarters which rang one gong for Chief Heck, two gongs for Assistant Chief Cal Hawkins, and three or more when there was trouble.

"We had one mounted policeman, Rufe LeForce. He was killed by the editor of one of the newspapers. We notified his folks to come for the body. After waiting a couple of days, we started to bury him. The funeral procession was four miles long. Just as we were lowering him into the grave a man drove up in a buggy. It was his brother, and he took the body back to Georgia. Before he left, he asked to see the man who had killed Rufe. We took him to the Fort Sill guardhouse, where we had the prisoner for safe-keeping, as sentiment was pretty high. Rufe's brother gazed at him a long time, as if he did not want to forget him. The editor was tried and sentenced to four years in prison, but got a new trial and came clear. He left immediately for the East, where he started another paper. Later he was murdered, and the mystery was never solved. We always thought Rufe's brother killed him. . . ."

Heck's operations were not confined to Lawton. He policed the whole county. Cattle thieves were as thick as Indians around the roulette tables. He had an Indian deputy who worked with him named Post Oak Jim. The Indians made good deputies, especially in rounding up cattle thieves, but they liked to drink and gamble. During a poker game, Jim got shot in the mouth. The bullet passed out the back of his neck. He then promised Heck never to drink or gamble again, and he kept his promise.

The biggest gang of rustlers was the Davis brothers. They stole cattle from the reservations and sold them back to the Government for the Indians. If the cattle were branded, they dumped the hides in a well. If not, they sold them.

Heck's posse caught them one night on the Neal ranch with fifteen stolen head. They found two wells full of hides, and sent the brothers to Fort Leavenworth. During the fight, Heck's Winchester was lost or stolen. He offered a $25 reward, but never recovered the weapon. The boys on the force made up a purse and bought him another, but he "never liked it as well as his old rifle."

He served seven years at Lawton. Toward the end of his second term, a "concourse of friends" presented him with a new badge—a golden star with a fine diamond in the center. His name was engraved upon the face of the star in black enameled letters.

Quoth the Lawton *Enterprise:* "Few men living have been presented a more beautiful emblem of esteem, and very few men could receive all the admiration and love that has been heaped upon him without getting the big head. . . . Long may you live, friend Heck, and may the happiest days of your past be the saddest of your future."

"These *were* the happiest days of his life," Matie related, in an interview just before her death at Tulsa in 1946. "He found time to visit old friends and relatives in Georgia. Some of them even came to see the 'wild' frontier he had described to Atlanta newspapers."

One summer morning, in 1905, he received a telegram announcing that Albert was coming for a visit. Since the war, Albert had been cashier of the Atlantic Coast Line Railroad, at Columbia, South Carolina. Heck went stepping high about police headquarters, warbling snatches from light and grand operas, and cutting up like a thoroughbred colt in a blue grass pasture.

"How do you like my singing?" he asked, and without waiting for an answer: "You ought to hear that boy of mine. When he gets here, I'll have him sing for you. Why, he trills like a bird, and is not only a cultured vocalist, but a composer. Just listen to this, one of his compositions:

> In Alabama folks eat peas,
> In Mississippi eat what you please;
> In North Carolina tar and rosin,
> Georgia girls love gubers and sorghum.

"I have sung that to Buck Lancaster (one of the policemen) until the great scalding tears coursed down his cheeks, and he howled like a coyote, Buck is so sympathetic. But I'll have the boy sing it for you when he gets here.

"When the Spanish-American war broke out and he went to the front as a Rough Rider, I came near going with him," Heck continued. "Governor Barnes offered me a commission as lieutenant, and I would have accepted, if I could have taken Bill Tilghman with me. But Bill was so old and decrepit that the government wouldn't have him, and I didn't have the heart to go and leave poor old Bill."

Then Heck threw out his chest and warbled a few bars from the prison scene of *Il Trovatore*.

226

Albert arrived to stay a few days, and stayed a whole month.

In December, Heck joined the famed wolf hunt in the Big Pasture country along Red River. Theodore Roosevelt, who had campaigned in Wichita Falls two years before, had been invited on the hunt by cattle barons Dan Waggoner, Tom and Burk Burnett. Sixteen wolves were bagged during the six-day chase, some of them captured alive and bare-handed by the renowned "wolf-catcher," John Abernathy. Heck never forgot the booming voice and squint-eyed sun-grin of the twenty-sixth President of the United States, who vied with the Westerners for endurance honors and loved every minute of it. The following February, Roosevelt appointed Abernathy the marshal for the Oklahoma Territory.

But Heck "seemed the happiest" the day he took Matie and little Beth and Harley on the train to Guthrie to see Oklahoma become a state, and Charles N. Haskell, whom he had known at Muskogee, inaugurated as first governor. He felt great pride in having served his Government well.

A few months after Roosevelt visited Oklahoma, he had signed into law a Congressional act dissolving the portion of the Comanche-Caddo holdings reserved from settlement in 1901 as common grazing grounds for the Indians, and the Big Pasture was attached to the white man's land. An act of April 21, 1904, had abolished the reservations of the Ponca, Otoe-Missouri, and Kaw Indians on the eastern border of the Cherokee Outlet. The areas were attached to the counties in which they were located, subject to territorial law. No opening to white settlement was involved. The lands were alloted to the tribesmen to dispose of or retain, as they saw fit.

The Osage holdings covered some 1,600,000 acres. They maintained an elaborate form of government. But two factions developed within the tribe. The half-breeds wanted allotments; the full bloods did not. The discovery of vast quantities of oil on the reservation and large sums of money owed white traders complicated matters. Political strife grew. The Indians fell prey to white shysters. Finally, on June 28, 1906, Congress provided for the division of the lands and funds individually to the Osage Indians.

Oklahoma was about evenly divided. The western half comprised the white man's land, the eastern half the lands of the Five Civilized Tribes. For a decade, it had been called the "Twin Territories." Since the first opening in 1889, the drift of whites into both territories had been torrential. Trends from the start pointed to the eventual doom of tribal government in these eastern lands. The Dawes Commission had been appointed by Congress in 1893 to negotiate with the Indians to resign their tribal titles and take allotments. By 1898, they had agreed to the plan and were brought under the United States laws.

From 1900 to 1907 had been a period of preparation for statehood for both regions. In the eastern half, counties had been created, existing towns incorporated, and new townsites reserved. New railroads had been built in Oklahoma Territory, and new rails built in Indian Territory connecting with them. On November 16, 1907, President Roosevelt signed into law a bill declaring the two areas a single state.

Law enforcement became the responsibility of constables, police departments, and sheriffs. For Federal purposes, Oklahoma was divided into two districts—a Western District at Guthrie and an Eastern District at Muskogee. It was the Day of Doom for the deputy marshals. When once hundreds of them roved the two regions, with their work dwindled now to small cases and routine, each marshal's force was reduced to a half dozen men.

Many of the old officers had spent their lives in Federal service. Few had saved anything. Some found jobs with the state or municipalities. Bill Tilghman served another term as sheriff of Lincoln County, became chief of police at Oklahoma City, then went to Cromwell in the oil boom of 1924 and was killed by a drunken prohibition officer. Bud Ledbetter served as sheriff of Muskogee County until he was an old man and died in the hills where he had captured the Jennings gang. Chris Madsen returned from the Spanish-American War as deputy marshal in the Southern District of Indian Territory at Ardmore until statehood, then as chief deputy under Abernathy until the latter resigned in 1910. He succeeded Abernathy until President Taft appointed

228

William S. Cade in 1911, and was chief deputy under Marshal Cade until 1913. He worked for the Government in some capacity until retirement in 1933, and died at Guthrie in 1947, aged 90.

Heck continued on as chief of police at Lawton. He was 57 now. His gray locks were turning white. The old wounds in his body were giving him trouble, and rheumatism from sleeping on the prairies and drinking from too many streams had set in. But he kept up a furious pace and told himself he was as good as ever.

Then it happened. As chief of police, he was in charge of the volunteer fire department. While making a run one night, he overtaxed the muscles of his heart. He was in an Oklahoma City hospital a long time before he came home.

In 1909, he ran an ad in a local paper: "To my Democratic friends. Some time ago I over-exerted myself and dilated part of my heart structure. I am much better now. All (of you) vote for me at the primary election on March 7th. . . ."

The voters, however, did not see fit to return him to office.

Undaunted, Heck called on Marshal Abernathy at Guthrie. On January 1, 1910, Abernathy appointed him deputy for the Western District of Oklahoma, with headquarters at Lawton.

He served process now from a buggy. On long trips, he took little Beth with him.

"If anything happens," he cautioned her, "just drive me home."

They covered an area slightly less than that of Connecticut. To the west lay the picturesque Wichita Mountains, their low granite peaks rising some 1,400 feet above the level plain. Among them lay beautiful parks and green valleys. Often he and Beth stopped to rest in the valleys or along the banks of the numerous streams which found their sources there, flowing north into the Washita, or south into Red River, clear and cool and fringed with cottonwood, elm, walnut, pecan, or hackberry. Most of the time they traveled over level country, coated with thick grass which had brought wealth to the cattleman of earlier years.

Sometimes they went east to the lands of the Chickasaws, where great crops of cotton and corn were produced from the fertile soil of the Washita Valley. And Heck would tell her tales of the many bad men he had captured there and hauled hundreds of miles in wagons to Fort Smith.

Or they traveled south to Red River and Texas, where he had trailed Sam Bass and killed Jim and Pink Lee, and got the first real start in his profession as express messenger and private detective.

Another year slipped by and Madsen became acting marshal at Guthrie. On New Year's night, five deputies took the oath of allegiance as soon as Chris was sworn in. One of the these was Heck Thomas.

Bill Tilghman came up from Oklahoma City. That night, the men had a little party. It was a close, genial affair. They talked over old times. Heck was dressed in a long Prince Albert. He looked a dandy. Chris twitted him and called him Scissor Tails.

"A funny outfit to vear," he said, "to go out to capture a bad man."

But under those tails was something more formidable—Heck's pearl-handled six-shooter.

It was the last time the Three Guardsmen were together. Back in Lawton, Heck's condition suddenly became worse. No more trips, even in a buggy. He walked unsteadily on the street. Finally, he couldn't walk at all.

On August 9, he wrote Chris:

"This malady is troubling me again, and I know I have not the strength to resist it, so no matter what happens don't you and Bill come down here, and no flowers. . . . No need to answer, for I will not be alive to receive it. Remember me to your children and good-bye forever. Your friend, Heck."

Six days later he lost consciousness and never recovered. Life passed from him at 4 o'clock in the morning, while a few friends, his wife, and daughters watched at his bedside.

Telegrams of sympathy poured in from everywhere. The Presbyterian church was too small to accommodate the hundreds who came to pay their final respects. The funeral cortege was the largest ever seen in Lawton. The burial was simple, the pallbearers were his old friends and Confederate veterans, and the service was as short and as clean-cut as the life that he had devoted to his state.

He lies buried in Highland cemetery. The stone is of native Oklahoma pink mountain granite. His photograph hangs in the State Historical Society alongside Chris Madsen and Bill Tilghman, and his Winchester and treasured small mementoes are displayed in Comanche County's Museum of the Great Plains, as a lasting tribute to the life of this man whose death was headlined in the August 15, 1912, issue of the Lawton *Constitution:* "The Name of Heck Thomas, Once A Terror to Outlaws."